THIRD EDITION

TOP NOTCH 2

ENGLISH FOR TODAY'S WORLD

JOAN SASLOW
ALLEN ASCHER

With *Top Notch Pop* Songs and Karaoke
by Rob Morsberger

Top Notch: English for Today's World Level 2, Third Edition

Pearson Education, 10 Bank Street, White Plains, NY 10606 USA

Staff credits: The people who made up the *Top Notch* team are Pietro Alongi, Rhea Banker, Peter Benson, Tracey Munz Cataldo, Rosa Chapinal, Aerin Csigay, Dave Dickey, Gina DiLillo, Nancy Flaggman, Irene Frankel, Shelley Gazes, Christopher Leonowicz, Kate McLoughlin, Julie Molnar, Laurie Neaman, Sherri Pemberton, Pamela Pia, Jennifer Raspiller, Charlene Straub, Paula Van Ells, and Kenneth Volcjak.

Cover photo: Sprint/Corbis
Text composition: TSI Graphics

Library of Congress Cataloging-in-Publication Data

Saslow, Joan M.
Top Notch : English for today's world. Fundamentals / Joan Saslow, Allen Ascher ; With Top Notch Pop Songs and Karaoke by Rob Morsberger. — Third Edition.
pages cm
Includes biographical references.
ISBN 978-0-13-354275-2 — ISBN 978-0-13-339348-4 — ISBN 978-0-13-354277-6 — ISBN 978-0-13-354278-3 1. English language—Textbooks for foreign speakers. 2. English language—Problems, exercises, etc. 3. English language—Sound recordings for foreign speakers. I. Ascher, Allen. II. Morsberger, Robert Eustis, 1929- III. Title. IV. Title: English for today's world.
PE1128.S2757 2015
428.2'4--dc23
2013044020

Printed in the United States of America

ISBN-10: 0-13-392894-2
ISBN-13: 978-0-13-392894-5
2 3 4 5 6 7 8 9 10—V003—19 18 17 16 15

ISBN-10: 0-13-354277-7 (with MyEnglishLab)
ISBN-13: 978-0-13-354277-6 (with MyEnglishLab)
3 4 5 6 7 8 9 10—V003—19 18 17 16 15

pearsonelt.com/topnotch3e

In Memoriam

Rob Morsberger (1959–2013)

The authors wish to acknowledge their memory of and gratitude to **Rob Morsberger**, the gifted composer and songwriter of the *Top Notch Pop* Songs and Karaoke that have provided learners both language practice and pleasure.

ABOUT THE AUTHORS

Joan Saslow

Joan Saslow has taught in a variety of programs in South America and the United States. She is author or coauthor of a number of widely used courses, some of which are *Ready to Go, Workplace Plus, Literacy Plus,* and *Summit.* She is also author of *English in Context,* a series for reading science and technology. Ms. Saslow was the series director of *True Colors* and *True Voices.* She has participated in the English Language Specialist Program in the U.S. Department of State's Bureau of Educational and Cultural Affairs.

Allen Ascher

Allen Ascher has been a teacher and teacher trainer in China and the United States, as well as academic director of the intensive English program at Hunter College. Mr. Ascher has also been an ELT publisher and was responsible for publication and expansion of numerous well-known courses including *True Colors, NorthStar,* the *Longman TOEFL Preparation Series,* and the *Longman Academic Writing Series.* He is coauthor of *Summit,* and he wrote the "Teaching Speaking" module of *Teacher Development Interactive,* an online multimedia teacher-training program.

Ms. Saslow and Mr. Ascher are frequent presenters at professional conferences and have been coauthoring courses for teens, adults, and young adults since 2002.

AUTHORS' ACKNOWLEDGMENTS

The authors are indebted to these reviewers, who provided extensive and detailed feedback and suggestions for *Top Notch,* as well as the hundreds of teachers who completed surveys and participated in focus groups.

Manuel Wilson Alvarado Miles, Quito, Ecuador • **Shirley Ando,** Otemae University, Hyogo, Japan • **Vanessa de Andrade,** CCBEU Inter Americano, Curitiba, Brazil • **Miguel Arrazola,** CBA, Santa Cruz, Bolivia • **Mark Barta,** Proficiency School of English, São Paulo, Brazil • **Edwin Bello,** PROULEX, Guadalajara, Mexico • **Mary Blum,** CBA, Cochabamba, Bolivia • **María Elizabeth Boccia,** Proficiency School of English, São Paulo, Brazil • **Pamela Cristina Borja Baltán,** Quito, Ecuador • **Eliana Anabel L. Buccia,** AMICANA, Mendoza, Argentina • **José Humberto Calderón Díaz,** CALUSAC, Guatemala City, Guatemala • **María Teresa Calienes Csirke,** Idiomas Católica, Lima, Peru • **Esther María Carbo Morales,** Quito, Ecuador • **Jorge Washington Cárdenas Castillo,** Quito, Ecuador • **Eréndira Yadira Carrera García,** UVM Chapultepec, Mexico City, Mexico • **Viviane de Cássia Santos Carlini,** Spectrum Line, Pouso Alegre, Brazil • **Centro Colombo Americano,** Bogota, Colombia • **Guven Ciftci,** Fatih University, Istanbul, Turkey • **Diego Cisneros,** CBA, Tarija, Bolivia • **Paul Crook,** Meisei University, Tokyo, Japan • **Alejandra Díaz Loo,** El Cultural, Arequipa, Peru • **Jesús G. Díaz Osío,** Florida National College, Miami, USA • **María Eid Ceneviva,** CBA, Bolivia • **Amalia Elvira Rodríguez Espinoza De Los Monteros,** Guayaquil, Ecuador • **María Argelia Estrada Vásquez,** CALUSAC, Guatemala City, Guatemala • **John Fieldeldy,** College of Engineering, Nihon University, Aizuwakamatsu-shi, Japan • **Marleni Humbelina Flores Urízar,** CALUSAC, Guatemala City, Guatemala • **Gonzalo Fortune,** CBA, Sucre, Bolivia • **Andrea Fredricks,** Embassy CES, San Francisco, USA • **Irma Gallegos Peláez,** UVM Tlalpan, Mexico City, Mexico • **Alberto Gamarra,** CBA, Santa Cruz, Bolivia • **María Amparo García Peña,** ICPNA Cusco, Peru • **Amanda Gillis-Furutaka,** Kyoto Sangyo University, Kyoto, Japan • **Martha Angelina González Párraga,** Guayaquil, Ecuador • **Octavio Garduño Ruiz** Business Training Consultant, Mexico City, Mexico • **Ralph Grayson,** Idiomas Católica, Lima, Peru • **Murat Gultekin,** Fatih University, Istanbul, Turkey • **Oswaldo Gutiérrez,** PROULEX, Guadalajara, Mexico • **Ayaka Hashinishi,** Otemae University, Hyogo, Japan • **Alma Lorena Hernández de Armas,** CALUSAC, Guatemala City, Guatemala • **Kent Hill,** Seigakuin University, Saitama-ken, Japan • **Kayoko Hirao,** Nichii Gakkan Company, COCO Juku, Japan • **Jesse Huang,** National Central University, Taoyuan, Taiwan • **Eric Charles Jones,** Seoul University of Technology, Seoul, South Korea • **Jun-Chen Kuo,** Tajen University, Pingtung , Taiwan • **Susan Krieger,** Embassy CES, San Francisco, USA • **Ana María de la Torre Ugarte,** ICPNA Chiclayo, Peru • **Erin Lemaistre,** Chung-Ang University, Seoul, South Korea • **Eleanor S. Leu,** Soochow University, Taipei, Taiwan • **Yihui Li (Stella Li),** Fooyin University, Kaohsiung, Taiwan • **Chin-Fan Lin,** Shih Hsin University, Taipei, Taiwan • **Linda Lin,** Tatung Institute of Technology, Taiwan • **Kristen Lindblom,** Embassy CES, San Francisco, USA • **Patricio David López Logacho,** Quito, Ecuador • **Diego López Tasara,** Idiomas Católica, Lima, Peru • **Neil Macleod,** Kansai Gaidai University, Osaka, Japan • **Adriana Marcés,** Idiomas Católica, Lima, Peru • **Robyn McMurray,** Pusan National University, Busan, South Korea • **Paula Medina,** London Language Institute, London, Canada • **Juan Carlos Muñoz,** American School Way, Bogota, Colombia • **Noriko Mori,** Otemae University, Hyogo, Japan • **Adrián Esteban Narváez Pacheco,** Cuenca, Ecuador • **Tim Newfields,** Tokyo University Faculty of Economics, Tokyo, Japan • **Ana Cristina Ochoa,** CCBEU Inter Americano, Curitiba, Brazil • **Tania Elizabeth Ortega Santacruz,** Cuenca, Ecuador • **Martha Patricia Páez,** Quito, Ecuador • **María de Lourdes Pérez Valdespino,** Universidad del Valle de México, Mexico • **Wahrena Elizabeth Pfeister,** University of Suwon, Gyeonggi-Do, South Korea • **Wayne Allen Pfeister,** University of Suwon, Gyeonggi-Do, South Korea • **Andrea Rebonato,** CCBEU Inter Americano, Curitiba, Brazil • **Thomas Robb,** Kyoto Sangyo University, Kyoto, Japan • **Mehran Sabet,** Seigakuin University, Saitama-ken, Japan • **Majid Safadaran Mosazadeh,** ICPNA Chiclayo, Peru • **Timothy Samuelson,** BridgeEnglish, Denver, USA • **Héctor Sánchez,** PROULEX, Guadalajara, Mexico • **Mónica Alexandra Sánchez Escalante,** Quito, Ecuador • **Jorge Mauricio Sánchez Montalván,** Quito, Universidad Politécnica Salesiana (UPS), Ecuador • **Letícia Santos,** ICBEU Ibiá, Brazil • **Elena Sapp,** INTO Oregon State University, Corvallis, USA • **Robert Sheridan,** Otemae University, Hyogo, Japan • **John Eric Sherman,** Hong Ik University, Seoul, South Korea • **Brooks Slaybaugh,** Asia University, Tokyo, Japan • **João Vitor Soares,** NACC, São Paulo, Brazil • **Silvia Solares,** CBA, Sucre, Bolivia • **Chayawan Sonchaeng,** Delaware County Community College, Media, PA • **María Julia Suárez,** CBA, Cochabamba, Bolivia • **Elena Sudakova,** English Language Center, Kiev, Ukraine • **Richard Swingle,** Kansai Gaidai College, Osaka, Japan • **Blanca Luz Terrazas Zamora,** ICPNA Cusco, Peru • **Sandrine Ting,** St. John's University, New Taipei City, Taiwan • **Christian Juan Torres Medina,** Guayaquil, Ecuador • **Raquel Torrico,** CBA, Sucre, Bolivia • **Jessica Ueno,** Otemae University, Hyogo, Japan • **Ximena Vacaflor C.,** CBA, Tarija, Bolivia • **René Valdivia Pereira,** CBA, Santa Cruz, Bolivia • **Solange Lopes Vinagre Costa,** SENAC, São Paulo, Brazil • **Magno Alejandro Vivar Hurtado,** Cuenca, Ecuador • **Dr. Wen-hsien Yang,** National Kaohsiung Hospitality College, Kaohsiung, Taiwan • **Juan Zárate,** El Cultural, Arequipa, Peru

LEARNING OBJECTIVES

	COMMUNICATION GOALS	VOCABULARY	GRAMMAR
UNIT 1 Getting Acquainted PAGE 2	• Get reacquainted with someone • Greet a visitor to your country • Discuss gestures and customs • Describe an interesting experience	• Tourist activities • The hand • Participial adjectives	• The present perfect ◦ Statements and yes / no questions ◦ Form and usage ◦ Past participles of irregular verbs ◦ With already, yet, ever, before, and never GRAMMAR BOOSTER • The present perfect ◦ Information questions ◦ Yet and already: expansion, common errors ◦ Ever, never, and before: use and placement
UNIT 2 Going to the Movies PAGE 14	• Apologize for being late • Discuss preferences for movie genres • Describe and recommend movies • Discuss effects of movie violence on viewers	• Explanations for being late • Movie genres • Adjectives to describe movies	• The present perfect ◦ With for and since ◦ Other uses • Wants and preferences: would like and would rather ◦ Form and usage ◦ Statements, questions, and answers GRAMMAR BOOSTER • The present perfect continuous • The present participle: spelling • Expressing preferences: review, expansion, and common errors
UNIT 3 Staying in Hotels PAGE 26	• Leave and take a message • Check into a hotel • Request housekeeping services • Choose a hotel	• Hotel room types and kinds of beds • Hotel room amenities and services	• The future with will ◦ Form and usage ◦ Statements and questions ◦ Contractions • The real conditional ◦ Form and usage ◦ Statements and questions GRAMMAR BOOSTER • Will: expansion • Can, should, and have to: future meaning • The real conditinal: factual and future; usage and common errors
UNIT 4 Cars and Driving PAGE 38	• Discuss a car accident • Describe a car problem • Rent a car • Discuss good and bad driving	• Bad driving habits • Car parts • Ways to respond (with concern / relief) • Phrasal verbs for talking about cars • Car types • Driving behavior	• The past continuous ◦ Form and usage ◦ Vs. the simple past tense • Direct objects with phrasal verbs GRAMMAR BOOSTER • The past continuous: other uses • Nouns and pronouns: review
UNIT 5 Personal Care and Appearance PAGE 50	• Ask for something in a store • Make an appointment at a salon or spa • Discuss ways to improve appearance • Define the meaning of beauty	• Salon services • Personal care products • Discussing beauty	• Indefinite quantities and amounts ◦ Some and any ◦ A lot of / lots of, many, and much • Indefinite pronouns: someone / no one / anyone GRAMMAR BOOSTER • Some and any: indefiniteness • Too many, too much, and enough • Comparative quantifiers fewer and less • Indefinite pronouns: something, anything, and nothing

CONVERSATION STRATEGIES	LISTENING / PRONUNCIATION	READING	WRITING
• Use "I don't think so." to soften a negative answer • Say "I know!" to exclaim that you've discovered an answer • Use "Welcome to ___." to greet someone in a new place • Say "That's great." to acknowledge someone's positive experience	**Listening Skills** • Listen to classify • Listen for details **Pronunciation** • Sound reduction in the present perfect	**Texts** • A poster about world customs • A magazine article about non-verbal communication • A travel poster • A photo story **Skills/strategies** • Identify supporting details • Relate to personal experience	**Task** • Write a description of an interesting experience **WRITING BOOSTER** • Avoiding run-on sentences
• Apologize and provide a reason when late • Say "That's fine." to reassure • Offer to repay someone with "How much do I owe?" • Use "What would you rather do . . . ? to ask about preference • Soften a negative response with "To tell you the truth, . . ."	**Listening Skills** • Listen for main ideas • Listen to infer • Dictation **Pronunciation** • Reduction of h	**Texts** • A movie website • Movie reviews • A textbook excerpt about violence in movies • A photo story **Skills/strategies** • Understand from context • Confirm content • Evaluate ideas	**Task** • Write an essay about violence in movies and on TV **WRITING BOOSTER** • Paragraphs • Topic sentences
• Say "Would you like to leave a message?" if someone isn't available • Say "Let's see." to indicate you're checking information • Make a formal, polite request with "May I ___?" • Say "Here you go." when handing someone something • Use "By the way, . . ." to introduce new information	**Listening Skills** • Listen to take phone messages • Listen for main ideas • Listen for details **Pronunciation** • Contractions with will	**Texts** • Phone message slips • A hotel website • A city map • A photo story **Skills/strategies** • Draw conclusions • Identify supporting details • Interpret a map	**Task** • Write a paragraph explaining the reasons for choosing a hotel **WRITING BOOSTER** • Avoiding sentence fragments with because or since
• Express concern about another's condition after an accident • Express relief when hearing all is OK • Use "only" to minimize the seriousness of a situation • Use "actually" to soften negative information • Empathize with "I'm sorry to hear that."	**Listening Skills** • Listen for details • Listen to summarize **Pronunciation** • Stress of particles in phrasal verbs	**Texts** • A questionnaire about bad driving habits • Rental car customer profiles • A feature article about defensive driving • A driving behavior survey • A photo story **Skills/strategies** • Understand from context • Critical thinking	**Task** • Write a paragraph comparing good and bad drivers **WRITING BOOSTER** • Connecting words and sentences: and, in addition, furthermore, and therefore
• Use "Excuse me." to initiate a conversation with a salesperson • Confirm information by repeating it with rising intonation • Use "No problem." to show you don't mind an inconvenience • Use "Let me check" to ask someone to wait while you confirm information	**Listening Skills** • Listen to recognize someone's point of view • Listen to take notes **Pronunciation** • Pronunciation of unstressed vowels	**Texts** • A spa and fitness center advertisement • A health advice column • A photo story **Skills/strategies** • Paraphrase • Understand from context • Confirm content • Apply information	**Task** • Write a letter on how to improve appearance **WRITING BOOSTER** • Writing a formal letter

	COMMUNICATION GOALS	VOCABULARY	GRAMMAR
UNIT 6 Eating Well PAGE 62	• Talk about food passions • Make an excuse to decline food • Discuss lifestyle changes • Describe local dishes	• Nutrition terminology • Food passions • Excuses for not eating something • Food descriptions	• Use to / used to • Negative yes / no questions GRAMMAR BOOSTER • Use to / used to: use and form, common errors • Be used to vs. get used to • Repeated actions in the past: would + base form, common errors • Negative yes / no questions: short answers
UNIT 7 About Personality PAGE 74	• Get to know a new friend • Cheer someone up • Discuss personality and its origin • Examine the impact of birth order on personality	• Positive and negative adjectives • Terms to discuss psychology and personality	• Gerunds and infinitives • Gerunds as objects of prepositions GRAMMAR BOOSTER • Gerunds and infinitives: other uses • Negative gerunds
UNIT 8 The Arts PAGE 86	• Recommend a museum • Ask about and describe objects • Talk about artistic talent • Discuss your favorite artists	• Kinds of art • Adjectives to describe art • Objects, handicrafts, and materials • Passive participial phrases	• The passive voice ◦ Form, meaning, and usage ◦ Statements and questions GRAMMAR BOOSTER • Transitive and intransitive verbs • The passive voice: other tenses • Yes / no questions in the passive voice: other tenses
UNIT 9 Living in Cyberspace PAGE 98	• Troubleshoot a problem • Compare product features • Describe how you use the Internet • Discuss the impact of the Internet	• Ways to reassure someone • The computer screen, components, and commands • Internet activities	• The infinitive of purpose • Comparisons with as . . . as ◦ Meaning and usage ◦ Just, almost, not quite, not nearly GRAMMAR BOOSTER • Expressing purpose with in order to and for • As . . . as to compare adverbs • Comparatives / superlatives: review • Comparison with adverbs
UNIT 10 Ethics and Values PAGE 110	• Discuss ethical choices • Return someone else's property • Express personal values • Discuss acts of kindness and honesty	• Idioms • Situations that require an ethical choice • Acknowledging thanks • Personal values	• The unreal conditional ◦ Form, usage, common errors • Possessive pronouns / Whose ◦ Form, usage, common errors GRAMMAR BOOSTER • should, ought to, had better • have to, must, be supposed to • Possessive nouns: review and expansion • Pronouns: summary

Grammar Readiness Self-Check .... **page x**
References .... **page 123**
Grammar Booster .... **page 126**
Writing Booster .... **page 143**
***Top Notch Pop* Lyrics** .... **page 153**

CONVERSATION STRATEGIES	LISTENING / PRONUNCIATION	READING	WRITING
• Provide an emphatic affirmative response with "Definitely." • Offer food with "Please help yourself." • Acknowledge someone's efforts by saying something positive • Soften the rejection of an offer with "I'll pass on the ___." • Use a negative question to express surprise • Use "It's not a problem." to downplay inconvenience	**Listening Skills** • Listen for details • Listen to personalize **Pronunciation** • Sound reduction: used to	**Texts** • A food guide • Descriptions of types of diets • A magazine article about eating habits • A lifestyle survey • Menu ingredients • A photo story **Skills/strategies** • Understand from context • Summarize • Compare and contrast	**Task** • Write a persuasive paragraph about the differences in present-day and past diets **WRITING BOOSTER** • Connecting ideas: subordinating conjunctions
• Clarify an earlier question with "Well, for example, . . ." • Buy time to think with "Let's see." • Use auxiliary do to emphasize a verb • Thank someone for showing interest. • Offer empathy with "I know what you mean."	**Listening Skills** • Listen for main ideas • Listen for specific information • Classify information • Infer information **Pronunciation** • Reduction of to in infinitives	**Texts** • A pop psychology website • A textbook excerpt about the nature / nurture controversy • Personality surveys • A photo story **Skills/strategies** • Understand vocabulary from context • Make personal comparisons	**Task** • Write an essay describing someone's personality **WRITING BOOSTER** • Parallel structure
• Say "Be sure not to miss ___." to emphasize the importance of an action • Introduce the first aspect of an opinion with "For one thing, . . ." • Express enthusiasm for what someone has said with "No kidding!" • Invite someone's opinion with "What do you think of ___?"	**Listening Skills** • Understand from context • Listen to take notes • Infer point of view **Pronunciation** • Emphatic stress	**Texts** • Museum descriptions • A book excerpt about the origin of artistic talent • An artistic survey • A photo story **Skills/strategies** • Recognize the main idea • Identify supporting details • Paraphrase	**Task** • Write a detailed description of a decorative object **WRITING BOOSTER** • Providing supporting details
• Ask for assistance with "Could you take a look at ___?" • Introduce an explanation with "Well, . . ." • Make a suggestion with "Why don't you try ___ing?" • Express interest informally with "Oh, yeah?" • Use "Everyone says . . ." to introduce a popular opinion • Say "Well, I've heard ___." to support a point of view	**Listening Skills** • Listen for the main idea • Listen for details **Pronunciation** • Stress in as . . . as phrases	**Texts** • A social network website • An internet user survey • Newspaper clippings about the Internet • A photo story **Skills/strategies** • Understand from context • Relate to personal experience	**Task** • Write an essay evaluating the benefits and problems of the Internet **WRITING BOOSTER** • Organizing ideas
• Say "You think so?" to reconfirm someone's opinion • Provide an emphatic affirmative response with "Absolutely." • Acknowledge thanks with "Don't mention it."	**Listening Skills** • Listen to infer information • Listen for main ideas • Understand vocabulary from context • Support ideas with details **Pronunciation** • Blending of d + y in would you	**Texts** • A personal values self-test • Print and online news stories about kindness and honesty • A photo story **Skills/strategies** • Summarize • Interpret information • Relate to personal experience	**Task** • Write an essay about someone's personal choice **WRITING BOOSTER** • Introducing conflicting ideas: On the one hand; On the other hand

TO THE TEACHER

What is *Top Notch?*

Top Notch is a six-level* communicative course that prepares adults and young adults to interact successfully and confidently with both native and non-native speakers of English.

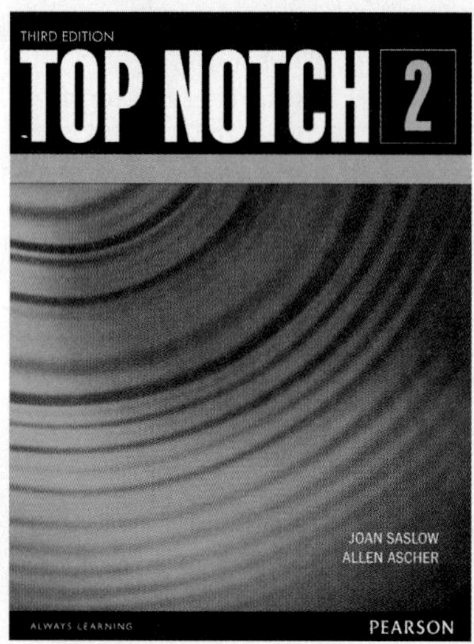

The goal of *Top Notch* is to make English unforgettable through:

- Multiple exposures to new language
- Numerous opportunities to practice it
- Deliberate and intensive recycling

The ***Top Notch*** course has two beginning levels—***Top Notch Fundamentals*** for true beginners and ***Top Notch 1*** for false beginners. ***Top Notch*** is benchmarked to the Global Scale of English and is tightly correlated to the Can-do Statements of the Common European Framework of Reference.

Each full level of ***Top Notch*** contains material for 60–90 hours of classroom instruction. In addition, the entire course can be tailored to blended learning with an integrated online component, *MyEnglishLab.*

NEW This third edition of ***Top Notch*** includes these new features: Extra Grammar Exercises, digital full-color Vocabulary Flash Cards, Conversation Activator videos, and Pronunciation Coach videos.

* ***Summit 1*** and ***Summit 2*** are the titles of the 5th and 6th levels of the ***Top Notch*** course.

Award-Winning Instructional Design*

Daily confirmation of progress

Each easy-to-follow two-page lesson begins with a clearly stated practical communication goal closely aligned to the Common European Framework's Can-do Statements. All activities are integrated with the goal, giving vocabulary and grammar meaning and purpose. *Now You Can* activities ensure that students achieve each goal and confirm their progress in every class session.

Explicit vocabulary and grammar

Clear captioned picture-dictionary illustrations with accompanying audio take the guesswork out of meaning and pronunciation. Grammar presentations containing both rules and examples clarify form, meaning, and use. The unique *Recycle this Language* feature continually puts known words and grammar in front of students' eyes as they communicate, to make sure language remains active.

High-frequency social language

Twenty memorable conversation models provide appealing natural social language that students can carry "in their pockets" for use in real life. Rigorous controlled and free discussion activities systematically stimulate recycling of social language, ensuring that it's not forgotten.

* ***Top Notch*** is the recipient of the Association of Educational Publishers' *Distinguished Achievement Award.*

Linguistic and cultural fluency

Top Notch equips students to interact with people from different language backgrounds by including authentic accents on the audio. Conversation Models, Photo Stories, and cultural fluency activities prepare students for social interactions in English with people from unfamiliar cultures.

Active listening syllabus

All Vocabulary presentations, Pronunciation presentations, Conversation Models, Photo Stories, Listening Comprehension exercises, and Readings are recorded on the audio to help students develop good pronunciation, intonation, and auditory memory. In addition, approximately fifty carefully developed listening tasks at each level of ***Top Notch*** develop crucial listening comprehension skills such as listen for details, listen for main ideas, listen to activate vocabulary, listen to activate grammar, and listen to confirm information.

*We wish you and your students enjoyment and success with **Top Notch 2**.*
We wrote it for you.

Joan Saslow and Allen Ascher

ActiveTeach

Maximize the impact of your ***Top Notch*** lessons. This digital tool provides an interactive classroom experience that can be used with or without an interactive whiteboard (IWB). It includes a full array of digital and printable features.

For class presentation . . .

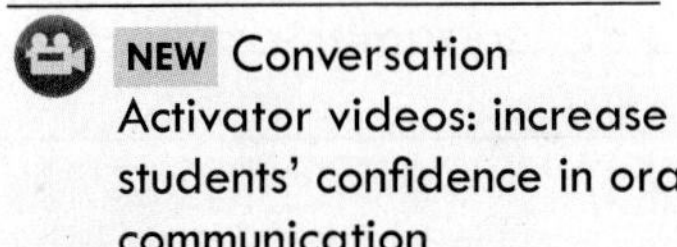

NEW Conversation Activator videos: increase students' confidence in oral communication

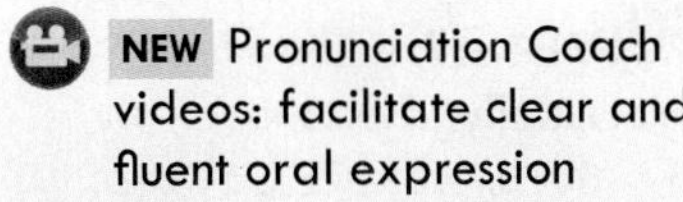

NEW Pronunciation Coach videos: facilitate clear and fluent oral expression

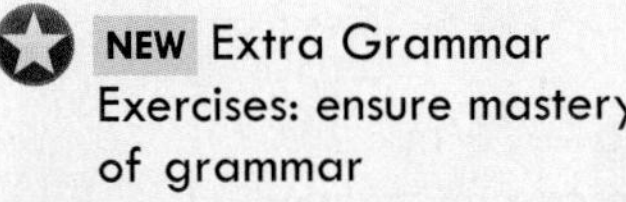

NEW Extra Grammar Exercises: ensure mastery of grammar

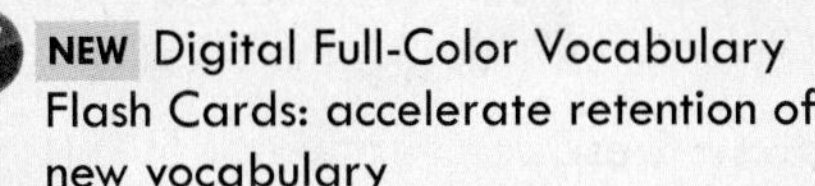

NEW Digital Full-Color Vocabulary Flash Cards: accelerate retention of new vocabulary

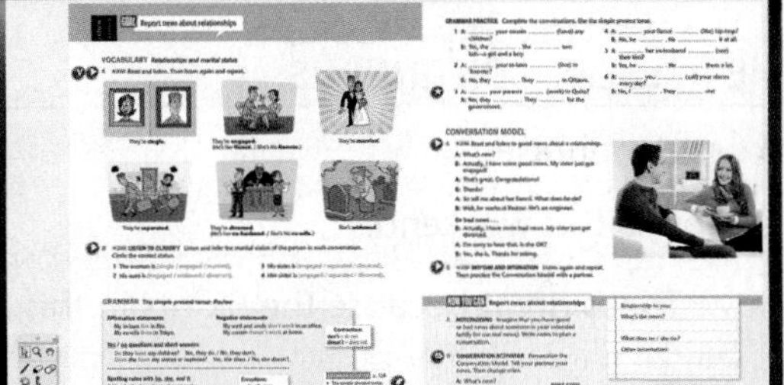

PLUS

- Clickable Audio: instant access to the complete classroom audio program
- *Top Notch TV* Video Program: a hilarious sitcom and authentic on-the-street interviews
- *Top Notch Pop* Songs and Karaoke: original songs for additional language practice

For planning . . .

- A *Methods Handbook* for a communicative classroom
- Detailed timed lesson plans for each two-page lesson
- *Top Notch TV* teaching notes
- Complete answer keys, audio scripts, and video scripts

For extra support . . .

- Hundreds of extra printable activities, with teaching notes
- *Top Notch Pop* language exercises
- *Top Notch TV* activity worksheets

For assessment . . .

- Ready-made unit and review achievement tests with options to edit, add, or delete items.

MyEnglishLab

An optional online learning tool

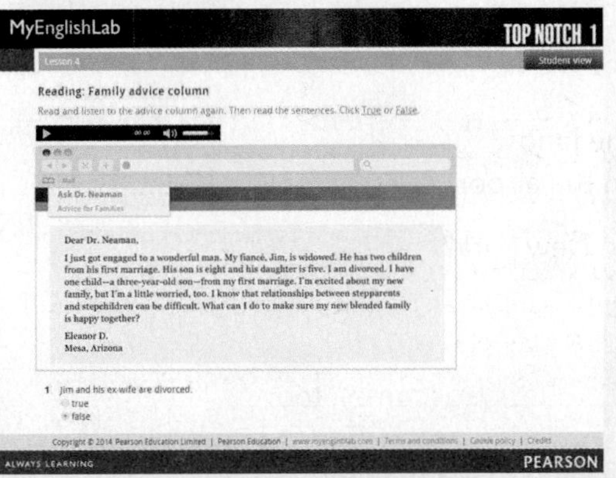

- NEW Grammar Coach videos, plus the Pronunciation Coach videos, and Digital Vocabulary Flash Cards
- NEW Immediate and meaningful feedback on wrong answers
- NEW Remedial grammar exercises
- Interactive practice of all material presented in the course
- Grade reports that display performance and time on task
- Auto-graded achievement tests

Workbook

Lesson-by-lesson written exercises to accompany the Student's Book

Full-Course Placement Tests

Choose printable or online version

Classroom Audio Program

- A set of Audio CDs, as an alternative to the clickable audio in the ActiveTeach
- Contains a variety of authentic regional and non-native accents to build comprehension of diverse English speakers
- NEW The entire audio program is available for students at www.english.com/topnotch3e. The mobile app *Top Notch Go* allows access anytime, anywhere and lets students practice at their own pace.

Teacher's Edition and Lesson Planner

- Detailed interleaved lesson plans, language and culture notes, answer keys, and more
- Also accessible in digital form in the ActiveTeach

For more information: www.pearsonelt.com/topnotch3e

Grammar Readiness

SELF-CHECK

The Grammar Readiness Self-Check is optional. Complete the exercises to confirm that you know this grammar previously taught in *Top Notch*.

THE SIMPLE PRESENT TENSE AND THE PRESENT CONTINUOUS

A **PRACTICE** Choose the correct verb or verb phrase.

1. We (take / are taking) a trip to California this weekend.
2. The flight (arrives / is arriving) now. That's great because the flights in this airport usually (arrive / are arriving) late.
3. Please drive slower! You (go / are going) too fast!
4. (Does it rain / Is it raining) often in March?
5. Brandon (goes / is going) skiing on his next vacation.
6. We (like / are liking) milk in both coffee and tea.

B **USE THE GRAMMAR** Complete each statement with the simple present tense or the present continuous.

1. In my family, we usually ....
2. Next weekend, I ....

BE GOING TO + BASE FORM FOR THE FUTURE

A **PRACTICE** Complete the conversations with be going to. Use contractions.

1. A: What .... (they / do) after English class?
   B: They .... (go) out to eat.
2. A: I .... (need) a rental car in Chicago.
   B: .... (you / make) a reservation online?
3. A: Who .... (you / call) when your plane lands?
   B: My wife. She .... (wait) for my call in the airport café.
4. A: What .... (you / do) when you get to New York?
   B: The first thing .... (we / do) is eat!
5. A: Who .... (be) at the meeting?
   B: My colleagues from the office. And my boss .... (come), too.

B **USE THE GRAMMAR** Write your own question and answer, using be going to + a base form.

Q: ....

....

A: ....

....

CAN, HAVE TO, COULD, AND SHOULD: MEANING AND FORM

A PRACTICE Choose the correct phrases.

1 We .... a reservation if we want a good room.
 a couldn't make b should make c should making

2 Susan doesn't have to wear formal clothes to the office. She .... jeans.
 a can't wear b can wearing c can wear

3 Dan can't go shopping this afternoon. He .... drive his children to school.
 a have to b has to c doesn't have to

4 They just missed the 3:12 express bus, but they .... the 3:14 local because it arrives too late. They should take a taxi.
 a could take b shouldn't to take c shouldn't take

5 The class has to end on time so the students .... the bus to the party.
 a can take b can to take c can't take

6 I can sleep late tomorrow. I .... go to the office.
 a have to b don't have to c doesn't have to

B USE THE GRAMMAR Write one statement with both can and have to. Write one statement with either should or could.

1 ....

2 ....

OBJECT PRONOUNS

A PRACTICE Rewrite each sentence, correcting the error.

1 Please call about it us. ....

2 She's buying for you it. ....

3 The brown shoes? She doesn't like on him them. ....

4 He wrote for her it. ....

5 They're giving to them it. ....

B USE THE GRAMMAR Rewrite each sentence, changing the two nouns to object pronouns.

1 I gave my sister the present yesterday. ....

2 The clerk gift-wrapped the sweaters for John. ....

COMPARATIVE ADJECTIVES

A PRACTICE Complete each sentence with the comparative form of the adjective.

1 I think very cold weather is .... (bad) than very hot weather.

2 A tablet is .... (convenient) than a laptop.

3 A T-shirt is .... (comfortable) than a sweatshirt in hot weather.

4 The clothes in a department store are usually .... (affordable) than ones in a small neighborhood store.

5 Orange juice is .... (good) for your health than orange soda.

6 Rio is pretty hot in the summer, but Salvador is .... (hot).

7 If you're getting dressed for the office, you should wear a .... (long) skirt.

B **USE THE GRAMMAR** Write your own two sentences, using one of these adjectives in comparative form in each sentence: cheap, popular, near, fast.

1 ....

2 ....

SUPERLATIVE ADJECTIVES

A **PRACTICE** Write statements with the superlative form of each adjective.

1 old *The oldest person in the world is 124 years old.*

2 good ....

3 funny ....

4 appropriate ....

5 unusual ....

6 large ....

7 beautiful ....

8 short ....

9 interesting ....

10 crazy ....

B **USE THE GRAMMAR** Write one statement about yourself, using a superlative adjective.

....

THE SIMPLE PAST TENSE: STATEMENTS

A **PRACTICE** Complete the paragraph with the simple past tense.

Chris .... (1 go) to New York at the end of the school year. His flight .... (2 get in) late, so he .... (3 take) a taxi directly to his hotel and .... (4 eat) something fast at the hotel café. Chris .... (5 have) tickets to a Broadway show, and he .... (6 not have) time to eat at a regular restaurant. Just before the show, he .... (7 meet) his friends in front of the theater. He really .... (8 love) the show. After the show, he .... (9 buy) a book about it. His friends .... (10 say) good night, and Chris .... (11 walk) back to the hotel, ... (12 drink) a big glass of cold juice, ... (13 go) to bed, and .... (14 sleep) for 10 hours.

B USE THE GRAMMAR Write four statements about what you did yesterday. Use one of these verbs in each statement: go, get dressed, eat, come home

1 ....

2 ....

3 ....

4 ....

THE SIMPLE PAST TENSE: YES / NO QUESTIONS

A PRACTICE Change each statement to a yes / no question.

1 Phil lost his luggage on the flight. ....

2 They drove too fast. ....

3 She wrote a letter to her uncle. ....

4 They found a wallet on the street. ....

5 Claire's husband spent a lot of money at the mall. ....

6 Ms. Carter taught her children to play the piano. ....

B USE THE GRAMMAR Write three yes / no questions. Use each of these verbs: bring, speak, break.

1 ....

2 ....

3 ....

THE SIMPLE PAST TENSE: INFORMATION QUESTIONS

A PRACTICE Complete each conversation with an information question in the simple past tense.

1 **A:** .... Chinese?
B: I studied in Shanghai.

2 **A:** .... your husband?
B: I met him two years ago.

3 **A:** .... about the problem?
B: I called my daughter. She always knows what to do.

4 **A:** .... your car?
B: My brother-in-law bought it. He needed a new car.

5 **A:** .... in Mexico?
B: My parents lived there for more than ten years.

B USE THE GRAMMAR Write two information questions in the simple past tense, one with How and one with What.

1 ....

2 ....

COMMUNICATION GOALS

1 Get reacquainted with someone.
2 Greet a visitor to your country.
3 Discuss gestures and customs.
4 Describe an interesting experience.

UNIT 1 Getting Acquainted

PREVIEW

CUSTOMS AROUND THE WORLD

Greetings

People greet each other differently around the world.

Some people bow.

Some people kiss once. Some kiss twice.

Some shake hands.

And some hug.

Exchanging Business Cards

People have different customs for exchanging business cards around the world.

Some customs are very formal. People always use two hands and look at the card carefully.

Other customs are informal. People accept a card with one hand and quickly put it in a pocket.

Getting Acquainted

What about small talk—the topics people talk about when they don't know each other well?

In some places, it's not polite to ask people about how much money they make or how old they are. But in other places, people think those topics are appropriate.

A **PAIR WORK** In your opinion, is there a right way and a wrong way to greet people? Explain.

B **DISCUSSION** In your country, are there any topics people should avoid during small talk? What about the topics below?

- the weather
- someone's job
- someone's religion
- someone's family
- someone's home
- (other) ___

ENGLISH FOR TODAY'S WORLD
Understand English speakers from different language backgrounds.
Leon = Spanish speaker
Taka = Japanese speaker

C ▶1:02 **PHOTO STORY** Read and listen to two people meeting in a hotel lobby.

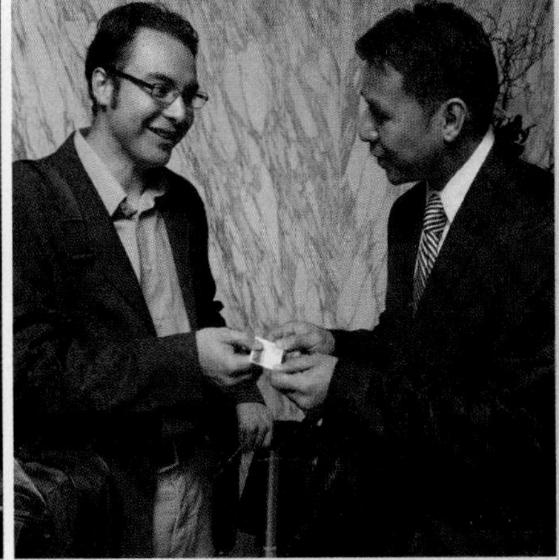

Leon: You look familiar. Haven't we met somewhere before?

Taka: I don't think so. I'm not from around here.

Leon: I know! Aren't you from Japan? I'm sure we met at the IT conference last week.

Taka: Of course! You're from Mexico, right?

Leon: That's right. I'm sorry. I've forgotten your name.

Taka: Kamura Takashi. But you can call me Taka.

Leon: Hi, Taka. Leon Prieto. Please call me Leon. So, what have you been up to since the conference?

Taka: Not much. Actually, I'm on my way to the airport now. I'm flying back home.

Leon: Hey, we should keep in touch. Here's my card. The conference is in Acapulco next year and I could show you around.

Taka: That would be great. I hear Acapulco's beautiful.

Leon: It was nice to see you again, Taka.

Taka: You, too.

D **FOCUS ON LANGUAGE** Find the underlined expression in the Photo Story that matches each explanation.

1 You say this when you want to offer to introduce someone to a new place.
2 You say this to suggest that someone call or e-mail you in the future.
3 You say this when you're not sure if you know someone, but you think you might.
4 You say this when you want to ask about someone's recent activities.

E **THINK AND EXPLAIN** Answer the questions, according to the Photo Story. Explain your answers.

1 Why does Leon begin speaking with Taka?
2 Has Taka been busy since the conference?
3 Why does Leon give Taka his business card?
4 What does Leon offer to do at the next conference?

"Because he thinks he knows Taka. He says, 'You look familiar.'"

SPEAKING

PAIR WORK With a partner, discuss and write advice for visitors about how to behave in your country. Then share your advice with the class.

Your advice
1
2
3

"Questions like *How old are you?* and *How much money do you make?* aren't polite. You shouldn't ask them."

"Don't exchange business cards with one hand! Always use two hands."

GOAL Get reacquainted with someone

GRAMMAR *The present perfect*

Use the present perfect to talk about an indefinite time in the past.
Form the present perfect with have or has and a past participle.

Affirmative and negative statements

We 've / haven't met them. She 's / hasn't called him.

Yes / no questions

A: Have you met them?
B: Yes, we have. / No, we haven't.

A: Has she called him?
B: Yes, she has. / No, she hasn't.

Remember: Use the simple past tense to talk about a definite or specific time.

present perfect: indefinite time	simple past tense: definite time
I've met Bill twice.	We met in 1999 and again in 2004.

Contractions

'**ve** met = have met
haven't met = have not met
'**s** met = has met
hasn't met = has not met

For regular verbs, the past participle form is the same as the simple past form.
open → opened
study → studied

Irregular verbs

base form	simple past	past participle
be	was / were	**been**
come	came	**come**
do	did	**done**
eat	ate	**eaten**
fall	fell	**fallen**
go	went	**gone**
have	had	**had**
make	made	**made**
meet	met	**met**
see	saw	**seen**
speak	spoke	**spoken**
take	took	**taken**
write	wrote	**written**

For more irregular verb forms, see page 123.

GRAMMAR BOOSTER p. 126
• The present perfect: information questions

A Choose the correct form to complete each sentence.

1 We've .... the 2:00 express train many times.
a take b took c taken

2 I had breakfast at 9:00, but I haven't .... lunch.
a have b had c having

3 Alison has .... to the mall.
a went b gone c go

4 My younger brother has .... home from work.
a come b came c comes

5 They posted some messages yesterday, but they haven't .... anything about their trip.
a written b write c wrote

B **PAIR WORK** Complete the conversations with the present perfect or the simple past tense. Then practice the conversations with a partner.

1 A: .... our new teacher? (Jake / meet)
B: Yes, ... He .... her in the office this morning. (meet)

2 A: .... to this class before? (they / be)
B: No, ... They're new at this school.

3 A: .... in the new school restaurant? (you / eat)
B: No, ... Is it good?

4 A: .... with the school director? (your classmates / speak)
B: Yes, ... They .... with her yesterday. (speak)

5 A: .... the new language lab? (Beth / see)
B: No, ... But she .... the library. (see)

C GRAMMAR PRACTICE Complete the message with the present perfect or the simple past tense.

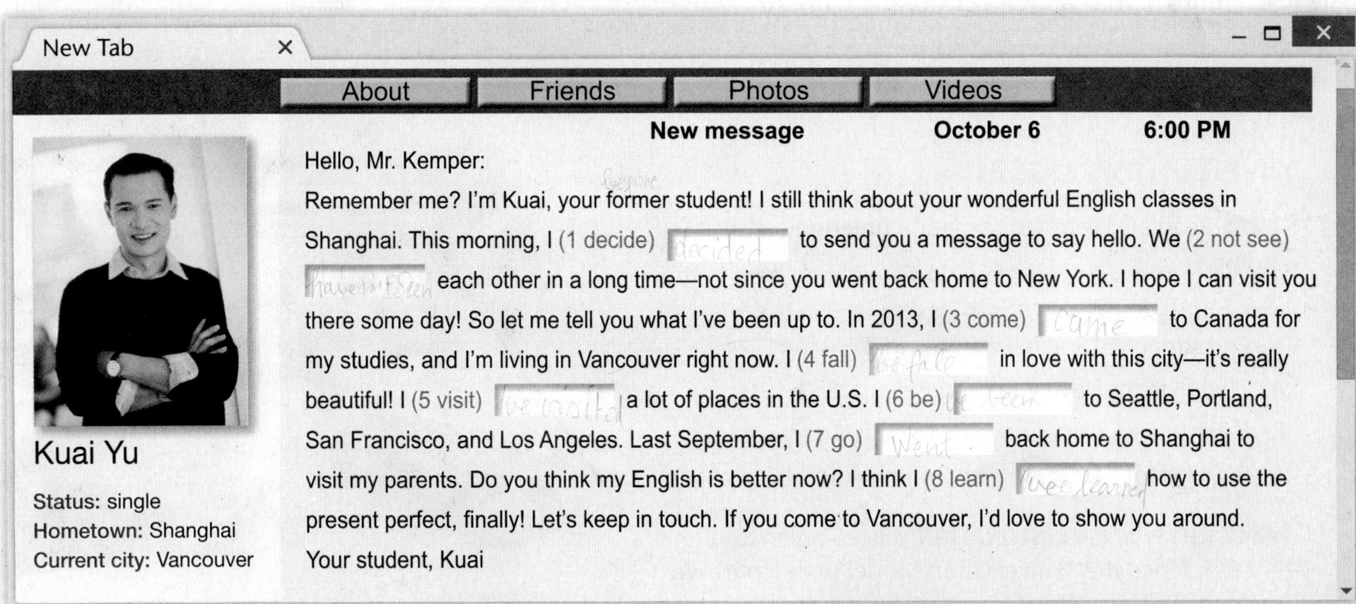

New Tab

About | Friends | Photos | Videos

New message **October 6** **6:00 PM**

Kuai Yu

Status: single
Hometown: Shanghai
Current city: Vancouver

Hello, Mr. Kemper:

Remember me? I'm Kuai, your former student! I still think about your wonderful English classes in Shanghai. This morning, I (1 decide) ______ to send you a message to say hello. We (2 not see) ______ each other in a long time—not since you went back home to New York. I hope I can visit you there some day! So let me tell you what I've been up to. In 2013, I (3 come) ______ to Canada for my studies, and I'm living in Vancouver right now. I (4 fall) ______ in love with this city—it's really beautiful! I (5 visit) ______ a lot of places in the U.S. I (6 be) ______ to Seattle, Portland, San Francisco, and Los Angeles. Last September, I (7 go) ______ back home to Shanghai to visit my parents. Do you think my English is better now? I think I (8 learn) ______ how to use the present perfect, finally! Let's keep in touch. If you come to Vancouver, I'd love to show you around.

Your student, Kuai

DIGITAL MORE EXERCISES

CONVERSATION MODEL

A 1:03 Read and listen to people getting reacquainted.

A: Audrey, have you met Hanah?
B: No, I haven't.
A: Hanah, I'd like you to meet Audrey.
C: Hi, Audrey. You look familiar. Have we met before?
B: I don't think so.
C: I know! Last month. You were at my sister Nicole's party.
B: Oh, that's right! How have you been?

B 1:04 **RHYTHM AND INTONATION** Listen again and repeat. Then practice the Conversation Model with a partner.

DIGITAL VIDEO COACH

PRONUNCIATION *Sound reduction in the present perfect*

A 1:05 Listen to how the sound /t/ of the negative contraction "disappears" in natural speech. Then listen again and repeat.

1 I haven't been to that class.
2 He hasn't met his new teacher.
3 They haven't taken the test.
4 She hasn't heard the news.

B Now practice saying the sentences on your own.

NOW YOU CAN Get reacquainted with someone

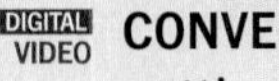

CONVERSATION ACTIVATOR With two other students, practice making introductions and getting reacquainted. Use your own names and the present perfect. Then change roles.

A: .... , have you met .... ?
B: No, I haven't.
A: .... , I'd like you to meet ....
C: .... You look familiar. Have we met before?
B: ....

DON'T STOP!

- Say how you have been.
- Say more about the time you met.
- Introduce other classmates.

Ideas

You met ...

- at a party
- at a meeting
- at a friend's house
- in another class
- (your own idea) ____

LESSON 2 **GOAL** Greet a visitor to your country

CONVERSATION MODEL

A ▶1:06 Read and listen to someone greeting a visitor.

A: Welcome to Beijing. Have you ever been here before?

B: No, it's my first time. But yesterday I went to the Forbidden Palace. It was fantastic!

A: That's great. Have you tried Beijing duck yet?

B: Beijing duck? No, I haven't. What's that?

A: It's a famous Chinese dish. I think you'll like it.

The Forbidden Palace

Beijing duck

B ▶1:07 **RHYTHM AND INTONATION** Listen again and repeat. Then practice the Conversation Model with a partner.

DIGITAL FLASH CARDS

VOCABULARY *Tourist activities around the world*

A ▶1:08 Read and listen. Then listen again and repeat.

climb Mt. Fuji

go sightseeing in New York

go to the top of the Eiffel Tower

try Korean food

take a tour of the Tower of London

take pictures of the Great Wall

B **PAIR WORK** Use the Vocabulary to say what you have and haven't done.

"I've climbed two famous mountains."

"I haven't tried Indian food."

GRAMMAR *The present perfect: already, yet, ever, before, and never*

Use ever or before in yes / no questions about *life experiences*.

Have you ever eaten Indian food? Has he been to Paris before?

Use yet or already in yes / no questions about *recent experiences*.

Have you toured Quito yet? Has she already been to the top of the Eiffel Tower?

In affirmative and negative statements

We've already seen the Great Wall.	We haven't tried Beijing duck yet.
They have never visited Mexico.	They haven't ever visited Mexico.
He's been to New York before.	He hasn't been to Boston before.

Always place before and yet at the end of statements and questions.

Be careful!

I **have never** (OR **haven't ever**) been there.
NOT I ~~haven't never~~ been there.

GRAMMAR BOOSTER p. 126

- Yet and already: expansion, common errors
- Ever, never, and before: use and placement

A **GRAMMAR PRACTICE** Use the words to write statements or questions in the present perfect.

1 (you / go sightseeing / in London / before)
2 (she / already / try / Guatemalan food)
3 (they / ever / be / to Buenos Aires)
4 (we / not take a tour of / Prague / yet)

B ▶1:09 **LISTEN TO ACTIVATE GRAMMAR** Listen and complete the questions, using the Vocabulary. Then listen again and complete the short answers.

Questions	Short Answers
1 Has she .... of the Taj Mahal yet?	.... , she ....
2 Has he .... in Kyoto yet?	.... , he ....
3 Has she ever .... ceviche?	.... , she ....
4 Has he already .... the Pyramid of the Sun?	.... , he ....
5 Has she ever .... to Rio de Janeiro before?	.... , she ....
6 Has she .... of Sugarloaf yet?	.... , she ....

The Taj Mahal • India

A temple • Kyoto, Japan

Ceviche • Peru

The Pyramid of the Sun • Mexico City

Sugarloaf • Rio de Janeiro, Brazil

C Write five questions about tourist activities in your city or country. Use yet, already, ever, and before.

Have you ever tried our seafood dishes?

1 ....
2 ....
3 ....
4 ....
5 ....

DIGITAL MORE EXERCISES

NOW YOU CAN Greet a visitor to your country

A **NOTEPADDING** On the notepad, write at least five activities for a tourist in your city or country.

Activity	Description
try Beijing duck	*It's a famous Chinese dish.*

Activity	Description

DIGITAL VIDEO

B **CONVERSATION ACTIVATOR** With a partner, change the Conversation Model to greet a visitor to your country. Use the present perfect. Suggest tourist activities in your city. Use your notepad. Then change roles.

A: Welcome to .... Have you ever been here before?
B: No, it's my first time. But yesterday I ....
A: .... Have you .... yet?
B: ....

DON'T STOP!

- Ask about other places and tourist activities.

C **CHANGE PARTNERS** Practice the conversation again, asking about other tourist activities on your notepad.

GOAL Discuss gestures and customs

BEFORE YOU READ

DIGITAL FLASH CARDS

1:10 **VOCABULARY • *The hand*** Read and listen. Then listen again and repeat.

1 thumb
2 index finger
3 middle finger
4 ring finger
5 pinkie
6 palm
7 fist

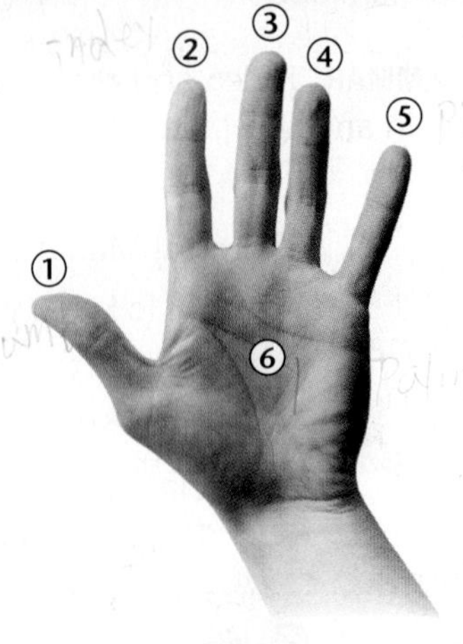
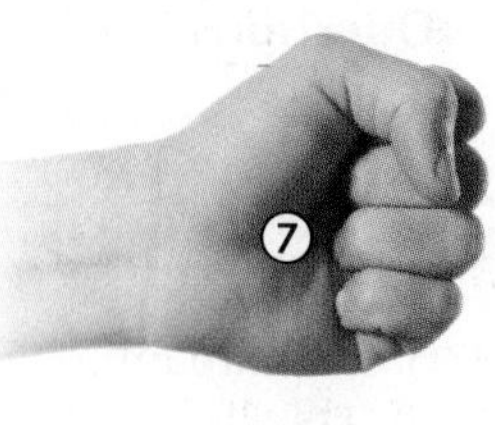

READING 1:11

We talked to June Galloway about her book,
Get off on the Right Foot: Don't Let the Wrong Gesture Ruin Your Day.

English is the world's international language. But in your book, you've focused on non-verbal communication. Why is that so important?
Well, gestures and other body language can have different meanings in different places. Something that you think is friendly or polite could come across as very rude in another culture. I've described many of these customs and cultural differences so my readers don't get off on the wrong foot when they meet people from places where the culture differs from their own.

Can greeting someone in the wrong way really lead to misunderstanding?
In some cases, yes. The firm handshake a North American expects may seem quite aggressive in other places. And a light handshake—which is normal in some countries—may seem unfriendly to a North American.

In what ways can hand gestures lead to misunderstanding?
Well, as an example, we assume all people indicate the numbers one to ten with their fingers the same way. But in fact, they don't. While North Americans usually use an index finger for "one," most Europeans use a thumb. North Americans extend all ten fingers for "ten." However, Chinese indicate the numbers one to ten all on one hand. For example, an extended thumb and pinkie means "six," and a fist means "ten." Imagine how confusing this can be when you're trying to communicate quantities and prices with your hands!

What other gestures can cause confusion?
Take the gesture for "come here," for example. In North America, people gesture with the palm up. Well, in southern Europe, that gesture means "good-bye"! And in many Asian countries, the palm-up gesture is considered rude. Instead, people there gesture with the palm down.

I've heard that, in Japan, pointing with the index finger is not polite. Is that right?
Yes. Japanese prefer to point with the palm open and facing up.

Surely there must be some gestures used everywhere, right? What about the thumbs-up sign for "great"?
Sorry. That's extremely rude in Australia and the Middle East. This is why it's so important to be aware of these cultural differences.

What gesture do you use . . .

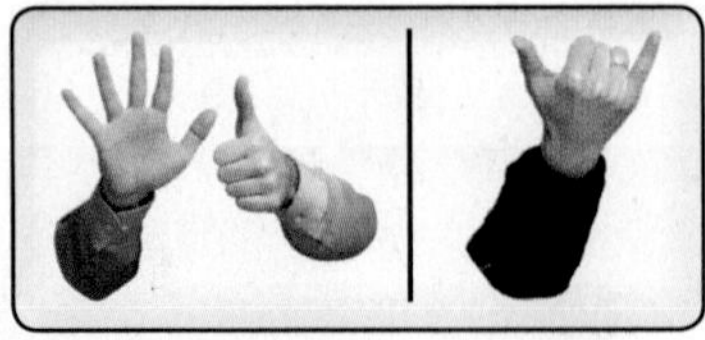

. . . for the number six?

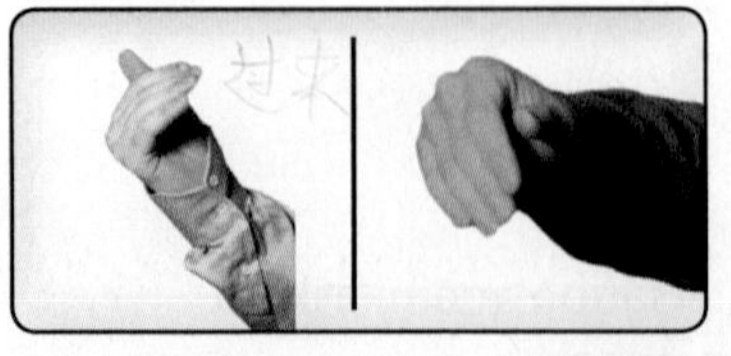

. . . for "Come here": palm up or down?

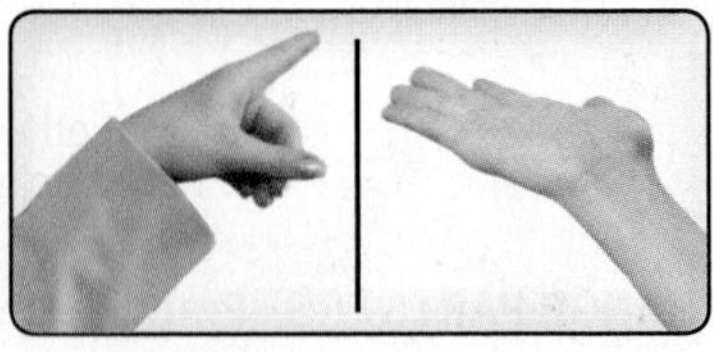

. . . for pointing? Do you use your index finger or an open palm?

A IDENTIFY SUPPORTING DETAILS Check the statements that are true, according to the article. Write ✗ next to the statements that are not true. Explain your answers.

- ☐ **1** In most of Europe, a thumb and an index finger mean "two."
- ☐ **2** In North America, a thumb and a pinkie mean "two."
- ☐ **3** Japanese point at pictures with an open palm facing up.
- ☐ **4** To be friendly, North Americans greet others with a light handshake.
- ☐ **5** Everyone uses the thumbs-up sign for "that's good."

"True. Galloway says most Europeans begin with the thumb. So the index finger is the next finger after that."

B RELATE TO PERSONAL EXPERIENCE Discuss the questions.

DIGITAL MORE EXERCISES

Have you ever been surprised by someone's gestures or body language on TV, in the movies, or in real life? What did you see? What do you think the action meant? Why were you surprised?

NOW YOU CAN Discuss gestures and customs

A PAIR WORK Read the travel tips about gestures and customs around the world. Compare your own gestures and customs with those described. Do any of them seem strange or rude?

Travel Tips

If someone gives you a gift, thank the person and open it right away. (Ecuador)

If you want to get a server's attention, it's more polite to use eye contact rather than hand gestures. (Kenya)

When a visitor is leaving your home, you should walk with that person out the door. (Korea)

When greeting people, older people should always be greeted first. (Mongolia)

If you are going to be more than 15 minutes late for a party, lunch, or dinner, you should call to explain. (United States)

Before you enter someone's home, you should take off your shoes. (Ukraine)

To gesture that something is good, hold your hand up, palm facing out, and slowly bring all your fingers to the thumb. (Turkey)

B NOTEPADDING With a partner, choose a topic and discuss your country's customs. Then write notes about your country on the notepad.

Topic: *showing respect for older people.*
Customs: *It's not polite to disagree with an older person.*

Topic:
Customs:

Are the rules the same for both men and women? How about for young people or older people? Explain.

Topics
- showing respect to older people
- do's and don'ts for gestures
- topics for polite small talk
- invitations
- visiting someone's home
- giving gifts
- offering or refusing food
- touching or not touching
- (your own topic) ___

Text-mining (optional)
Find and underline three words or phrases in the Reading that were new to you. Use them in your Discussion.
For example: "body language."

C DISCUSSION Tell your classmates about the customs you described on your notepad. Does everyone agree?

LESSON 4 **GOAL** Describe an interesting experience

BEFORE YOU LISTEN

DIGITAL FLASH CARDS **A** 1:12 **VOCABULARY • *Participial adjectives*** Read and listen. Then listen again and repeat.

The safari was **fascinating**. (They were **fascinated**.)

The ski trip was **thrilling**. (They were **thrilled**.)

The sky-dive was **frightening**. (They were **frightened**.)

The food was **disgusting**. (They were **disgusted**.)

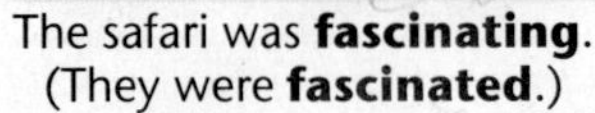

B Write lists of things you think are fascinating, thrilling, frightening, or disgusting.

C **PAIR WORK** Compare your lists.

"I've never eaten snails. I think they're disgusting!"

"Really? I've tried them, and I wasn't disgusted at all. They're good!"

LISTENING COMPREHENSION

A 1:13 **LISTEN TO CLASSIFY** Listen to the three interviews. Then listen again and write the number of the speaker described by each statement.

.... **a** travels to have thrilling experiences
.... **b** describes differences in body language
.... **c** was disgusted by something
.... **d** is fascinated by other cultures
.... **e** tries to be polite
.... **f** does things that other people think are frightening

2 Andrew Barlow

1 Nancy Sullivan

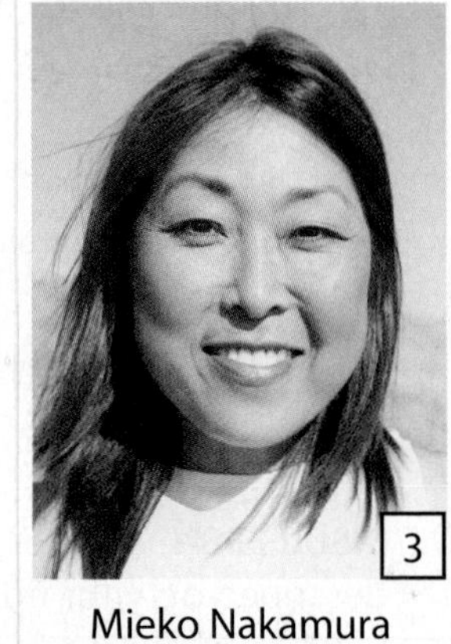

3 Mieko Nakamura

B 1:14 **LISTEN FOR DETAILS** Listen again and answer the questions in complete sentences.

1 Nancy Sullivan

a How many countries has she visited? ....

b What did she notice about gestures in India? ....

2 Andrew Barlow

c What did the people in the village do to thank him? ....

d Why did he eat something he didn't want to? ....

3 Mieko Nakamura

e What has she done twice? ....

f How did she get to "the top of the world"? ....

NOW YOU CAN Describe an interesting experience

A **NOTEPADDING** Answer the questions. Explain what happened. Write as many details as you can.

Have you ever been someplace that was really fascinating?

Have you ever eaten something that was really strange or disgusting?

Have you ever done something that was really thrilling or frightening?

B **PAIR WORK** Ask your partner about the experiences on his or her notepad.

DON'T STOP!

- Ask more questions.
- Ask about other experiences: "Have you ever . . ."

RECYCLE THIS LANGUAGE.

climb [a mountain]
go sightseeing in [Italy]
go to the top of [the Eiffel Tower]
try [snails]
take a tour of [New York]
take pictures of [the Taj Mahal]

C **GROUP WORK** Choose one of the experiences your partner told you about. Tell your classmates about your partner's experience.

"My partner went hang gliding last year. She was frightened, but it was really thrilling."

hang gliding

REVIEW

A ▶1:15 Listen to the conversation with a tourist in Vancouver and check Yes or No. Then listen again and write the answers to the questions, using yet or already.

Has she. . .	**Yes**	**No**	
1 been to the Vancouver Aquarium?	☑	☐	*Yes. She's already been to the aquarium.*
2 visited Gastown?	☐	☐	....
3 been to the top of Grouse Mountain?	☐	☐	....
4 seen the Capilano Suspension Bridge?	☐	☐	....
5 tried dim sum?	☐	☐	....
6 gone to the top of the Harbour Centre Tower?	☐	☐	....

B Use the photos to write questions using the present perfect with ever or before. Don't use the same verb more than once.

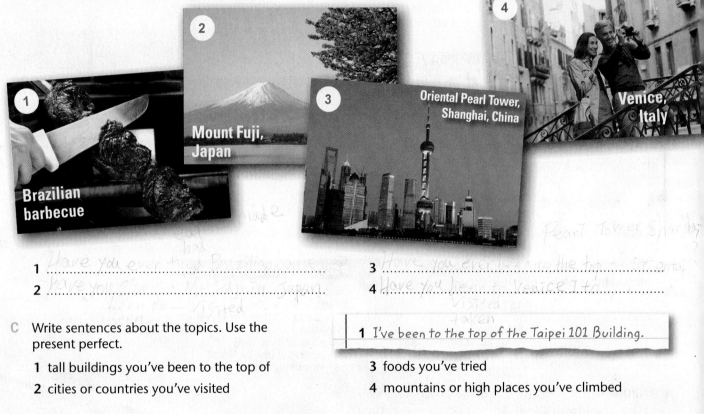

1 Brazilian barbecue

2 Mount Fuji, Japan

3 Oriental Pearl Tower, Shanghai, China

4 Venice, Italy

1 .... **3** ....

2 .... **4** ....

C Write sentences about the topics. Use the present perfect.

1 I've been to the top of the Taipei 101 Building.

1 tall buildings you've been to the top of

2 cities or countries you've visited

3 foods you've tried

4 mountains or high places you've climbed

WRITING

Write about one of the interesting experiences you talked about in Lesson 4. Describe what happened, where you were, who you were with, and how you felt.

I've had a few frightening experiences in my life.
Last year, I was on vacation in . . .

WRITING BOOSTER p. 143
- Avoiding run-on sentences
- Guidance for this writing exercise

For additional language practice . . .

♫ TOP NOTCH POP • Lyrics p. 153
"Greetings and Small Talk"

DIGITAL SONG   DIGITAL KARAOKE

DIGITAL GAMES

ORAL REVIEW

PAIR WORK

1 Create a conversation for the man and woman in photo 1. Imagine the man is welcoming the woman to his city. Choose one of the cities in the travel brochure.

Welcome to Paris. Have you been here before?

2 Create a conversation for the three people in photo 2. Imagine they get reacquainted during a tour of Europe.

A: Have you met __?
B: Actually, you look familiar. Have we met before?
C: Yes, I think we have. We were at the ...

3 Look at the brochure and imagine that you are on one of these tours. Ask and answer questions, using the present perfect.

Have you tried tapas yet?

Tour **Europe**

SPAIN | FRANCE | ITALY | THE U.K. | RUSSIA

Madrid, Spain

The Prado Museum

Tapas

London, the U.K.

The Millennium Wheel

Carnaby Street

Paris, France

The Eiffel Tower

Tour boat on the Seine River

Moscow, Russia

Borscht

Ballet at the Bolshoi Theater

Rome, Italy

The Colosseum

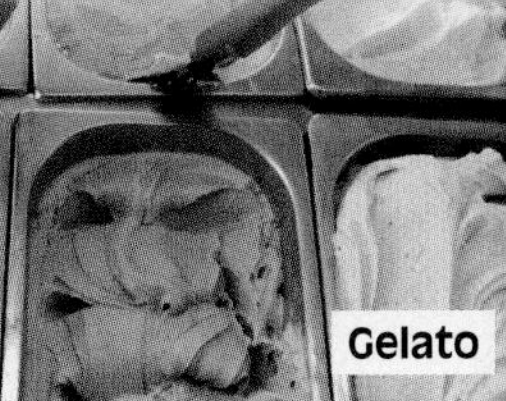

Gelato

NOW I CAN

- ☐ Get reacquainted with someone.
- ☐ Greet a visitor to my country.
- ☐ Discuss gestures and customs.
- ☐ Describe an interesting experience.

COMMUNICATION GOALS

1 Apologize for being late.
2 Discuss preferences for movie genres.
3 Describe and recommend movies.
4 Discuss effects of violence on viewers.

UNIT 2 Going to the Movies

PREVIEW

Log In | Your account | Help

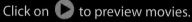

WebFlicks Stream to watch instantly or add disc to your wish list

Leonardo DiCaprio Click on ▶ to preview movies.

Titanic 3D 1997 (3D 2012)
194 minutes
This 1997 blockbuster disaster movie (11 Oscars!) is the true story of the ill-fated ocean liner *Titanic*. But it's also a 194-minute love story. Rose (Kate Winslet), an unhappy young woman, falls in love with Jack (DiCaprio), a poor artist who gives her life meaning. The scenes of the sinking of the magnificent *Titanic* are truly frightening. An epic classic romance!
Genre: Romantic drama, disaster

★★★★★
Stream
Add disc to your wish list

Blood Diamond 2006
143 minutes
DiCaprio stars as an ex-criminal involved in the violent diamond trade during the 1999 civil war in Sierra Leone. He joins up with a fisherman (Djimon Hounsou) to try to find a pink diamond that they think can change both of their lives. This thrilling action movie will keep you sitting on the edge of your seat.
Genre: Action, drama

Stream
Add disc to your wish list

The Great Gatsby 2013
143 minutes
This beautiful adaptation of F. Scott Fitzgerald's fascinating 1925 novel of the same name tells the story of neighbors from the fictional town of West Egg on New York's Long Island in the summer of 1922. The main character, a mysterious millionaire, Jay Gatsby (DiCaprio), falls in love with the beautiful Daisy Buchanan (Carey Mulligan), but the story ends in tragedy.
Genre: Romantic drama

★★★★★

Stream
Add disc to your wish list

More DiCaprio movies

BY GENRE
comedy, crime, drama, romance, action, disaster

BY TITLE
The Man in the Iron Mask (1998)
The Beach (2000)
Gangs of New York (2002)
Catch Me If You Can (2002)
The Aviator (2004)
The Departed (2006)
Body of Lies (2008)
Shutter Island (2010)
Inception (2010)
The Wolf of Wall Street (2013)

A **PAIR WORK** Did you see any of these DiCaprio movies when they were in the theater? If so, tell your partner about them. If not, is there one you would like to see now? Explain why.

B **DISCUSSION** Where do you like to see movies: at home or in a movie theater? Explain your reasons.

C ▶1:18 **PHOTO STORY** Read and listen to a conversation at a movie theater.

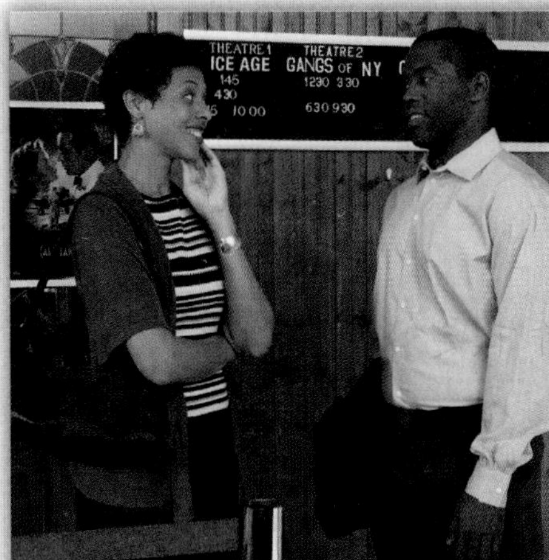

Anna: So, what are you in the mood for? They've got a bunch of great classic movies tonight.

Peter: They sure do. Hey, you're a big DiCaprio fan. I missed *Gangs of New York* when it was playing. Have you ever seen it?

Anna: Nope, I haven't. I've heard it's pretty violent. Frankly, I just can't take all that fighting.

Peter: Yeah. It *is* supposed to be pretty bloody. . . . What else?

Anna: Well, there's *Ice Age*. They say it's spectacular. What do you think?

Peter: Hmm. To tell you the truth, I can't stand animated films. Sorry. I've just never liked them. I think I'd rather see something . . .

Peter: Hey! What about *Casablanca*?

Anna: *Casablanca*? Now you're talking! And by the way, it's my treat. You paid last time. What do you say?

Peter: It's a deal! I'll get the popcorn.

D **FOCUS ON LANGUAGE** Find underlined words or phrases in the Photo Story that have almost the same meaning as the ones below.

1 "I'll pay."
2 "really don't like"
3 "To tell you the truth, . . ."
4 "a lot of"
5 "I didn't see . . ."
6 "They say . . ."

E **INFER MEANING** With a partner, discuss, find, and underline . . .

1 a noun that has the same meaning as "movie."
2 two different adjectives that are related to "fighting" or "killing."
3 an adjective that means "really great."

F **THINK AND EXPLAIN** First answer each question. Then explain your answer with a quotation from the Photo Story.

1 What actor does Anna like? Leonardo DiCaprio
How do you know?
Peter says, "Hey, you're a big DiCaprio fan."

2 Did Anna see *Gangs of New York*? ....
How do you know?
....

3 What movie does Anna suggest? ....
How do you know?
....

4 Who is going to pay for the popcorn? ....
How do you know?
....

SPEAKING

PAIR WORK Make a list of movies playing in your town. Which movies would you like to see? Which movies would you not like to see? Give reasons for your answers.

LESSON 1 **GOAL** Apologize for being late

GRAMMAR *The present perfect: for and since; Other uses of the present perfect*

Use for and since to describe periods of time that began in the past. Use for to describe a length of time. Use since with a specific time or date in the past.

How long have you been here? | I've been here for ten minutes. (a length of time)
I've been here for many years. (a length of time)
I've been here since eight o'clock. (a specific time in the past)

Be careful!
They've lived here since **2013**.
NOT They've lived here ~~since five years~~.

Other uses:

- with always: I've always wanted to see *Car Planet*.
- with ordinals and superlatives: This is the third time I've seen *Ping Pong*. It's the best movie I've ever seen.
- with lately, recently, or just: Have you seen a good movie recently (or lately)? I've just seen *The Beach*—what a great movie!
- with still or so far: You still haven't seen *Tomato Babies*? I've seen it three times so far!

GRAMMAR BOOSTER p. 127
- The present perfect continuous: unfinished actions
- Spelling rules for the present participle: review, common errors

A GRAMMAR PRACTICE Choose the correct words to complete the paragraph.

I've been a big fan of Penélope Cruz (1 for / since) more than twenty years. I've followed her career (2 since / so far) I was in high school. That means I've watched every movie she's made (3 for / since) 1993, except for *Vicky Cristina Barcelona*. I (4 yet / still) haven't seen that one, but I plan to see it soon. I've (5 still / always) loved Penélope's work. I've (6 since / always) been the first person in line at the theater when her movies open. Of the movies Penélope has made (7 lately / always), the most interesting ones to me are *To Rome with Love* and *I'm So Excited*. I think they're the (8 best / just) movies she's made (9 so far / still). I've (10 always / already) seen them twice!

B PAIR WORK Take turns asking and answering the questions. Use the present perfect in all your answers.

1 Is there a movie you've always wanted to see?
2 Have you seen any good movies recently?
3 What's the best movie you've ever seen?
4 What's the worst movie you've ever seen?
5 How many movies have you seen so far this month?
6 Is there a classic movie that you still haven't seen?

DIGITAL MORE EXERCISES

VOCABULARY *Explanations for being late*

DIGITAL FLASH CARDS

A 1:19 Read and listen. Then listen again and repeat.

I overslept.

I missed the bus.

I couldn't get a taxi.

I couldn't find a parking space.

I got stuck in traffic.

B PAIR WORK Think of two other explanations for being late.

C ▶1:20 **LISTEN TO ACTIVATE VOCABULARY** Listen to the conversations. Complete the sentences, inferring the information and using the Vocabulary.

1 Ted's late because he ....
2 Maude probably ....
3 They're going to be late because they ....
4 First they .... Then they probably ....

PRONUNCIATION *Reduction of h*

▶1:21 Notice how the sound /h/ often disappears in natural speech. Read and listen. Then listen again and repeat.

1 How long have you waited?
2 Where have you been?
3 What has he read about the film?
4 When did he buy the tickets?
5 What's her favorite movie?
6 Who's his favorite star?

CONVERSATION MODEL

A ▶1:22 Read and listen to someone apologize for being late.

A: Have you been here long?
B: For about ten minutes.
A: Sorry I'm late. I got stuck in traffic. Did you get tickets?
B: Yes. But the 8:00 show for *The Love Boat* is sold out. I got tickets for *Paradise Island.* I hope that's OK.
A: That's fine. How much do I owe?
B: Nothing. It's on me.
A: Well, thanks! Next time it's my treat.

B ▶1:23 **RHYTHM AND INTONATION** Listen again and repeat. Then practice the Conversation Model with a partner.

NOW YOU CAN Apologize for being late

A Add four more movies to the showtimes.

Stuck in Traffic	7:00	9:00	11:00
	7:30	9:35	[7:30 sold out]
	7:45	10:20	midnight
	8:00	11:00	[8:00 sold out]
	7:50	10:10	

B **CONVERSATION ACTIVATOR** With a partner, personalize the Conversation Model with your movies and explanations. Then change roles.

A: Have you been here long?
B: For ....
A: Sorry I'm late. I .... Did you get tickets?
B: Yes. But .... I hope that's OK.
A: ....

DON'T STOP!

- Say more about the movie.
- Offer to pay.
- Discuss what to do after the show.

RECYCLE THIS LANGUAGE.

[Titanic 3] is sold out.
We missed __.
It started __ minutes ago.
I've already seen __.
That's past my bedtime!
I'm not a [Naomi Watts] fan.
I've heard [it's spectacular].
They say [it's pretty violent].
How much do I owe?
It's on me.
It's my treat.

C **CHANGE PARTNERS** Practice the conversation again, making other changes.

LESSON 2 GOAL Discuss preferences for movie genres

DIGITAL FLASH CARDS VOCABULARY *Movie genres*

A ▶1:24 Read and listen. Then listen again and repeat.

an action film

a horror film

a science-fiction film

an animated film

a comedy

a drama

a documentary

a musical

B **PAIR WORK** Compare your favorite movies for each genre.

"My favorite animated film is *Frozen*."

C ▶1:25 **LISTEN TO INFER** Listen and write the genre for each movie in the chart. Then circle the movie if the people decided to see it.

D **DISCUSSION** Which movies sound good to you? Listen again if necessary. Explain your choices.

Movie	Genre
1 *The Bottom of the Sea*	
2 *Tango in Tap Shoes*	
3 *The Ant Who Wouldn't Die*	
4 *Chickens Never Wear Shoes*	
5 *Goldilocks Grows Up*	
6 *The Equalizer*	
7 *Twelve Angry Women*	
8 *City Under the Sea*	

GRAMMAR *Ways to express wants and preferences*

Would like

Use would like + an infinitive (to + a base form) to politely express or ask about wants.

I'd like to go to the movies.
Would she like to see *The Dancer*?
What would your friends like to do?

I / She / We / They	'd like	to see a comedy.

Would rather

Use would rather + a base form to express or ask about a preference between two or more activities.

Would your children rather see an animated film or an action film?
What would you rather do: go to a movie or a play?
She'd rather see a less violent film than *Gangs of New York*.

I / He / We / They	'd rather	see a drama.

Use would rather not + a base form to express a negative preference.

We'd rather not watch TV tonight.

Yes / no questions	short answers
Would you like to see a documentary?	Yes, I would. / No, I wouldn't.
Would they rather stay home?	Yes, they would. / No, they wouldn't. OR No, they'd rather not.

Be careful!

Would you rather see *Titanic*? Yes, **I would.**
NOT Yes, I ~~would rather~~.
Would they like to go out tonight? Yes, **they would.**
NOT Yes, they ~~would like~~.
Would your parents like to go to the early show?
Yes, **they would.** NOT Yes, ~~they'd~~.

GRAMMAR BOOSTER p. 128
- Expressing preferences: review, expansion, and common errors.

A **GRAMMAR PRACTICE** Complete the conversations about wants and preferences.

1 A: (I like / I'd like) to see *Star Wars X* again. Would you? It's at the CineMax.
B: Actually, (I'd rather. / I'd rather not.) Let's stay home.

2 A: (Do you like / Would you like) to stream something on TV?
B: Yes, (I'd like. / I would.)

3 A: What would you rather (see / to see): a science fiction film or a comedy?
B: Me? (I'd rather / I rather) see a science fiction movie.

4 A: There's a musical and a horror movie on TV. (Would / Does) your husband rather see the horror movie?
B: Yes, (he would rather. / he would.)

5 A: My sister (would like to / would like) go to the movies on Friday.
B: Great. (I would / I would like), too.

B **PAIR WORK** Use would like and would rather to ask your partner about movies he or she would like to see and his or her preferences.

"Would you like to see *Boomerang*?"

"What would you rather see: a documentary or a drama?"

CONVERSATION MODEL

A 1:26 Read and listen to people discussing their movie preferences.

A: What would you rather do: stay home and stream a movie or go to the theater?
B: I'd rather go out. Is that OK?
A: Sure! . . . Would you rather see *Horror City* or *Love in Paris*?
B: Are you kidding? I can't stand horror movies, and to tell you the truth, I'm not that big on love stories.
A: Well, how about a documentary? *The Great Wall of China* is playing, too. I've heard it's great.
B: That works for me!

1:28 Ways to agree on a plan
That works for me.
It's a deal!
Great idea!

B 1:27 **RHYTHM AND INTONATION** Listen again and repeat. Then practice the Conversation Model with a partner.

NOW YOU CAN Discuss preferences for movie genres

A **CONVERSATION ACTIVATOR** Write the names of some movies. With a partner, change the Conversation Model, using your own movies. Then change roles.

A: What would you rather do: stay home and stream a movie or go to the theater?
B: I'd rather .... Is that OK?
A: .... Would you rather see .... or .... ?
B: Are you kidding? I can't stand .... , and to tell you the truth, I ....
A: Well, how about .... ?

DON'T STOP!

- Say more about the movies and express more movie preferences.

I don't like / hate / love __s.
Have you ever seen __?
I missed it.
Frankly, __ .
I'm not that big on __s.
I've heard / They say it's [fascinating, thrilling, frightening, disgusting].

B **CHANGE PARTNERS** Change the conversation again, using different movies.

LESSON 3 GOAL **Describe and recommend movies**

BEFORE YOU LISTEN

DIGITAL FLASH CARDS

A 1:29 **VOCABULARY • *Adjectives to describe movies*** Read and listen. Then listen again and repeat.

funny something that makes you laugh

hilarious very, very funny

silly not serious; almost stupid

boring not interesting

weird very strange or unusual, in a negative way

unforgettable something you are going to remember

romantic about love

thought-provoking something that makes you think

violent bloody; with a lot of fighting and killing

B **PAIR WORK** Write the title of a movie for each adjective. Then tell your partner about your choices.

a funny movie	
a hilarious movie	
a silly movie	
a boring movie	
a weird movie	
an unforgettable movie	
a romantic movie	
a thought-provoking movie	
a violent movie	

LISTENING COMPREHENSION

A 1:30 **LISTEN FOR MAIN IDEAS** Listen to the movie reviewer. Write a check next to the movies he recommends, and write an ✗ next to the ones he doesn't.

1 ☐ *Popcorn* 2 ☐ *The Vacation* 3 ☐ *Aquamundo* 4 ☐ *Wolf Babies*

B 1:31 **LISTEN TO INFER** Listen carefully to each movie review again. Based on the reviewer's opinion, circle one or more adjectives to describe each movie.

1 *Popcorn* (weird / funny / boring)

2 *The Vacation* (romantic / violent / unforgettable)

3 *Aquamundo* (boring / violent / thought-provoking)

4 *Wolf Babies* (violent / boring / hilarious)

C 1:32 **LISTENING: DICTATION** Listen to the following excerpts from the reviews. Complete each statement, based on what you hear.

POPCORN ★

① First up is *Popcorn*, a new .... starring David Bodine and Judy Crabbe. ② Unfortunately, *Popcorn* is a complete waste of ....

THE VACATION ★ ★ ★ ★ ★

③ Our next film, *The Vacation*, is a well-acted and .... ④ I highly .... wonderful ....

AQUAMUNDO ★ ★ ★

⑤ *Aquamundo* is no .... film; it's based on real scientific research. ⑥ A .... film. Don't ....

WOLF BABIES ★ ★ ★

⑦ Adults will find the story ...., but children won't forget these .... , scary scenes for a long time.

NOW YOU CAN Describe and recommend movies

A **PAIR WORK** Read the short movie reviews and choose the movie you think sounds the most interesting. Then compare movie choices. Explain your reasons.

WHAT'S YOUR ALL-TIME FAVORITE MOVIE?

Phil Ito Toronto, CANADA

I've just seen *Tootsie*. What a great movie—perhaps one of the most hilarious romantic comedies of all time. Before I saw the movie, I thought the plot sounded both weird and silly, but it wasn't. Dustin Hoffman stars as out-of-work actor Michael Dorsey, who dresses as a woman to get a part on a TV drama. But problems begin when he falls in love with his co-star, Jessica Lange, who doesn't know Michael is a man. If you want a good laugh, be sure to see this funny, funny film!

Angela Teixeira Fortaleza, BRAZIL

When someone says that documentaries are boring, I say, "You have to see *Grizzly Man*," one of the most thought-provoking documentaries of all time. This 2005 movie by German director Werner Herzog tells the true story of the life and death of Timothy Treadwell, who lived for 13 years among bears in the Alaska wilderness. Treadwell believed that he could live near bears without danger. In the end, however, Treadwell and his girlfriend are killed by bears. Even if you would rather avoid violence, go to see *Grizzly Man* because there is no actual violence on screen.

Rebecca Lane Miami, USA

I've just seen *Casablanca* for the hundredth time. It's the most romantic movie in the world, and there's no movie I would rather see. Humphrey Bogart and Ingrid Bergman star as former lovers who meet after many years. They're still in love and have to make some difficult choices. The ending is unforgettable and always makes me cry. This movie was made in 1942, but it's always "new." I guess that's what makes it a classic.

B **NOTEPADDING** Write notes about a movie you've seen recently. (It's OK if you don't have all the information.)

Title of film:

Genre:

Stars:

Director or producer:

Adjectives that describe the movie:

What the movie is about:

C **GROUP WORK** Describe and recommend the movies on your notepads. Use adjectives from the Vocabulary and other adjectives you know.

DON'T STOP!

- Ask questions.

RECYCLE THIS LANGUAGE.

Questions	More adjectives	
Was it [funny / silly / scary]?	thrilling	exciting
Who was in it?	fascinating	great
What kind of movie was it?	frightening	interesting
Do you recommend it?	disgusting	bloody
What was it about?	scary	unusual
	popular	terrific
	awful	pretty good

Text-mining (optional)
Look at the reviews in Exercise A. Find and underline three words or phrases that were new to you. Use them in your Group Work. For example: "falls in love with . . ."

LESSON 4 GOAL Discuss effects of violence on viewers

BEFORE YOU READ

WARM-UP At what age do you think it's safe to permit children to see violent movies and TV shows? Explain.

READING ▶1:33

Can Violent Movies or TV Programs Harm Children?

Many people say that children have become more aggressive in recent years—that is, they are more likely to fight with their friends, sisters, and brothers. A number of scientific studies have reported that watching violence can, in fact, cause a growth in aggression. According to the research, two kinds of programs and movies encourage aggressive behavior in young children more than others: (1) realistic violent action programs and movies, and (2) violent cartoons.

One disturbing conclusion is that the effects of violent viewing last for many years. One study showed that children who watched violent TV programs when they were 8 years old were more likely to behave aggressively at age 18. Furthermore, as adults they were more likely to be convicted of violent crimes, such as child abuse and murder.

Studies have also demonstrated that watching violent movies and TV shows can affect children's attitudes towards violence in the world around them. Children who watch a lot of fighting and bloodshed tend to find it "normal" and may accept more violence in society. They may even begin to commit violent acts themselves.

Very often, characters in movies and on television who commit violent crimes are not sorry for their actions and don't face consequences or punishment. When children see fictional characters who are criminals like these, they learn that doing bad things is OK. For children, who are growing and developing, this is a bad message. It's important for them to see that our society doesn't tolerate crime.

So what can we do? With young children, we have the power to control the TV programs and movies they watch, so we can protect them from seeing any violence at all. However, with older children it's impossible to completely prevent their exposure to violence. But we can try to limit the number of hours they spend watching it. And when children have seen a violent film or TV show, it's important to discuss it with them, to help them understand that violence is not a normal part of life.

A UNDERSTAND FROM CONTEXT Circle the correct word or phrase to complete each statement, according to the information in the article.

1 (A realistic / An aggressive) person is someone who is likely to fight with others.

2 Scientific studies have reported that some kinds of movies and TV programs can (limit / encourage) aggressive behavior.

3 One kind of violent crime is (murder / bad behavior).

4 A word that means almost the same thing as hurt is (help / harm).

5 It's difficult to (permit / prevent) older children from seeing any violence on TV and in movies.

6 Research has suggested that (a consequence / an advantage) of watching violent films is aggressive behavior.

B **CONFIRM CONTENT** Discuss the questions, using the information in the article. Then share your answers with the class.

1 According to the article, what are some ways that viewing violence can affect children?
2 What kinds of programs and movies are most harmful?
3 According to the article, some studies show that viewing violence can have effects that last for many years. What are some of these long-term effects?
4 What bad "message" can come from violent programs and movies?
5 What suggestions does the article make to help parents prevent the bad effects of violent TV programs and movies in very young children? In older children?

DIGITAL MORE EXERCISES

C **EVALUATE IDEAS** Do you agree with the article that "violence is not a normal part of life"? Explain your answer.

NOW YOU CAN Discuss effects of violence on viewers

A Complete the chart with three films or television shows you know. Rate the level of violence from 0 to 3, with 3 being the most violent.

Title	Medium	Level of Violence
The Dark Knight Rises	film	2

0 = not violent, 1 = somewhat violent, 2 = violent, 3 = ultra violent

B **NOTEPADDING** Write notes about the most violent film or TV show on your chart.

Should children see it? Why? / Why not?

Is it OK for adults to see it? Why? / Why not?

C **DISCUSSION** Discuss the effects of violence on viewers. Use the information from your notepad to help you express your ideas. Here are some questions to consider in your discussion:

- In your opinion, are there some people who should not see violent movies? If so, who?
- Is the effect of viewing violence the same in children and adults?
- Does violence encourage adults to behave aggressively?

"**I think** violent movies can make people violent. They see violence, and they go out and do the same thing they see in the movie."

"**I agree . . .**"

"**I disagree. I feel that . . .**"

Text-mining (optional)
Find and underline three words or phrases in the Reading that were new to you. Use them in your Discussion.
For example: "a bad message."

REVIEW

A ▶1:34 Listen to the conversation about movies. Check the correct description of each movie.

1

☐ a romantic film
☐ a documentary about Brazil
☐ a horror movie

2

☐ an animated police story
☐ a weird love story
☐ an unforgettable comedy

3

☐ an unforgettable movie
☐ a weird police story
☐ an animated children's film

4

☐ a documentary about cooking ham
☐ a musical tragedy
☐ a silly comedy

5

☐ a documentary
☐ a movie only for adults
☐ an animated musical

6

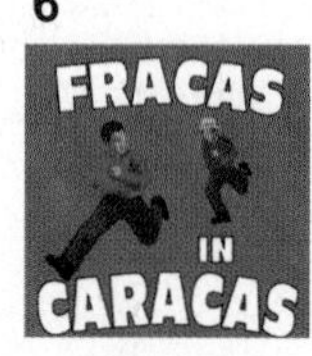

☐ a comedy
☐ an animated film
☐ a drama

B Complete the conversations. Choose the correct verbs and adverbial expressions, and write the movie genres.

1 A: (Have you seen / Did you see) a good .... (just / lately)?
B: To tell you the truth, no. But last night (we've seen / we saw) a great ....

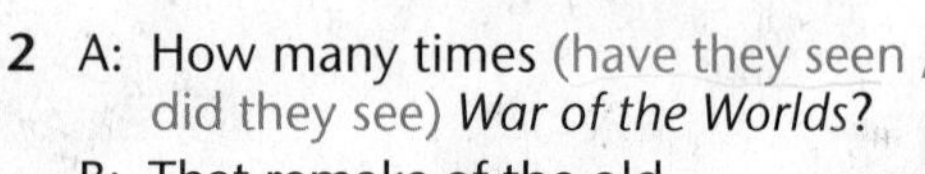

2 A: How many times (have they seen / did they see) *War of the Worlds*?
B: That remake of the old .... movie? I think (they saw it / they've seen it) twice (still / so far).

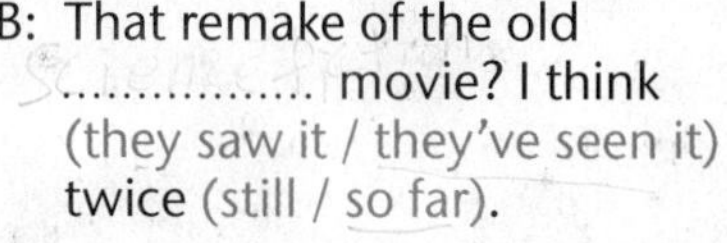

3 A: Sally is such a .... fan. How long (has she waited / did she wait) for this film to come out on DVD?
B: She's waited (for / since) at least six months.

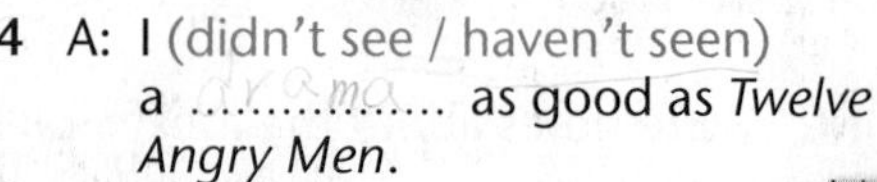

4 A: I (didn't see / haven't seen) a .... as good as *Twelve Angry Men*.
B: Really? I (lately / still) (didn't see / haven't seen) it.

C Complete each statement or question with <u>for</u> or <u>since</u>.

1 That film has played at the Metroplex .... two weeks.
2 *The Talking Parrot* has been available to stream online .... last Tuesday.
3 I've loved animated movies .... I was a child.
4 Have you been here .... more than an hour?
5 I've been a fan of science fiction movies .... over thirty years.
6 I've been in the ticket line .... 6:30!

For additional language practice . . .
TOP NOTCH POP
• Lyrics p. 153
"Better Late Than Never"
DIGITAL SONG
DIGITAL KARAOKE

WRITING

Write two paragraphs about violence in movies and on TV. Explain why some people think it's harmful and why others think it isn't.

WRITING BOOSTER p. 144
- Paragraphs
- Topic sentences
- Guidance for this writing exercise

ORAL REVIEW

PAIR WORK

1 With a partner, guess the genre of the three movies. Imagine what the movies are about and choose actors to star in the movies. Present your ideas to the class. Use the following as a model.

We think "Love in Paradise" is a romantic movie. It's about a man and a woman who meet and fall in love in Hawaii.

2 Create a conversation for one of the couples. Say as much as you can. For example:

It's 7:30. Did we miss "Love in Paradise"?

SOLD OUT

Cult of Blood
7:20 9:00 Midnight

Love in Paradise
7:15 9:45

Ticket to the Moon
8:00 10:00

Ticket to the Moon

Love in Paradise

Cult of Blood

7:30

NOW I CAN

- ☐ Apologize for being late.
- ☐ Discuss preferences for movie genres.
- ☐ Describe and recommend movies.
- ☐ Discuss effects of violence on viewers.

COMMUNICATION GOALS

1 Leave and take a message.
2 Check into a hotel.
3 Request housekeeping services.
4 Choose a hotel.

UNIT 3 Staying in Hotels

PREVIEW

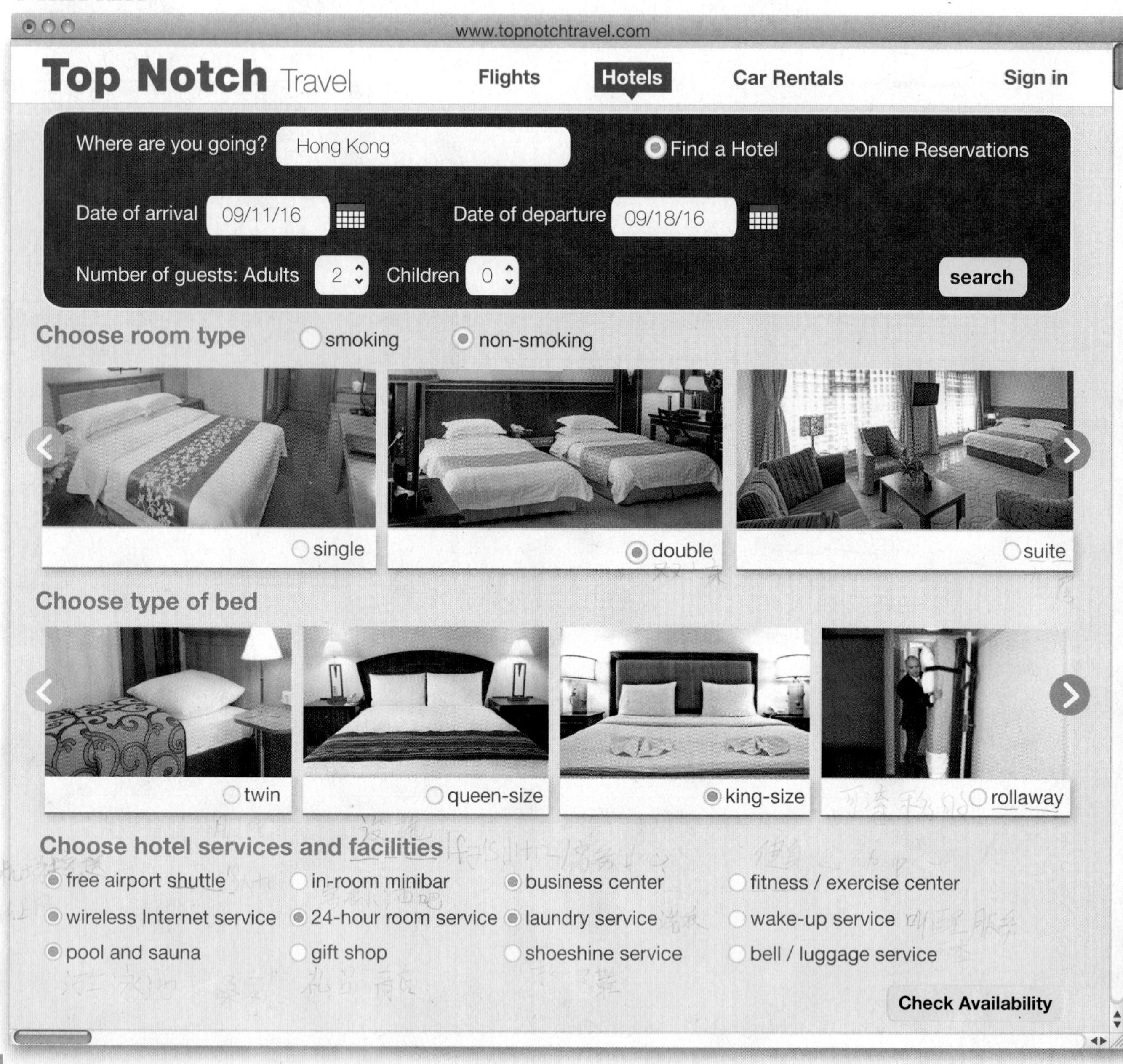

DIGITAL FLASH CARDS **A** 2:02 **VOCABULARY • *Hotel room types and kinds of beds*** Read and listen. Then listen again and repeat.

1 a single room	**4** a smoking room	**7** a queen-size bed
2 a double room	**5** a non-smoking room	**8** a king-size bed
3 a suite	**6** a twin bed	**9** a rollaway bed

B **PAIR WORK** Have you—or has someone you know—ever stayed at a hotel? Tell your partner about it, using the Vocabulary and the facilities from the website.

C ▶2:03 **PHOTO STORY** Read and listen to someone checking out of a hotel.

Guest: Good morning. I'm checking out of Room 604.

Clerk: I'll be happy to help you with that. Was your stay satisfactory?

Guest: Yes. Very nice. Thanks.

Clerk: Did you have anything from the minibar last night?

Guest: Just a bottle of water.

Clerk: OK. Let me add that to your bill.

Clerk: And would you like to put this on your Vista card?

Guest: Yes, I would, please. By the way, I need to go to the airport.

Clerk: Certainly. If you're in a hurry, I'll call you a taxi. But if you'd rather take the free airport shuttle, there's one leaving in twenty minutes.

Guest: Great. I'll take the shuttle. Why pay for a taxi? And that'll give me time to pick up a few things at the gift shop before I leave.

Clerk: No problem. I'll ask the bellman to give you a hand with your luggage. He'll let you know when the shuttle's here.

Guest: Thanks so much.

Clerk: You're welcome. Have a safe trip, and we hope to see you again.

D **FOCUS ON LANGUAGE** Find underlined words and phrases in the Photo Story with the same meaning.

1 pay with **2** help **3** leaving **4** OK **5** don't have much time

E **THINK AND EXPLAIN** Explain why each statement is false, using information from the Photo Story.

1 The guest is staying for a few more days.
2 The guest has complaints about the hotel.
3 The guest pays the bill in cash.
4 The shuttle is arriving in an hour.

SPEAKING

Match each picture with a hotel service from the list. Which services are important to you? Explain why.

1 ....

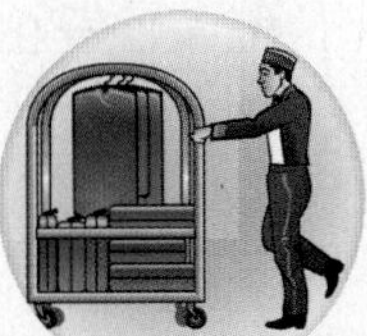

2 ....

3 ....

4 ....

5 ....

6 ....

7 ....

▶2:04 **Hotel services**
airport shuttle
bell service
laundry service
minibar
room service
shoeshine service
wake-up service

" Wake-up service is important to me. When I travel for business, we usually have very early meetings. "

LESSON 1 **GOAL** Leave and take a message

CONVERSATION MODEL

A ▶2:05 Read and listen to someone leaving a message.

A: Hello? I'd like to speak to Anne Smith. She's a guest.

B: I'll ring that room for you . . . I'm sorry. She's not answering. Would you like to leave a message?

A: Yes. Please tell her Tim Klein called. I'll meet her at the hotel at three this afternoon.

B: Is that all?

A: Yes, thanks.

B ▶2:06 **RHYTHM AND INTONATION** Listen again and repeat. Then practice the Conversation Model with a partner.

GRAMMAR *The future with will*

You can use will or won't + a base form to talk about the future.

Affirmative statements

He **will call** back tomorrow.

Negative statements

We **won't be** at the hotel this afternoon.

Questions

Will she **meet** us at the restaurant? — Yes, she will. / No, she won't.
Will they **take** a taxi to the hotel? — Yes, they will. / No, they won't.

When **will** the shuttle **arrive**? (In about ten minutes.)
What **will** you **do** in New York? (Visit the Empire State Building.)
Where **will** they **go** on their next vacation? (Probably Los Angeles.)

Who **will** Ana **call** when she arrives? (She'll call the front desk.)
BUT
Who **will call** the front desk? (Ana will.)

Contractions
will = **'ll**
will not = **won't**

Remember: You can also talk about the future with be going to, the present continuous, or the simple present tense.
I'**m going to call** again at 4:00.
They'**re meeting** at noon at the hotel.
She **arrives** on PanAir Flight 24 tonight.

GRAMMAR BOOSTER p. 129
- Will: expansion
  - Will and be going to
  - other uses of will
- Can, should, and have to: future meaning

A **FIND THE GRAMMAR** Look at the Conversation Model again. Circle two uses of will.

B **GRAMMAR PRACTICE** Complete the statements and questions in the messages, using will or won't. Use contractions when possible.

1. Message for Ms. Yalmaz: Ms. Calloway called. .... back later this evening. (she / call)
2. Message for Mr. Ballinger: .... at the Clayton Hotel until after 5:00. (your colleagues / not / be)
3. Message for John Torrence: Your boss called. .... a recommendation for a nice restaurant for tonight. (he / need)
4. Message from Mark Smith: .... us to the airport after the meeting? (who / take)
5. Message for Ms. Harris: .... at the airport before 6:00. (your brother / not / arrive)
6. Message from Janis Torres: .... at 3:00 tomorrow, London time. (the conference call / start)
7. Message from Mrs. Park: .... come in to the office early tomorrow? (I / have to)
8. Message for Ms. Grady: .... us tomorrow? (where / you / meet)

C ▶2:07 **LISTEN FOR DETAILS** Listen to the phone messages. Then listen again and complete each message slip, according to the information you hear. Use the future with will in each message.

1

PHONE MESSAGE

FOR: Judy Diller

FROM: ☑ Mr. ☐ Ms. ☐ Mrs. ☐ Miss Pearl

☑ Please call ☐ Will call again

☐ Wants to see you ☐ Returned your call

Message: He'll be . . .

2

PHONE MESSAGE

FOR: Hank Pitt

FROM: ☐ Mr. ☐ Ms. ☐ Mrs. ☐ Miss

☐ Please call ☐ Will call again

☐ Wants to see you ☐ Returned your call

Message:

3

PHONE MESSAGE

FOR: Collin Mack

FROM: ☐ Mr. ☐ Ms. ☐ Mrs. ☐ Miss

☐ Please call ☐ Will call again

☐ Wants to see you ☐ Returned your call

Message:

4

PHONE MESSAGE

FOR: Patricia Carlton

FROM: ☐ Mr. ☐ Ms. ☐ Mrs. ☐ Miss

☐ Please call ☐ Will call again

☐ Wants to see you ☐ Returned your call

Message:

DIGITAL VIDEO COACH

PRONUNCIATION *Contractions with will*

A ▶2:08 Notice that each contraction is one syllable. Read and listen. Then listen again and repeat.

1 I'll call back later.
2 She'll be at the Frank Hotel.
3 He'll bring his laptop to the meeting.
4 We'll need a taxi.
5 You'll have to leave at 6:30.
6 They'll meet you in twenty minutes.

B Look at the message slips you wrote in Exercise C above. Read each message aloud, using the correct pronunciation of the contracted form of will.

NOW YOU CAN Leave and take a message

A **FRAME YOUR IDEAS** On a separate sheet of paper, write four messages you could leave someone.

DIGITAL VIDEO

B **CONVERSATION ACTIVATOR** With a partner, change the Conversation Model. Leave your own messages. Your partner completes the message slip. Then change roles.

A: Hello? I'd like to speak to ....
B: I'll ring that room for you . . . I'm sorry. .... Would you like to leave a message?
A: Yes. Please tell ....
B: Is that all?
A: ....

WHILE YOU WERE OUT . . .

FOR: ____

☐ Mr. ☐ Ms. ☐ Mrs. ☐ Miss ____ called.

Phone: ____

☐ Please call back

☐ Will call again

Message: ____

DON'T STOP!

- Leave another message.
- Confirm that you've understood the message correctly.
- Ask for more information.

RECYCLE THIS LANGUAGE.

How do you spell your last name?
Could you please spell that for me?
Could you please repeat that?
What's your ___?

C **CHANGE PARTNERS** Leave other messages.

LESSON 2 **GOAL** Check into a hotel

GRAMMAR *The real conditional*

Conditional sentences express the results of actions or conditions.

<u>if</u> clause (the condition)	result clause (the result)
If the business center is still open,	I'll check my e-mail.

Real conditional sentences express factual or future results. When the result is future, use <u>will</u> in the result clause.

(A factual result: Use present tense in both clauses.)
If a hotel room has wireless Internet, guests don't have to go to a business center to check e-mail.
(A future result: Use present tense in the <u>if</u> clause and future with <u>will</u> in the result clause.)
If she checks in early, she'll get the room she wants.

Questions

If they don't have a non-smoking room, will you stay at a different hotel?
Where will you go if they don't have a room for tonight?
If there are no rental cars at the airport, what will they do?

Be careful!
Never use <u>will</u> in the <u>if</u> clause.
If you hurry, you'll catch the shuttle. NOT If you ~~will hurry~~, you'll catch the shuttle.

In conditional sentences, the clauses can be reversed with no change in meaning.
In writing, use a comma when the <u>if</u> clause comes first.
If the fitness center is still open, I'll go swimming.
I'll go swimming if the fitness center is still open.

GRAMMAR BOOSTER p. 130
- The real conditional: present and future; usage and common errors

A UNDERSTAND THE GRAMMAR Write <u>factual</u> if the conditional sentence expresses a fact. Write <u>future</u> if it expresses a future result.

.... 1 If you make your reservation in advance, you save a lot of money.
.... 2 She'll miss the 11:00 shuttle if she doesn't check out early today.
.... 3 If a guest is in a hurry, a taxi is faster than the shuttle.
.... 4 We will call your room this evening if there are any messages.
.... 5 If you request a suite, you usually get free breakfasts.
.... 6 You'll have to pay a daily fee if you want wireless service.

B GRAMMAR PRACTICE Complete the real conditional statements and questions with correct forms of the verbs.

1 .... (you / not / be able) to order breakfast at the restaurant if .... (you / not / hurry) .
2 If .... (they / get) a suite on their next cruise, ... (they / be) a lot more comfortable.
3 .... (you / reserve) a room with a king-size bed if .... (it / be) affordable?
4 .... (someone / give) me a hand if .... (I / need) help with my luggage?
5 Who .... (we / call) if .... (we / need) laundry service?
6 .... (I / have to) pay if .... (I / use) wireless Internet service?
7 If .... (you / request) a rollaway bed, ... (someone / bring) it to your room.
8 Where .... (she / go) if .... (she / need) to make copies?

DIGITAL MORE EXERCISES

CONVERSATION MODEL

A ▶2:09 Read and listen to someone checking into a hotel.

A: Hi. I'm checking in. The name's Baker.
B: Let's see. That's a double for two nights. Non-smoking?
A: That's right.
B: May I have your credit card?
A: Here you go. By the way, is the restaurant still open?
B: It closes at 9:00. But if you hurry, you'll make it.
A: Thanks.

B ▶2:10 **RHYTHM AND INTONATION** Listen again and repeat. Then practice the Conversation Model with a partner.

C ▶2:11 **LISTEN FOR DETAILS** Listen to guests check into a hotel. Complete the information about what each guest needs.

	Type of bed(s)	Non-smoking room?	Bell service?
1		☐	☐
2		☐	☐
3		☐	☐
4		☐	☐

NOW YOU CAN Check into a hotel

A **CONVERSATION ACTIVATOR** With a partner, role-play checking into a hotel. Change the room and bed type, and ask about a hotel facility from the pictures. Then change roles.

A: Hi, I'm checking in. The name's ....
B: Let's see. That's a .... for .... night(s). Non-smoking?
A: ....
B: May I have your credit card?
A: Here you go. By the way, is the .... still open?
B: It closes at .... But if you hurry, you'll make it.
A: ....

- Ask about other services and facilities.

Gift Shop Hours
8 AM to 9 PM

B **CHANGE PARTNERS** Practice the conversation again. Discuss other room and bed types and hotel facilities.

LESSON 3 GOAL Request housekeeping services

BEFORE YOU LISTEN

DIGITAL FLASH CARDS

A ▶2:12 **VOCABULARY • *Hotel room amenities and services*** Read and listen. Then listen again and repeat.

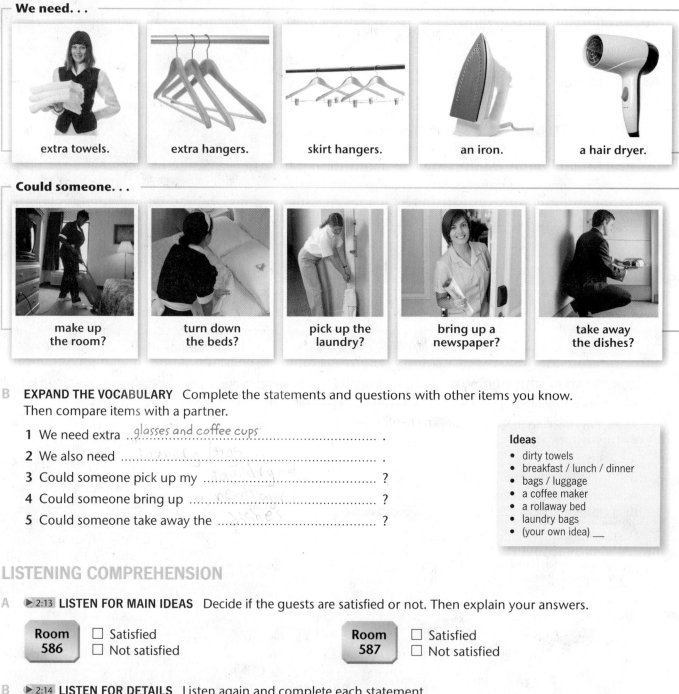

We need. . .

extra towels.

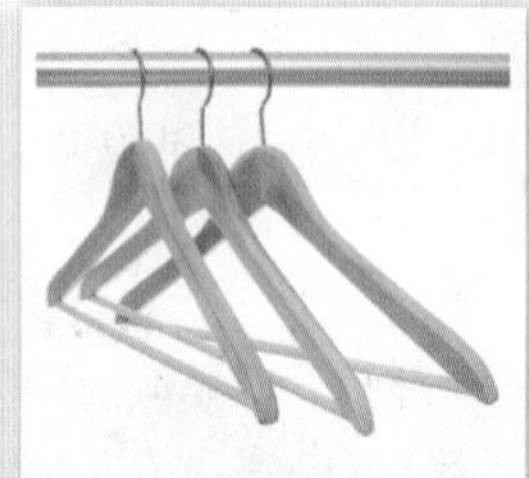
extra hangers.

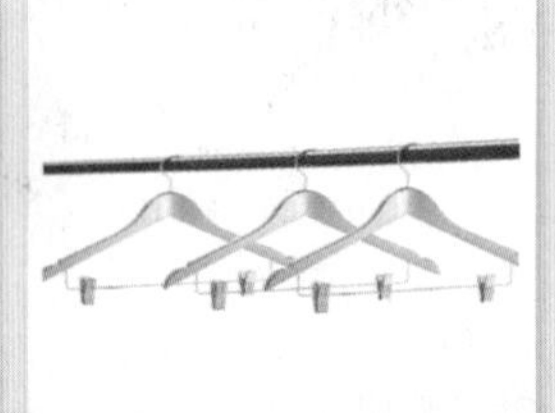
skirt hangers.

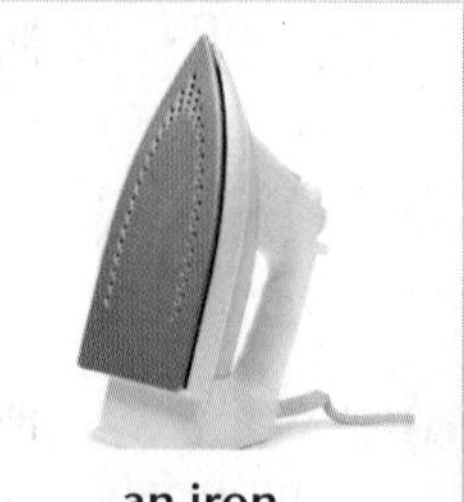
an iron.

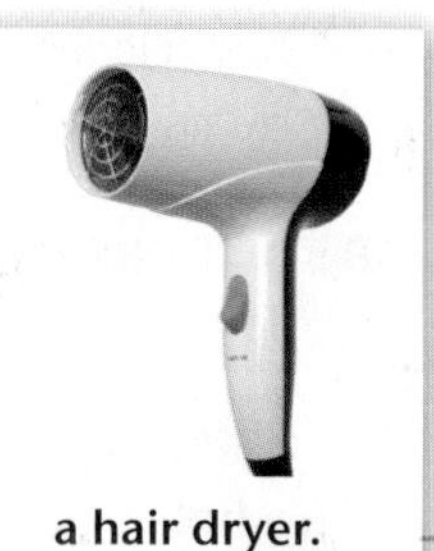
a hair dryer.

Could someone. . .

make up the room?

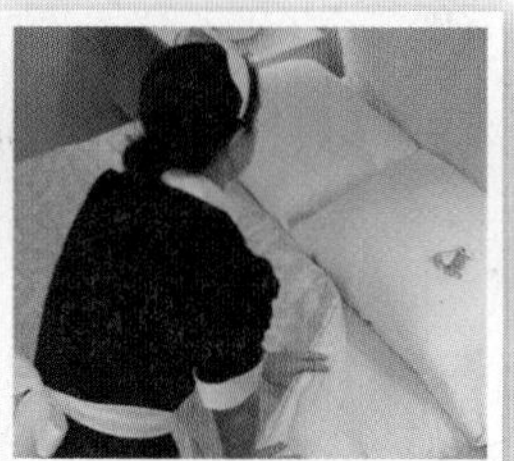
turn down the beds?

pick up the laundry?

bring up a newspaper?

take away the dishes?

B **EXPAND THE VOCABULARY** Complete the statements and questions with other items you know. Then compare items with a partner.

1 We need extra glasses and coffee cups .
2 We also need ....
3 Could someone pick up my .... ?
4 Could someone bring up .... ?
5 Could someone take away the .... ?

Ideas
- dirty towels
- breakfast / lunch / dinner
- bags / luggage
- a coffee maker
- a rollaway bed
- laundry bags
- (your own idea) __

LISTENING COMPREHENSION

A ▶2:13 **LISTEN FOR MAIN IDEAS** Decide if the guests are satisfied or not. Then explain your answers.

Room 586
☐ Satisfied
☐ Not satisfied

Room 587
☐ Satisfied
☐ Not satisfied

B ▶2:14 **LISTEN FOR DETAILS** Listen again and complete each statement.

Room 586
The guest wants someone to take away .... , bring up .... and .... , and pick up ....

Room 587
The guest wants someone to .... the .... , bring up .... , and .... the ....

NOW YOU CAN Request housekeeping services

A **PAIR WORK** Look at the pictures. With a partner, discuss what you think each hotel guest is saying.

B **PAIR WORK** Role-play a telephone conversation between one of the guests and hotel staff. Use your ideas from Exercise A. Then change roles. Start like this:

A: Hello. Room Service. How can I help you?
B: Hi, I'd like to order . . .

DON'T STOP!

- Complain about other problems.
- Ask about the hotel facilities and services.
- Leave a message for another hotel guest.

RECYCLE THIS LANGUAGE.

Hotel staff
Hello, [Gift Shop].
Is everything OK?
I'm sorry to hear that.
Let me check.
Certainly.
I'll be happy to help you with that.

Hotel guest
Is the [sauna] still open?
What time does the [business center] close / open?
Could someone __?
The __ isn't / aren't working.
The __ won't turn on.
I need __.
I'd like to order [room service].
I'd like to leave a message for __.

LESSON 4 GOAL Choose a hotel

BEFORE YOU READ

EXPLORE YOUR IDEAS What do you think is the best way to get information about a hotel?

- ☐ by word of mouth
- ☐ from an online hotel booking service
- ☐ from a travel guide book
- ☐ from a travel agency
- ☐ other ....

READING ▶2:15

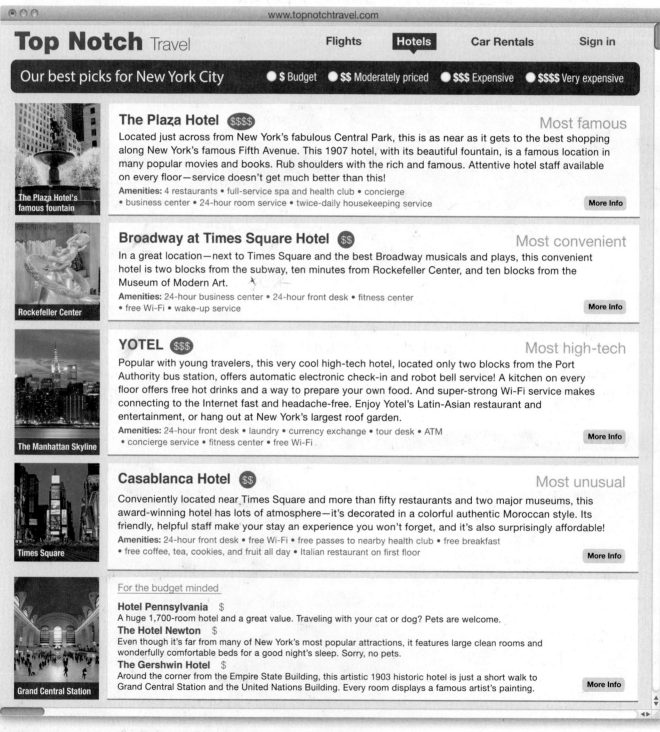

www.topnotchtravel.com

Top Notch Travel — Flights | Hotels | Car Rentals | Sign in

Our best picks for New York City — $ Budget · $$ Moderately priced · $$$ Expensive · $$$$ Very expensive

The Plaza Hotel's famous fountain

The Plaza Hotel $$$$ — Most famous

Located just across from New York's fabulous Central Park, this is as near as it gets to the best shopping along New York's famous Fifth Avenue. This 1907 hotel, with its beautiful fountain, is a famous location in many popular movies and books. Rub shoulders with the rich and famous. Attentive hotel staff available on every floor—service doesn't get much better than this!

Amenities: 4 restaurants • full-service spa and health club • concierge • business center • 24-hour room service • twice-daily housekeeping service

More Info

Rockefeller Center

Broadway at Times Square Hotel $$ — Most convenient

In a great location—next to Times Square and the best Broadway musicals and plays, this convenient hotel is two blocks from the subway, ten minutes from Rockefeller Center, and ten blocks from the Museum of Modern Art.

Amenities: 24-hour business center • 24-hour front desk • fitness center • free Wi-Fi • wake-up service

More Info

The Manhattan Skyline

YOTEL $$$ — Most high-tech

Popular with young travelers, this very cool high-tech hotel, located only two blocks from the Port Authority bus station, offers automatic electronic check-in and robot bell service! A kitchen on every floor offers free hot drinks and a way to prepare your own food. And super-strong Wi-Fi service makes connecting to the Internet fast and headache-free. Enjoy Yotel's Latin-Asian restaurant and entertainment, or hang out at New York's largest roof garden.

Amenities: 24-hour front desk • laundry • currency exchange • tour desk • ATM • concierge service • fitness center • free Wi-Fi

More Info

Times Square

Casablanca Hotel $$ — Most unusual

Conveniently located near Times Square and more than fifty restaurants and two major museums, this award-winning hotel has lots of atmosphere—it's decorated in a colorful authentic Moroccan style. Its friendly, helpful staff make your stay an experience you won't forget, and it's also surprisingly affordable!

Amenities: 24-hour front desk • free Wi-Fi • free passes to nearby health club • free breakfast • free coffee, tea, cookies, and fruit all day • Italian restaurant on first floor

More Info

Grand Central Station

For the budget minded

Hotel Pennsylvania $
A huge 1,700-room hotel and a great value. Traveling with your cat or dog? Pets are welcome.

The Hotel Newton $
Even though it's far from many of New York's most popular attractions, it features large clean rooms and wonderfully comfortable beds for a good night's sleep. Sorry, no pets.

The Gershwin Hotel $
Around the corner from the Empire State Building, this artistic 1903 historic hotel is just a short walk to Grand Central Station and the United Nations Building. Every room displays a famous artist's painting.

More Info

A **DRAW CONCLUSIONS** Complete each statement with the name of a hotel (or hotels) from the Reading. Then compare choices and reasons with a partner.

1 On his vacations, Carl Ryan, 43, likes to stay near the Theater District. If he stays at the Broadway at Times Square Hotel or the Casablanca Hotel , he'll be near the Theater District.

2 Stella Korman, 35, doesn't like the beds in most hotels. However, if she stays at .... , her room will definitely have a great bed.

3 Mark and Nancy Birdsall (22 and 21) are always online. If they stay at the .... , the Wi-Fi service is not only free, but it's really fast.

4 Lucy Lee, 36, will pay more for a hotel that is very comfortable and offers a lot of services. If she stays at .... , she'll be very happy.

5 Brenda Rey prefers hotels that are different and interesting. If she stays at .... , she'll find them different from other hotels.

6 James Kay always travels with his dog, Louie. If he stays at .... , Louie will have to stay home.

DIGITAL MORE EXERCISES

B **IDENTIFY SUPPORTING DETAILS** Compare responses in Exercise A with a partner. If you disagree, explain why you chose a particular hotel.

NOW YOU CAN Choose a hotel

A **FRAME YOUR IDEAS** What's important to you in choosing a hotel? Rate the following factors on a scale of 1 to 5.

	not important ← → very important
price	1 – 2 – 3 – 4 – 5
room size	1 – 2 – 3 – 4 – 5
cleanliness	1 – 2 – 3 – 4 – 5
location	1 – 2 – 3 – 4 – 5
service	1 – 2 – 3 – 4 – 5
amenities	1 – 2 – 3 – 4 – 5
atmosphere	1 – 2 – 3 – 4 – 5

B **PAIR WORK** Find each hotel from the Reading on the map. Discuss the advantages and disadvantages of each. Then choose a hotel.

"The Casablanca Hotel sounds like it has a lot of atmosphere. It's affordable, and the location is good."

Text-mining (optional)
Find three words or phrases in the Reading that were new to you. Use them in your Pair Work.
For example: "conveniently located."

C **SURVEY AND DISCUSSION** Take a survey of how many classmates chose each hotel. Discuss and explain your choices.

"Most of us chose the Hotel Newton because . . ."

REVIEW

A 2:16 Listen to the phone conversations in a hotel. Then listen again and complete each statement, using words from the box.

bell	room	dinner	hangers	make up the room
laundry	shoeshine	towels	wake-up	turn down the beds

1 She wants someone to bring up .... She also needs .... service.
2 He needs .... service, and he wants someone to bring up extra ....
3 She wants someone to .... , and she wants someone to bring up extra ....
4 He needs .... service and .... service.

B What hotel room or bed type should each guest ask for?

1 Ms. Gleason is traveling alone. She doesn't need much space. *a single room*
2 Mr. and Mrs. Vanite and their twelve-year-old son Boris are checking into a room with one king-size bed. ....
3 Mike Krause plans to use his room for business meetings with important customers. ....
4 George Nack is a big man, and he's very tall. He needs a good night's sleep for an important meeting tomorrow. ....
5 Paul Krohn's company wants him to save some money by sharing a room with a colleague. ....

C Write real conditional statements and questions. Use the correct forms of the verbs and correct punctuation.

1 if / it / rain this morning / Mona / not go / to the beach
If it rains this morning, Mona won't go to the beach.
2 if / you / walk to the restaurant / you / be there in fifteen minutes
....
3 Mr. Wang / get a better job / if / he / do well on the English test tomorrow
....
4 what / Karl / do / if / the airline / cancels his flight
.... ?
5 if / you / not like / your room / who / you / call
.... ?

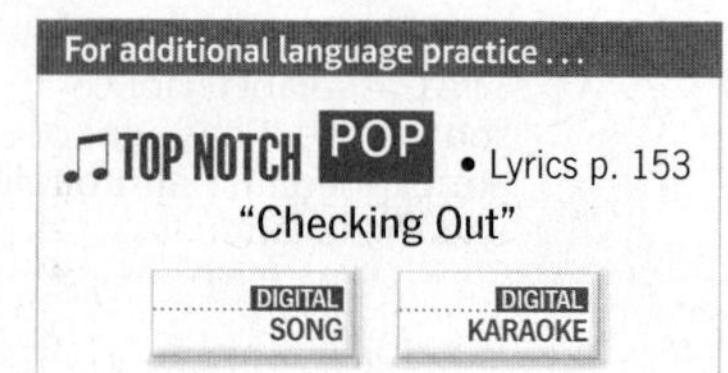

For additional language practice . . .
TOP NOTCH POP • Lyrics p. 153
"Checking Out"
DIGITAL SONG
DIGITAL KARAOKE

WRITING

Write a paragraph about the hotel you chose in Lesson 4. Explain why you would like to stay there. What are its advantages and disadvantages?

I would like to stay at the Hotel Casablanca. Atmosphere is very important to me and . . .

WRITING BOOSTER p. 145
- Avoiding sentence fragments with because or since
- Guidance for this writing exercise

DIGITAL GAMES

ORAL REVIEW

PAIR WORK

1 Create a conversation between the hotel guest in Room 816 and the woman at the front desk. Ask for hotel services or complain about a problem. Start like this:

Hello? Is this the front desk?

2 Create a conversation between the man at the front desk and the caller. Use will. Complete the message slip. Start like this:

A: Front desk. Can I help you?
B: Yes, thanks. I'd like to leave a message for . . .

3 Create a conversation between the two men at the front desk. Check into or check out of the hotel. Discuss hotel amenities, services, and schedules. Start like this:

Hi. I'm checking in. The name's ....

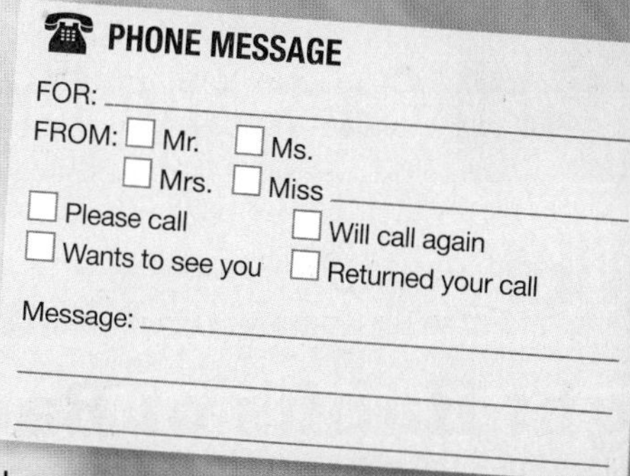

PHONE MESSAGE

FOR: ______________________

FROM: ☐ Mr. ☐ Ms. ☐ Mrs. ☐ Miss ______________

☐ Please call ☐ Will call again

☐ Wants to see you ☐ Returned your call

Message: ______________________

✓ NOW I CAN

- ☐ Leave and take a message.
- ☐ Check into a hotel.
- ☐ Request housekeeping services.
- ☐ Choose a hotel.

UNIT 4 Cars and Driving

COMMUNICATION GOALS

1 Discuss a car accident.
2 Describe a car problem.
3 Rent a car.
4 Discuss good and bad driving.

PREVIEW

Eight Habits of Bad Drivers

How many drivers in your city . . .

1 speed?
☐ none ☐ some ☐ most ☐ all

2 tailgate?
☐ none ☐ some ☐ most ☐ all

3 talk on the phone?
☐ none ☐ some ☐ most ☐ all

4 text while driving?
☐ none ☐ some ☐ most ☐ all

5 weave through traffic?
☐ none ☐ some ☐ most ☐ all

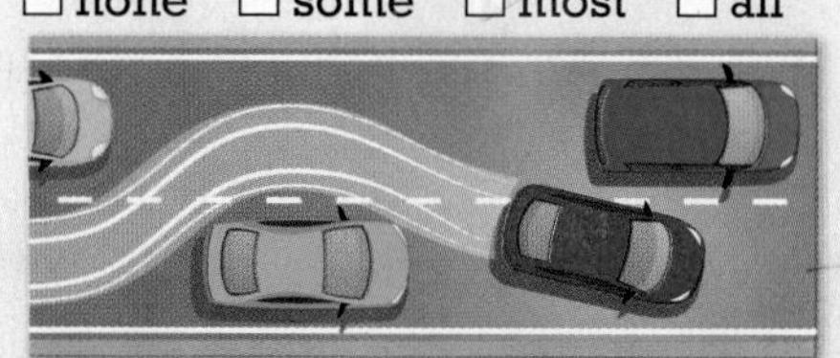

6 don't stop at red lights?
☐ none ☐ some ☐ most ☐ all

7 don't signal when turning?
☐ none ☐ some ☐ most ☐ all

8 pass in a no-passing zone?
☐ none ☐ some ☐ most ☐ all

DIGITAL FLASH CARDS

A ▶2:19 **VOCABULARY • *Bad driving habits*** Read and listen. Then listen again and repeat.

speed
tailgate
talk on the phone
text while driving
weave through traffic
not stop at red lights
not signal when turning
pass in a no-passing zone

B PAIR WORK Compare surveys with a partner. Discuss and explain your answers.

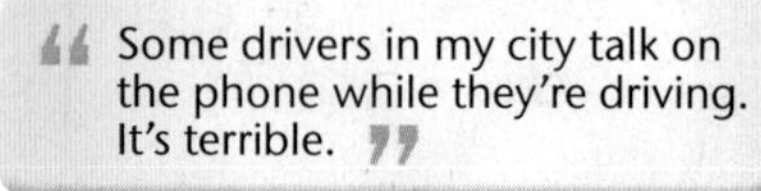

“Some drivers in my city talk on the phone while they're driving. It's terrible.”

“Lots of taxi drivers turn without signaling. I don't like that.”

C ▶2:20 **PHOTO STORY** Read and listen to a conversation between two old friends.

Mason: Brad! Long time no see.

Brad: Mason! You're right. It *has* been a long time. How've you been?

Mason: I can't complain. What about you? How's the family?

Brad: Great! I was just going in here to pick up a present for Marissa. Tomorrow's our fifth anniversary.

Mason: Congratulations! . . . Hey! Let's have a cup of coffee and catch up on old times. There's a nice coffee place right around the corner.

Brad: You won't believe what I just saw.

Mason: What?

Brad: This taxi was coming around the corner, and he hit a bus! Someone said the guy was texting while he was driving.

Mason: You've got to be kidding! Was anyone hurt?

Brad: I don't think so.

Mason: Thank goodness for that.

Brad: I just can't stop thinking about that accident.

Mason: I know. The driving in this city has always been bad, but now everyone's texting and talking on the phone instead of paying attention to the road.

Brad: You can say that again! You shouldn't multitask while you're driving a car.

D **FOCUS ON LANGUAGE** Match each numbered sentence with one of the quotations from the Photo Story.

1 I've been fine.
2 I totally agree with you.
3 I'm so happy for you!
4 I'm glad nothing terrible happened.
5 Really? That's unbelievable.
6 It's great to see you again.

a "Congratulations!"
b "I can't complain."
c "Long time no see."
d "Thank goodness for that."
e "You can say that again!"
f "You've got to be kidding!"

E **THINK AND EXPLAIN** Discuss with a partner.

1 What did Mason mean when he said, "Let's have a cup of coffee and catch up on old times."?
2 What did Brad mean when he said, "You shouldn't multitask while you're driving a car"?

SPEAKING

DISCUSSION Discuss an accident you know about. Answer the questions.

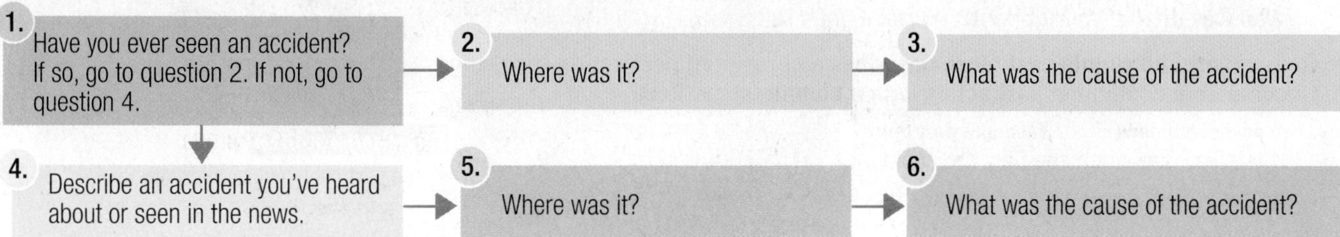

1. Have you ever seen an accident? If so, go to question 2. If not, go to question 4.
2. Where was it?
3. What was the cause of the accident?
4. Describe an accident you've heard about or seen in the news.
5. Where was it?
6. What was the cause of the accident?

GOAL Discuss a car accident

DIGITAL FLASH CARDS

VOCABULARY *Car parts*

A ▶2:21 Read and listen. Then listen again and repeat.

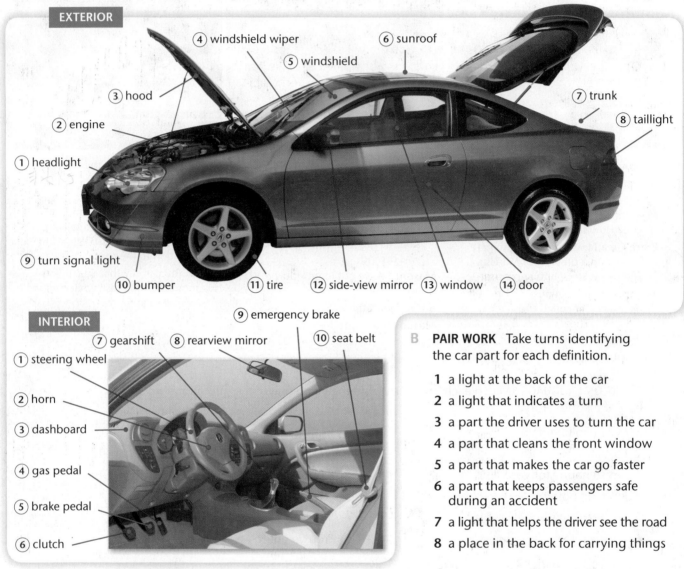

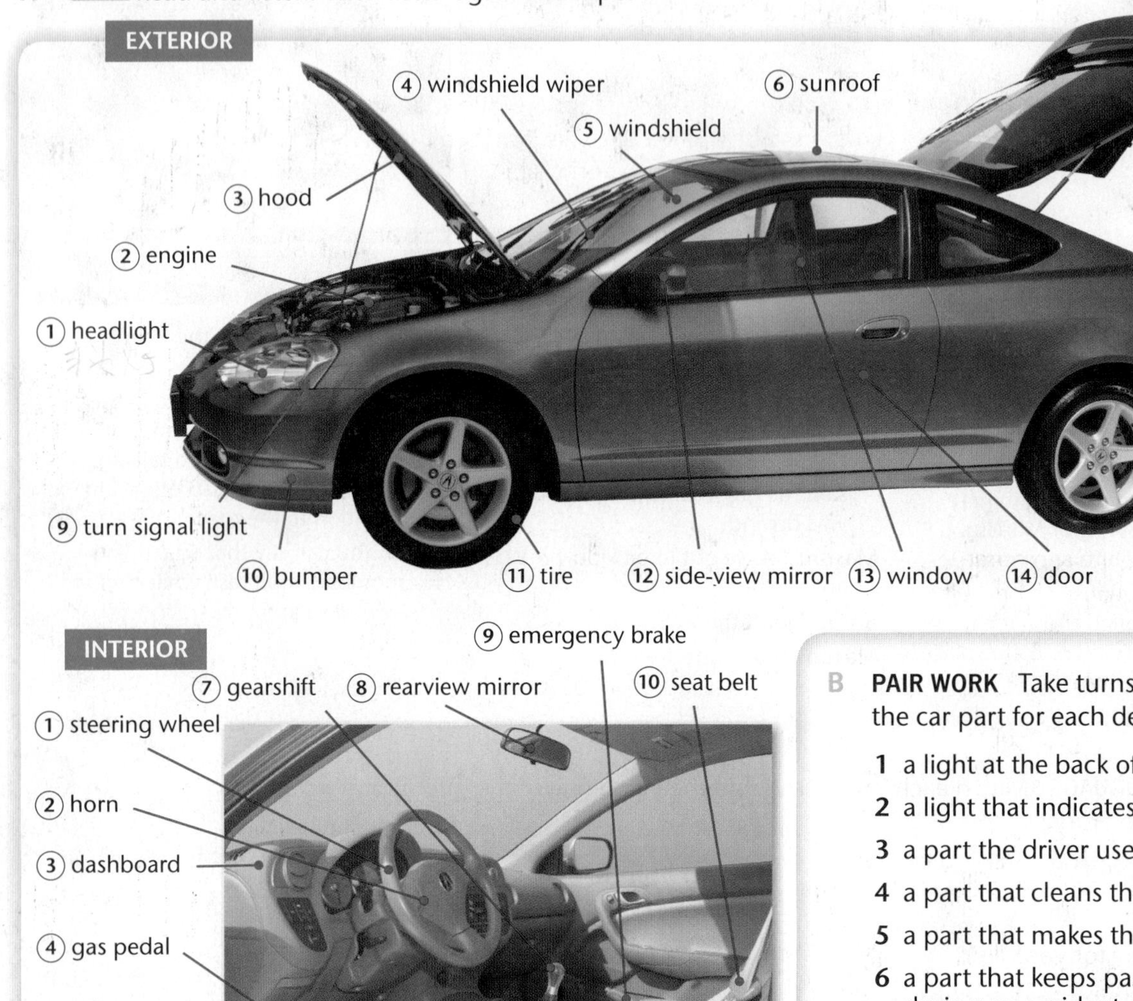

B **PAIR WORK** Take turns identifying the car part for each definition.

1 a light at the back of the car
2 a light that indicates a turn
3 a part the driver uses to turn the car
4 a part that cleans the front window
5 a part that makes the car go faster
6 a part that keeps passengers safe during an accident
7 a light that helps the driver see the road
8 a place in the back for carrying things

GRAMMAR *The past continuous*

The past continuous describes an activity that continued during a period of time in the past or at a specific time in the past.

The car **was making** a funny sound while they **were driving**.
Were the headlights **working**? (Yes, they were. / No, they weren't.)
Who **was driving** your car at 10:00 last night?

Remember: The simple past tense describes a completed past action. Use when to combine a continuing past action with a completed action.

past continuous	simple past tense
It **was raining**	when she **had** the accident.

Form the past continuous with was or were and a present participle.
The other driver **was speeding**.

GRAMMAR BOOSTER p. 131
• The past continuous: other uses

A GRAMMAR PRACTICE Complete the paragraph with the past continuous and the simple past tense.

I .... (1 have) an accident yesterday. I .... (2 drive) slowly and I'm sure I .... (3 pay) attention. But I .... (4 wait) for a phone call. When the phone .... (5 ring), I .... (6 answer) it. Suddenly, the car in front of me .... (7 stop), and I .... (8 hit) it. I certainly .... (9 learn) my lesson! Luckily, I .... (10 not speed) when I .... (11 have) the accident.

DIGITAL MORE ERCISES

B 2:22 **LISTEN TO ACTIVATE VOCABULARY** Listen to the conversations about accidents. Write the number of each conversation in the box under the picture. Then listen again and write the car part or parts that were damaged in each accident.

☐ .... ☐ .... ☐ .... ☐ ....

CONVERSATION MODEL

A 2:23 Read and listen to a conversation about a car accident.

A: I had an accident.
B: I'm so sorry. Are you OK?
A: I'm fine. No one was hurt.
B: Thank goodness. How did it happen?
A: Well, the other driver was tailgating, and he hit my car.
B: Oh, no! Was there much damage?
A: No. I'll only have to replace a taillight.

2:25 **Ways to respond**

With concern	With relief
I'm so sorry.	Thank goodness.
Oh, no!	What a relief!
How awful!	That's good.
I'm sorry to hear that.	
That's terrible.	

B 2:24 **RHYTHM AND INTONATION** Listen again and repeat. Then practice the Conversation Model with a partner.

NOW YOU CAN Discuss a car accident

A Write what the driver was doing. Use the past continuous.

The driver wasn't paying attention.

SPEED LIMIT 80

kph

DIGITAL VIDEO

B CONVERSATION ACTIVATOR With a partner, change the Conversation Model, using the pictures. Then change roles.

A: I had an accident.
B: .... Are you OK?
A: ....
B: .... How did it happen?
A: Well, ... , and .... hit my car.
B: .... Was there much damage?
A: ....

DON'T STOP!

- Ask more questions about location, other damage, the other driver, etc.

C CHANGE PARTNERS Discuss other accidents.

GOAL Describe a car problem

VOCABULARY *Phrasal verbs for talking about cars*

DIGITAL FLASH CARDS

A 2:26 Read and listen. Then listen again and repeat.

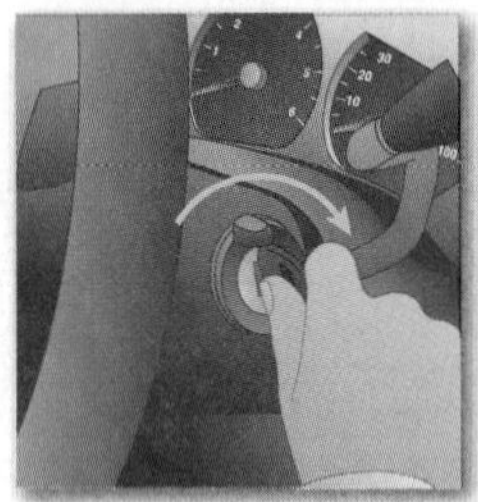
turn on

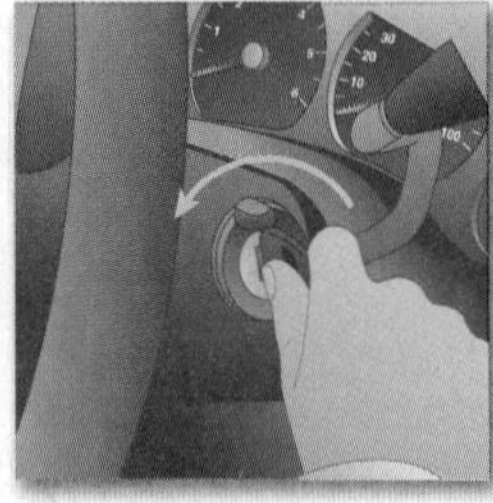
turn off

pick up

fill up

drop off

B Complete the sentences with the two parts of each phrasal verb.

1 The car's almost out of gas. Let's go in here so I can .... it ....
2 It's raining, and I can't .... the windshield wipers .... They aren't working.
3 Can I use your car this afternoon? I can .... it .... at 3:30 if you don't need it then.
4 We have to return the rental car before 6:00. Let's .... it .... early at the airport and get something to eat, OK?
5 I can't .... the air conditioning .... It's freezing in here!

GRAMMAR *Placement of direct objects with phrasal verbs*

Phrasal verbs contain a verb and a particle that together have their own meaning.

main verb		particle		
turn	+	on	=	start (a machine)

Many phrasal verbs are separable. This means that a direct object noun can come before or after the particle. Turn on, turn off, pick up, drop off, and fill up are separable.

I'll **drop off** the car. (direct object) OR I'll drop the car (direct object) off.

Be careful! With a separable phrasal verb, if the direct object is a pronoun, it must come before the particle.

I'll **drop** it **off**. (NOT I'll ~~drop off it~~.)
Did you **fill** them **up**? (NOT Did you ~~fill up them~~?)
Where will they **pick** us **up**? (NOT Where will they ~~pick up us~~?)

GRAMMAR BOOSTER p. 131
• Nouns and pronouns: review

PRONUNCIATION *Stress of particles in phrasal verbs*

DIGITAL VIDEO COACH

A 2:27 Stress changes when an object pronoun comes before the particle. Read and listen. Then listen again and repeat.

1 A: I'd like to pick up my car.
B: OK. What time can you pick it up?

2 A: They need to drop off the keys.
B: Great. When do they want to drop them off?

B **GRAMMAR / VOCABULARY PRACTICE** Write statements or questions, placing the direct objects correctly. Then practice reading the sentences aloud with a partner. Use correct stress.

1 The taillights aren't working. (can't / I / on / them / turn) ....

2 They're expecting the car at 10:00. (off / drop / 10:00 / at / I'll / it) ....

3 It's too cold for air conditioning. (button / which / off / it / turns) .... ?

4 Thanks for fixing the car. (it / pick / what time / I / can / up) .... ?

DIGITAL MORE RCISES

5 The car is almost out of gas. (up / please / fill / it) ....

CONVERSATION MODEL

A ▶2:28 Read and listen to someone describing a car problem.

A: I'm dropping off my car.
B: Was everything OK?
A: Well, actually, the windshield wipers aren't working.
B: I'm sorry to hear that. Any other problems?
A: No. That's it.
B: Is the gas tank full?
A: Yes. I just filled it up.

B ▶2:29 **RHYTHM AND INTONATION** Listen again and repeat. Then practice the Conversation Model with a partner.

C **FIND THE GRAMMAR** Find and underline two direct objects in the Conversation Model.

NOW YOU CAN Describe a car problem

A **NOTEPADDING** Write two or more possible car parts for each car problem.

won't open / close:	*the sunroof, the hood . . .*
won't turn on / off:	
(is / are) making a funny sound:	
(isn't / aren't) working:	

DIGITAL VIDEO

B **CONVERSATION ACTIVATOR** With a partner, change the Conversation Model. Report a problem with a car. Use your notepad for ideas. Then change roles and problems.

A: I'm dropping off my car.
B: Was everything OK?
A: Well, actually ....
B: .... Any other problems?
A: ....

C **CHANGE PARTNERS** Describe other car problems.

D **OPTION** Role-play a conversation in which you report an accident when you drop off a rental car. Describe the accident. Say what you were doing when you had the accident, using the past continuous. Then change roles. Start like this:

A: I'm dropping off my car. I had an accident . . .

RECYCLE THIS LANGUAGE.

Oh, no! How did it happen? Is there any damage? Was anyone hurt?	Yes, the [taillight] is broken. isn't working. won't turn on / off. is making a funny sound.

LESSON **3** **GOAL** Rent a car

BEFORE YOU LISTEN

DIGITAL FLASH CARDS

A ▶ 2:30 **VOCABULARY • *Car types*** Read and listen. Then listen again and repeat.

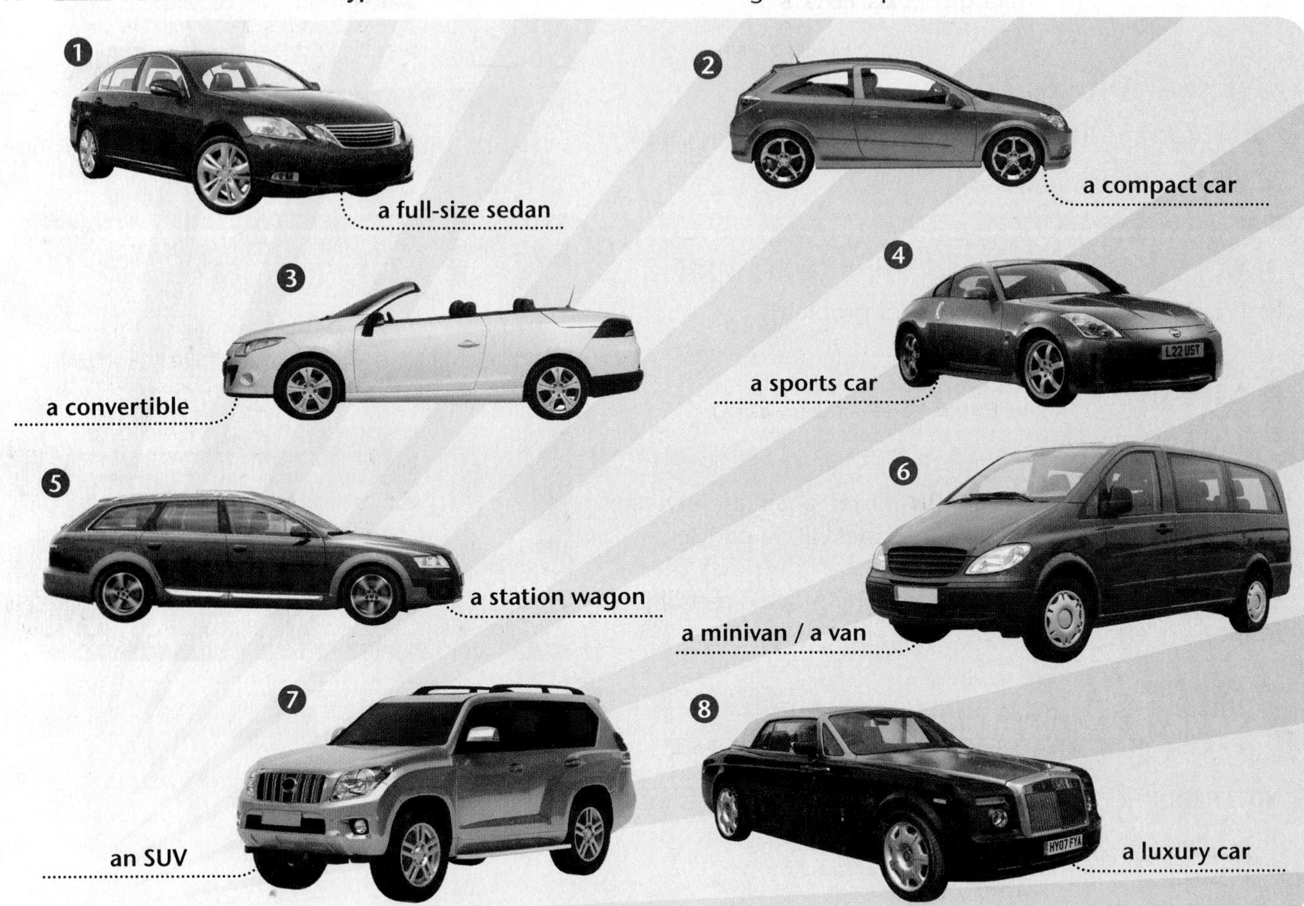

B **PAIR WORK** Which car would you like to drive? Which car would you *not* like to drive? Discuss with a partner, using the Vocabulary.

“I'd like to drive the luxury car because people will think I have a lot of money.”

“Really? I'd rather drive the convertible. It's really cool.”

LISTENING COMPREHENSION

A ▶ 2:31 **LISTEN FOR DETAILS** Listen. Write the car type that the speakers discuss in each conversation.

1 .... 2 .... 3 .... 4 ....

B ▶ 2:32 **LISTEN TO SUMMARIZE** Listen again. Write a check mark if the caller rented a car. Then listen again. Write the reasons the other callers didn't rent a car.

☐ 1 ....

☐ 2 ....

☐ 3 ....

☐ 4 ....

NOW YOU CAN Rent a car

A **PAIR WORK** Read about each customer at Wheels Around the World, an international car rental company. Choose the best type of car for each person. Discuss reasons with your partner.

> "A compact car is good for driving in a big city. It is easier to park in a small parking space."

1

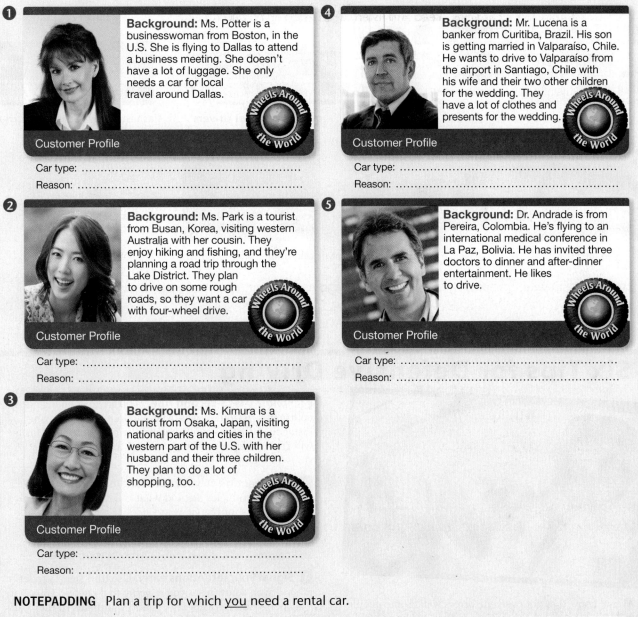

Background: Ms. Potter is a businesswoman from Boston, in the U.S. She is flying to Dallas to attend a business meeting. She doesn't have a lot of luggage. She only needs a car for local travel around Dallas.

Wheels Around the World

Customer Profile

Car type: ....

Reason: ....

2

Background: Ms. Park is a tourist from Busan, Korea, visiting western Australia with her cousin. They enjoy hiking and fishing, and they're planning a road trip through the Lake District. They plan to drive on some rough roads, so they want a car with four-wheel drive.

Wheels Around the World

Customer Profile

Car type: ....

Reason: ....

3

Background: Ms. Kimura is a tourist from Osaka, Japan, visiting national parks and cities in the western part of the U.S. with her husband and their three children. They plan to do a lot of shopping, too.

Wheels Around the World

Customer Profile

Car type: ....

Reason: ....

4

Background: Mr. Lucena is a banker from Curitiba, Brazil. His son is getting married in Valparaíso, Chile. He wants to drive to Valparaíso from the airport in Santiago, Chile with his wife and their two other children for the wedding. They have a lot of clothes and presents for the wedding.

Wheels Around the World

Customer Profile

Car type: ....

Reason: ....

5

Background: Dr. Andrade is from Pereira, Colombia. He's flying to an international medical conference in La Paz, Bolivia. He has invited three doctors to dinner and after-dinner entertainment. He likes to drive.

Wheels Around the World

Customer Profile

Car type: ....

Reason: ....

B **NOTEPADDING** Plan a trip for which <u>you</u> need a rental car.

Destination	Pickup date	Drop off date	Number of companions	Activities

C **ROLE PLAY** With a partner, role-play a phone call to Wheels Around the World to rent a car for the trip you planned on your notepad. Choose one of the car types from the Vocabulary on page 44. Discuss the trip and your needs. Then change roles.

RECYCLE THIS LANGUAGE.

Agent

Hello. Wheels Around the World.
What kind of car [do you need / would you like]?
How many people are you traveling with?
When will you [pick up / drop off] the car?
Where will you drop off the car?
Would you rather rent [a full-sized sedan] or [an SUV]?

Caller

I'd like to make a reservation.
I'd like a [compact car].
I'd rather have a [van].
I'm traveling with [my husband].
It's a [business trip / vacation].
I [have / don't have] a lot of luggage.
Do you accept credit cards?

LESSON 4 GOAL Discuss good and bad driving

BEFORE YOU READ

DIGITAL FLASH CARDS

A ▶2:33 **VOCABULARY • *Driving behavior*** Read and listen. Then listen again and repeat.

Bad or aggressive drivers . . .

honk their horns

stare at other drivers

gesture at other drivers

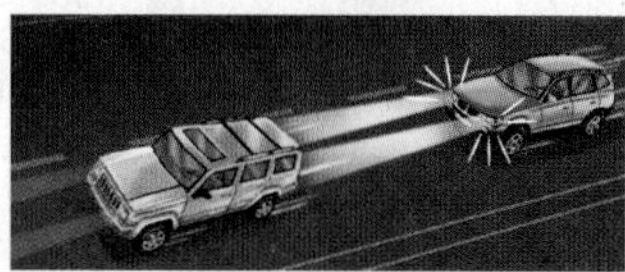
flash their lights at other drivers

Good drivers . . .

pay attention

observe the speed limit

maintain a safe following distance

And don't forget . . .
speed
tailgate
talk on the phone
text while driving
weave through traffic
not stop at stoplights
not signal while turning
pass in a no-passing zone

B **WARM-UP** In your opinion, which of the bad and aggressive driving habits are the most dangerous? Why?

READING ▶2:34

FEATURE ARTICLE

Six Tips for Defensive Driving

We all know that not everyone drives well. Some people tailgate, gesture, weave through traffic, and honk—classic signs of the aggressive driving that causes one third of all car crashes. But more and more people are now talking on the phone, eating, and even watching TV as they drive—examples of the multitasking and inattentive driving that is a growing cause of accidents. Although we can't control the actions of other drivers, the following defensive driving tips can help us reduce the risks caused by our own driving and the bad driving of others.

1 Slow down. Driving too fast for weather or road conditions gives you less time to react to dangers on the road ahead of you. Also, as you increase your speed, your car becomes harder to control and takes longer to come to a stop.

2 Follow the "3-second rule." The greatest chance of a collision is in front of you. Maintaining a safe following distance of three seconds behind the car in front of you will give you enough time to react if that car slows or stops suddenly.

3 Pay attention to your surroundings. Be aware of where other vehicles are and what is happening on the road. Check your rearview and side-view mirrors frequently. Before changing lanes, always look over your shoulder to check your "blind spots"—areas to the side and rear of your car that aren't visible in your mirrors.

4 Signal your intentions early. Use turn signals to let other drivers know what you're going to do before you do it. This helps other drivers understand your plans so they can make their own defensive driving decisions.

5 Expect the unexpected. Assume that other drivers will make mistakes. Plan ahead what you will do if another driver breaks a traffic law or cuts you off. For example, don't assume that a vehicle coming to a stop sign or a red light is going to stop. Be prepared to stop your own car if necessary.

6 Don't take others' aggressive driving personally. Other people will drive badly. They're not thinking about you. If you permit them to make you angry, it can affect your own driving and lead to an accident. When other drivers show signs of aggressive driving, just slow down or pull over to let them pass.

A **UNDERSTAND FROM CONTEXT** Circle the correct word or phrase to complete each statement.

1 A person who is doing more than one activity at the same time is (multitasking / driving defensively).

2 Following the "3-second rule" means maintaining a safe (road condition / following distance).

3 Tailgating, gesturing, and honking are three examples of (inattentive / aggressive) driving.

4 Not paying attention is an example of (inattentive / aggressive) driving.

5 *Collision* and *crash* are two words that mean (danger / accident).

6 A part of the road that you can't see in your mirrors is called a (blind spot / lane).

B **CRITICAL THINKING** How can defensive driving help drivers avoid accidents? Explain your opinion, using the Vocabulary and examples from the Reading or from your own experience.

NOW YOU CAN Discuss good and bad driving

A **PAIR WORK** Complete the survey and then compare surveys with a partner.

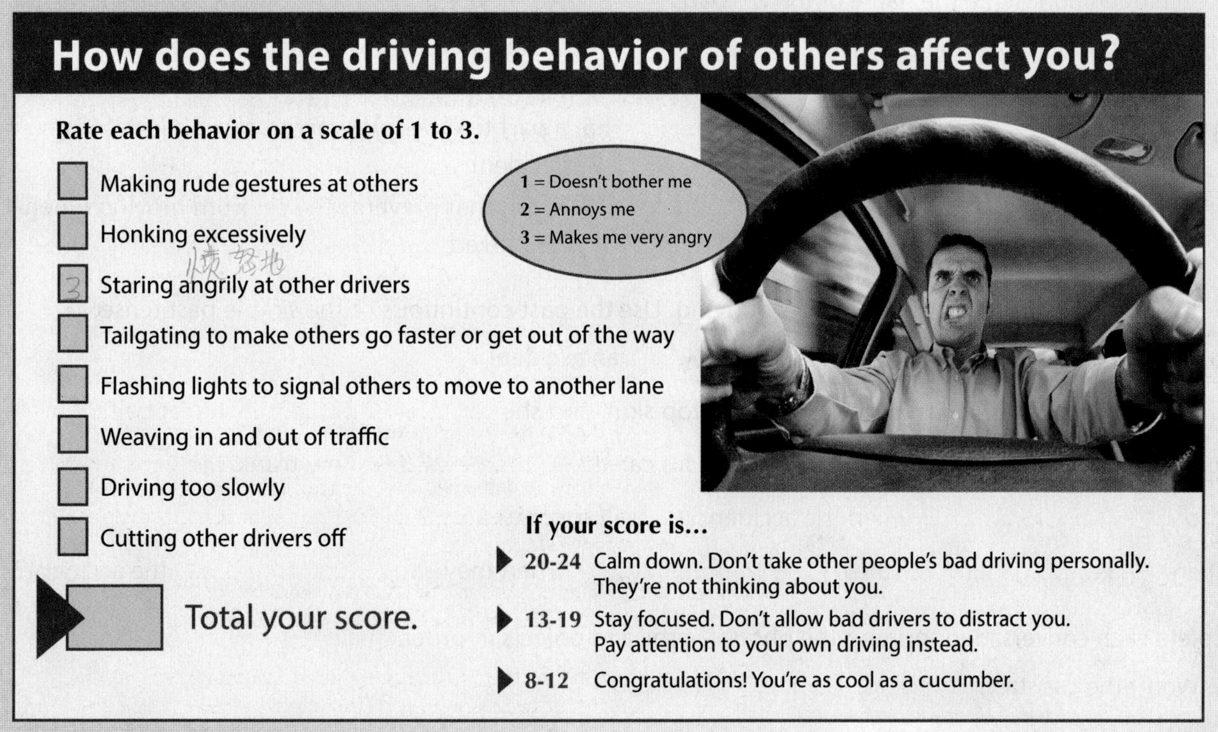

How does the driving behavior of others affect you?

Rate each behavior on a scale of 1 to 3.

1 = Doesn't bother me
2 = Annoys me
3 = Makes me very angry

- ☐ Making rude gestures at others
- ☐ Honking excessively
- ☐ Staring angrily at other drivers
- ☐ Tailgating to make others go faster or get out of the way
- ☐ Flashing lights to signal others to move to another lane
- ☐ Weaving in and out of traffic
- ☐ Driving too slowly
- ☐ Cutting other drivers off

☐ Total your score.

If your score is...

- **20-24** Calm down. Don't take other people's bad driving personally. They're not thinking about you.
- **13-19** Stay focused. Don't allow bad drivers to distract you. Pay attention to your own driving instead.
- **8-12** Congratulations! You're as cool as a cucumber.

B **NOTEPADDING** Describe what good and bad drivers do. Use the Vocabulary.

Good drivers . . .	Aggressive drivers . . .
use their turn signals	*flash their lights at others*

C **DISCUSSION** Discuss good and bad driving. What percentage of drivers do you think are bad or aggressive? Use your notepad for support.

Text-mining (optional)
Find and underline three words or phrases in the Reading that were new to you. Use them in your Discussion.
For example: "slow down."

REVIEW

A 2:35 Listen to the conversations. Then complete the statements with words and phrases for bad or aggressive driving.

1 The other driver just .... them ....
2 Jim's mother says he's ....
3 The driver behind them is .... at them.
4 The driver opened his window and .... at them.
5 The driver is .... because he wants to pass.
6 The driver is ....
7 The driver is .... at them.

B Read each definition. Write the name of the car part.

1 a window on the top of the car: ....
2 a part that stops the car: ....
3 a window the driver looks through to see the cars in front: ....
4 a place where the driver can find information about speed and amount of gas: ....
5 a part that people wear to avoid injuries in an accident: ....
6 a part that prevents the car from moving when it's parked: ....

C Complete each statement or question about driving. Use the past continuous or the simple past tense.

1 I .... (not pay attention), and I .... (have) an accident.
2 The other driver .... (not stop) at the stop sign, and she .... (not wear) a seat belt.
3 He .... (talk) on a cell phone, and his car .... (damage) my trunk.
4 Who .... (drive) when the accident .... (occur)?
5 Where .... they .... (stand) when they .... (see) the accident?

D Complete each conversation, putting the phrasal verbs and objects in order.

1 A: Won't the car start?
B: No. I can't .... (it / turn / on) .
2 A: Do you need gas?
B: Yes. Please .... (up / fill / it) .
3 A: Hey, you haven't turned on your headlights.
B: Oops. Thanks. I can't believe I forgot to .... (turn / on / them) .
4 A: Can All Star Limo drive us to the airport?
B: Yes. They'll .... (us / pick / up) at 5:30.

For additional language practice . . .
TOP NOTCH POP • Lyrics p. 153
"Wheels around the World"
DIGITAL SONG
DIGITAL KARAOKE

WRITING

Write a short paragraph about the differences between good and bad drivers. Include language from pages 38, 44, and 46 in your paragraph.

WRITING BOOSTER p. 146
- Connecting words and sentences: And, In addition, Furthermore, and Therefore
- Guidance for this writing exercise

ORAL REVIEW

GROUP STORY Together, create a story about the pictures. Each person adds one sentence to the story. Begin with January 16. Use the past continuous and the simple past tense in your story. Start like this:

They picked up their rental car in Temuco on January 16 . . .

PAIR WORK

1 Create conversations for the people in the first three pictures. For example:

A: We'd like to rent a car.
B: Certainly. What kind of a car do you need?

2 Create a phone conversation for the fourth picture. The woman reports the accident to Multi Car Rentals. The agent responds. Say as much as you can. For example:

We had an accident. My husband was . . .

NOW I CAN

- ☐ Discuss a car accident.
- ☐ Describe a car problem.
- ☐ Rent a car.
- ☐ Discuss good and bad driving.

COMMUNICATION GOALS

1 Ask for something in a store.
2 Make an appointment at a salon or spa.
3 Discuss ways to improve appearance.
4 Define the meaning of beauty.

UNIT 5 Personal Care and Appearance

PREVIEW

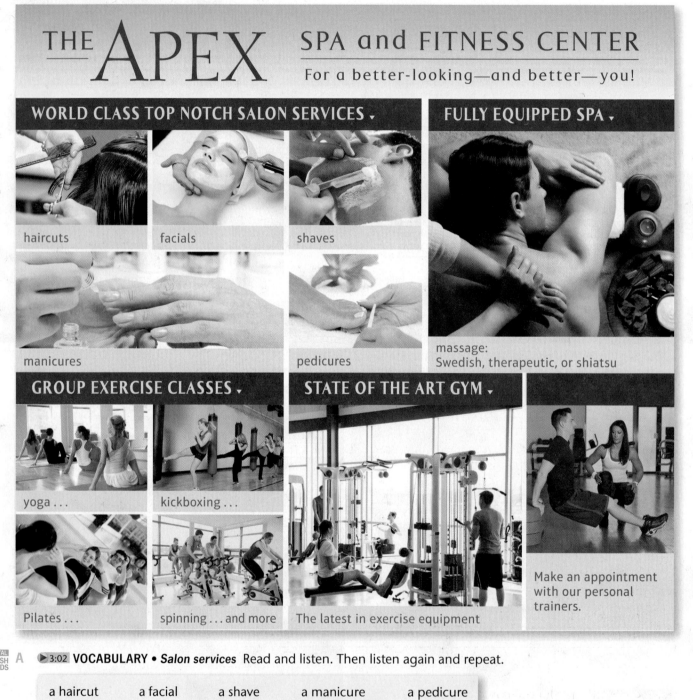

THE APEX SPA and FITNESS CENTER

For a better-looking—and better—you!

WORLD CLASS TOP NOTCH SALON SERVICES

haircuts

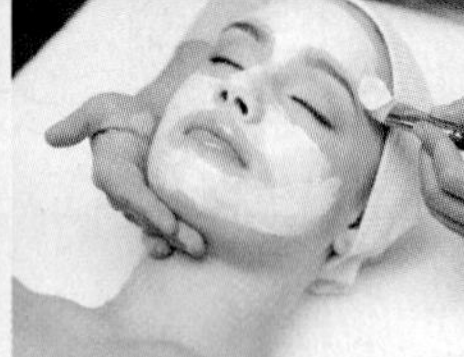

facials

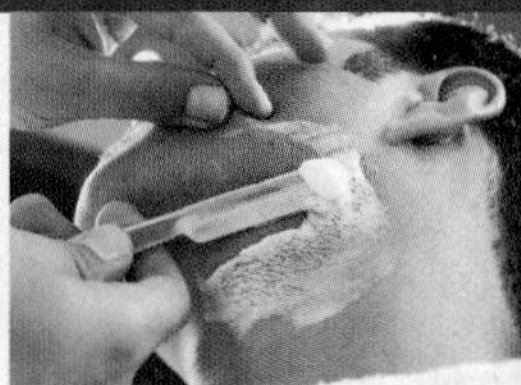

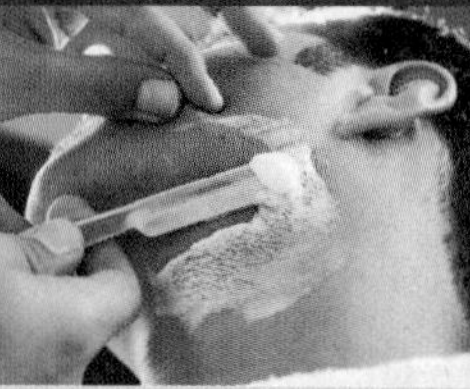

shaves

manicures

pedicures

FULLY EQUIPPED SPA

massage: Swedish, therapeutic, or shiatsu

GROUP EXERCISE CLASSES

yoga . . .

kickboxing . . .

Pilates . . .

spinning . . . and more

STATE OF THE ART GYM

The latest in exercise equipment

Make an appointment with our personal trainers.

DIGITAL FLASH CARDS

A 3:02 **VOCABULARY • *Salon services*** Read and listen. Then listen again and repeat.

a haircut	a facial	a shave	a manicure	a pedicure

B **PAIR WORK** With a partner, discuss the Apex Club services. What are the advantages of combining exercise and fitness with spa and massage services in one club?

ENGLISH FOR TODAY'S WORLD
Understand English speakers from different language backgrounds.
Receptionist = French speaker

C ▶3:03 **PHOTO STORY** Read and listen to a conversation in a spa salon.

Receptionist: Can I help you, sir?
Client: Would it be possible to get a massage? I don't have an appointment.
Receptionist: Well, actually, you're in luck. Our eleven o'clock just called to cancel his appointment.
Client: Terrific.
Receptionist: Let me show you to the dressing area.

Client: Thanks. Oh, while I'm at it, do you think I could get a haircut, too?
Receptionist: Yes. But you might have to wait a bit. We don't have anything until 12:00.
Client: Not a problem. By the way, how much will the massage and haircut come to?
Receptionist: Let's see . . . it will be 110 euros in all.

Client: Great. One more question. Is it customary to tip the staff?
Receptionist: Well, that's up to you. But most clients give the stylist and the masseuse a euro or two each.

D **FOCUS ON LANGUAGE** Answer the questions, using language from the Photo Story.

1 How does the client ask for a massage?
2 How does the receptionist indicate that the client can have a massage without an appointment?
3 How does the client ask about the price of a massage and a haircut?
4 What phrase does the receptionist use to tell the client the total cost of the salon services?
5 How does the client say "That's OK"?
6 What expression does the receptionist use to tell the client that the amount to tip is his decision?

SPEAKING

A **PERSONALIZE** Check the word or phrase that best describes how often you get these salon services. Then compare charts with a partner.

	weekly	monthly	once in a while	never	I do this for myself!
haircut	☐	☐	☐	☐	☐
facial	☐	☐	☐	☐	☐
shave	☐	☐	☐	☐	☐
manicure	☐	☐	☐	☐	☐
pedicure	☐	☐	☐	☐	☐
massage	☐	☐	☐	☐	☐

B **PAIR WORK** In your opinion, what is the value of each service? Compare opinions with a partner.

"I think massages are great for backaches. A massage helps me feel better."

"A shave? Are you kidding? I do that myself. I don't go to salons!"

LESSON 1 **GOAL** Ask for something in a store

DIGITAL FLASH CARDS

VOCABULARY *Personal care products*

A ▶3:04 Read and listen. Then listen again and repeat.

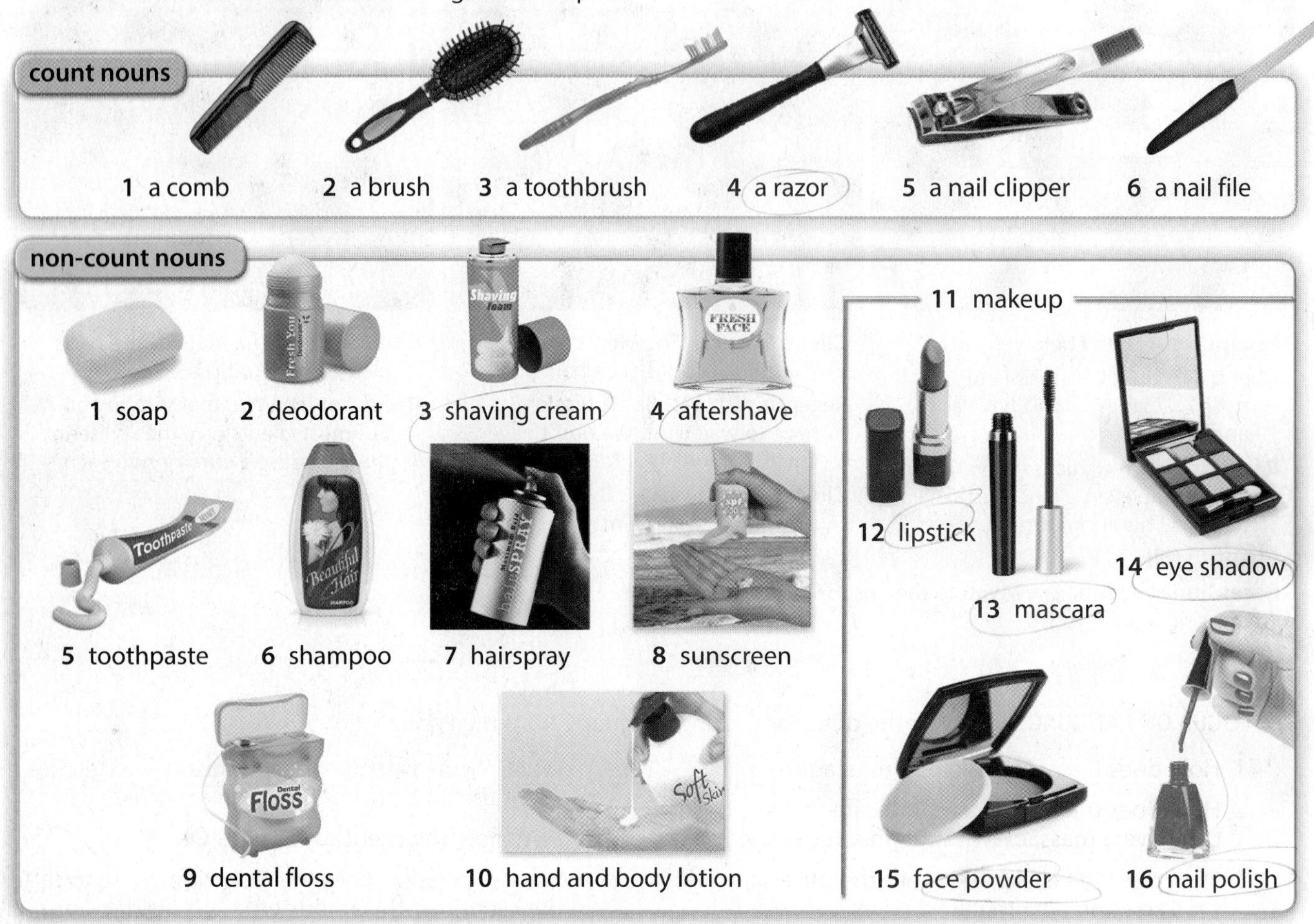

B ▶3:05 **LISTEN TO INFER** Listen and circle the kind of product each ad describes.

1 Spring Rain (shampoo / deodorant)
2 Rose (soap / nail polish)
3 Pro-Tect (sunscreen / hand and body lotion)
4 All Over (face powder / hand and body lotion)
5 Scrubbie (toothpaste / shaving cream)
6 Maximum Hold (hairspray / shampoo)

GRAMMAR *Quantifiers for indefinite quantities and amounts*

Use some and any with both plural count nouns and non-count nouns.

some: affirmative statements

We bought some combs. Now we have some.
They need some soap. We have some.

any: negative statements

I don't have any razors. I don't want any.
We don't want any makeup. We don't need any.

some or any: questions

Do you want any aftershave? OR Do you want some aftershave?
Does she have any nail files? OR Does she have some nail files?

Use a lot of or lots of with both plural count nouns and non-count nouns in statements and questions. They have the same meaning.

That store has a lot of (or lots of) razors. They don't have a lot of (or lots of) sunscreen.
Do they have a lot of (or lots of) makeup?

Use many and much in negative statements.

many: with plural count nouns	much: with non-count nouns
They don't have many brands of makeup.	The store doesn't have much toothpaste.

GRAMMAR BOOSTER p. 132

- Some and any: indefiniteness
- Too many, too much, and enough
- Comparative quantifiers fewer and less

GRAMMAR PRACTICE Complete the conversation between a husband and wife packing for a trip.

Dana: Do we have (1 any / many) shampoo?

Neil: Yes. We have (2 many / lots of) shampoo.

Dana: And Maggie uses (3 much / a lot of) sunscreen. Is there (4 many / any)?

Neil: No, there isn't (5 some / any). And we don't have (6 much / many) toothpaste, either. I can pick (7 some / any) up on my way back from work.

Dana: Hey, Adam's shaving now. Does he need (8 any / many) shaving cream?

DIGITAL MORE ERCISES

Neil: He doesn't shave every day. He can use mine!

CONVERSATION MODEL

A ▶3:06 Read and listen to someone looking for personal care products in a store.

A: Excuse me. Where would I find sunscreen?

B: Sunscreen? Have a look in the cosmetics section, in aisle 2.

A: Actually, I did, and there wasn't any.

B: I'm sorry. Let me get you some from the back. Anything else?

A: Yes. I couldn't find any razors either.

B: No problem. There are some over there. I'll show you.

B ▶3:07 **RHYTHM AND INTONATION** Listen again and repeat. Then practice the Conversation Model with a partner.

C **FIND THE GRAMMAR** Find and underline the four quantifiers in the Conversation Model.

NOW YOU CAN Ask for something in a store

A **CONVERSATION ACTIVATOR** With a partner, use the store directory to change the Conversation Model. Use the Vocabulary and quantifiers. Then change roles.

A: Excuse me. Where would I find .... ?

B: .... ? Have a look in ....

A: Actually, I did, and there .... any.

B: I'm sorry. Let me get you .... from the back. Anything else?

A: ....

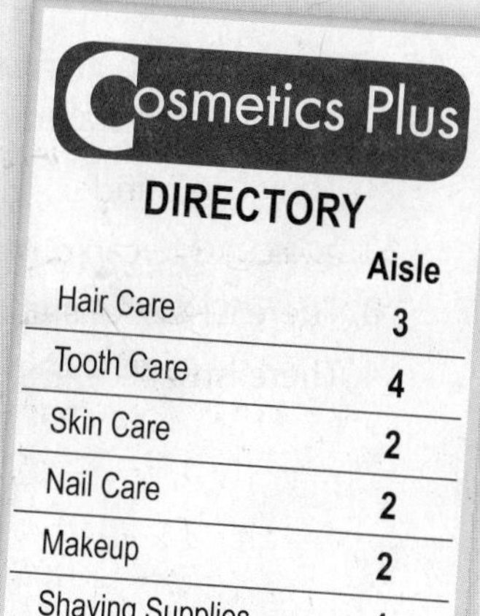

Cosmetics Plus
DIRECTORY
Aisle
Hair Care 3
Tooth Care 4
Skin Care 2
Nail Care 2
Makeup 2
Shaving Supplies 1

DON'T STOP!

- Ask about other personal care products.

RECYCLE THIS LANGUAGE.

How much [is that aftershave / are those nail clippers]?
Can I get this [shampoo] in a larger / smaller size?
Can I get this lipstick in [black]?
Do you have any cheaper [razors]?

B **CHANGE PARTNERS** Practice the conversation again, asking for other products.

GOAL Make an appointment at a salon or spa

CONVERSATION MODEL

A ▶3:08 Read and listen to someone make an appointment for a haircut.

A: Hello. Classic Spa and Salon.

B: Hello. This is Monica Morgan. I'd like to make an appointment for a haircut.

A: When would you like to come in, Ms. Morgan?

B: Today, if possible.

A: Let me check. . . . Sean has an opening at 2:00.

B: Actually, that's a little early for me. Is someone available after 4:00?

A: Yes. Yelena can see you then.

B ▶3:09 **RHYTHM AND INTONATION** Listen again and repeat. Then practice the Conversation Model with a partner.

GRAMMAR *Indefinite pronouns: someone / no one / anyone*

Someone, no one, and anyone are indefinite pronouns. Each refers to an unnamed person. Use indefinite pronouns when the identity of the person is unknown or unimportant.

Affirmative statements

Someone / No one	is available.
Someone / No one	is waiting for the manicurist.

I saw someone at the front desk.

Questions

Can	anyone / someone	wash my hair?
Is there	anyone / someone	at the front desk?
Did you see	anyone / someone	waiting for a shave?

Negative statements

There isn't anyone waiting.
I didn't see anyone at the salon.

Be careful!
Use anyone, not no one, with the negative form of a verb.
I didn't speak to **anyone**.
NOT I didn't speak to ~~no one~~.

GRAMMAR BOOSTER p. 133
- Indefinite pronouns: something, anything, everything, and nothing

A ▶3:10 **LISTEN TO ACTIVATE VOCABULARY AND GRAMMAR** Listen to the conversations. Complete each statement with someone or anyone and the salon service(s).

1 They can't find .... to give her a .... this afternoon.
2 .... can give him a .... and a .... at 4:00.
3 There is .... who can give her a .... and a .... at 6:30.
4 There isn't .... who can give him a .... today.

B GRAMMAR PRACTICE Complete each statement or question with <u>someone</u>, <u>no one</u>, or <u>anyone</u>. In some cases, more than one answer is correct.

1. There's someone (or no one) at the front desk.
2. They didn't tell .... it would be a long wait.
3. Did you see .... giving a manicure?
4. I didn't ask .... about the price.
5. There will be .... here to give you a pedicure in a few minutes.
6. .... can cut your hair at 12:30 if you can wait.
7. Please don't tell .... the price. It was very expensive!
8. .... called and left you this message while you were getting your shampoo.
9. There wasn't .... there when she called for an appointment.
10. I didn't speak to .... about the bad haircut.
11. .... told me the salon offers shiatsu massage now.
12. I don't have the nail file. I gave it to ....

DIGITAL MORE EXERCISES

DIGITAL VIDEO COACH

PRONUNCIATION *Pronunciation of unstressed vowels*

A ▶ 3:11 The vowel in an unstressed syllable is often pronounced /ə/. Read and listen, paying attention to the syllable or syllables marked with /ə/. Then listen again and repeat.

1	2	3	4	5
• ●	● •	● • •	● • •	• ● • •
ma ssage	fa cial	ma ni cure	pe di cure	de o do rant
/ə/	/ə/	/ə/	/ə/	/ə/ /ə/

B Now practice saying the words on your own.

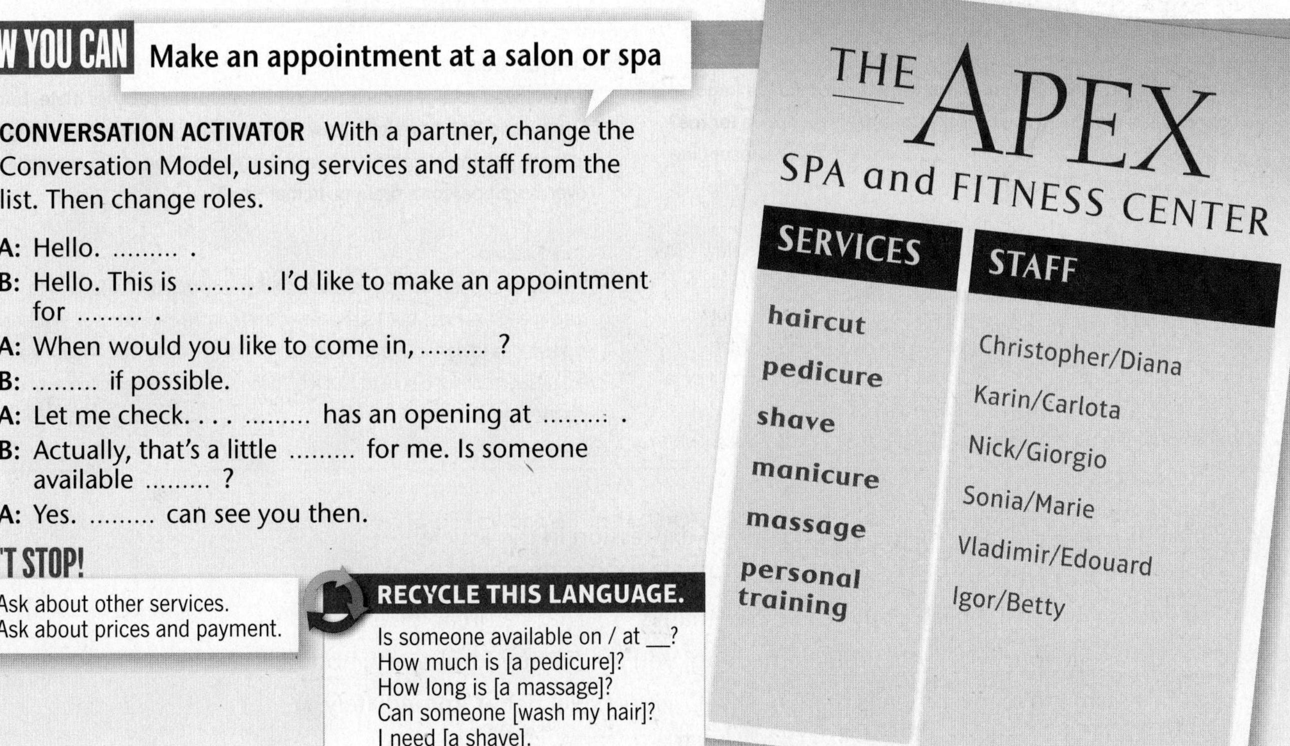

THE APEX
SPA and FITNESS CENTER
SERVICES
STAFF
haircut
pedicure
shave
manicure
massage
personal training
Christopher/Diana
Karin/Carlota
Nick/Giorgio
Sonia/Marie
Vladimir/Edouard
Igor/Betty

NOW YOU CAN Make an appointment at a salon or spa

DIGITAL VIDEO

A CONVERSATION ACTIVATOR With a partner, change the Conversation Model, using services and staff from the list. Then change roles.

A: Hello. ....
B: Hello. This is .... I'd like to make an appointment for ....
A: When would you like to come in, ... ?
B: .... if possible.
A: Let me check. . . . . has an opening at ....
B: Actually, that's a little .... for me. Is someone available .... ?
A: Yes. .... can see you then.

DON'T STOP!

- Ask about other services.
- Ask about prices and payment.

RECYCLE THIS LANGUAGE.

Is someone available on / at __?
How much is [a pedicure]?
How long is [a massage]?
Can someone [wash my hair]?
I need [a shave].
Is the tip included?
Do you accept credit cards?

B CHANGE PARTNERS Practice the conversation again, making an appointment for other services.

LESSON 3 GOAL Discuss ways to improve appearance

BEFORE YOU READ

PREDICT Look at the photos and title of the article. What questions do you think the people will ask Dr. Weiss?

READING ▶3:12

Cosmetic surgery
... for everyone?

Q&A

Contact Doctor Weiss at Personal Health Magazine: weiss@personalhealth.rx

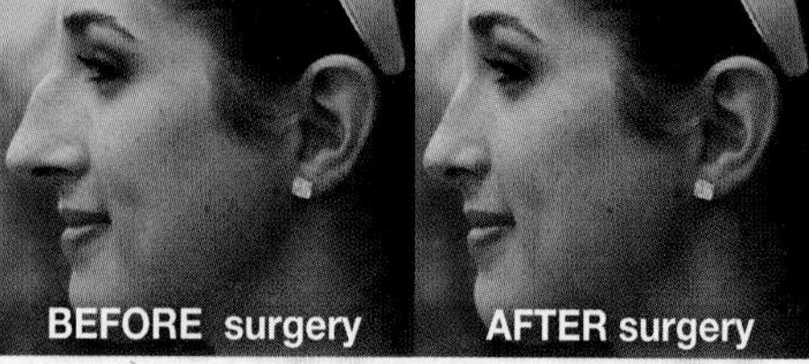
BEFORE surgery AFTER surgery

Some people consider cosmetic surgery no more serious than visiting a spa or a salon. But others say, "I think I'll pass." They're aware that cosmetic surgery is, in fact, surgery, and surgery should never be taken lightly. Fitness editor Dr. Gail Weiss answers readers' questions about cosmetic surgery.

Dear Dr. Weiss:
I'm at my wits' end with my face. I have wrinkles and sun damage. I'm only 30, but I look 50. Do you think a face-lift is an option for me?
Josephine

Dear Josephine:
This popular and effective surgery lifts the face and the neck in one operation. But a face-lift is surgery, and afterwards you will have to stay home for a number of days. It takes time to recover. Before you decide to have a face-lift, ask your dermatologist or a cosmetic surgeon about a chemical peel. A chemical peel removes the top layer of skin and can improve the appearance of the skin without surgery. Compared to surgery, a half-hour visit to your dermatologist would be a piece of cake! Good luck!
Gail Weiss, M.D

Dear Dr. Weiss:
I'm a 24-year-old man who is already losing his hair. Dr. Weiss, I'm looking for a wife, and I'm afraid no woman will want to marry a 25-year-old bald guy. I need some advice.
Calvin

Dear Calvin:
There are several surgical procedures which a cosmetic surgeon can perform to help treat hair loss and restore hair for both men and women. But if that's not practical, remember that some of the world's most attractive men are bald!
Gail Weiss, M.D.

Dear Dr. Weiss:
When I was young, I was a chocoholic. I ate a lot of chocolate, but I never gained any weight. Now that I'm older, I can't eat anything without gaining weight! I've heard that liposuction is the answer to an overweight person's dreams. Is that true?
Dawson

Dear Dawson:
It's true that liposuction can remove fat deposits that don't respond to dieting and exercise, but it's expensive and can be dangerous. It would be a good idea to ask your doctor for some help in dieting first. Then, if you are unsuccessful, be sure to find a surgeon with a lot of experience before deciding on liposuction.
Gail Weiss, M.D.

A PARAPHRASE Find and circle each underlined expression in the article. Then circle the correct word or phrase to complete each statement.

1 If you say I think I'll pass, you mean ("No, thanks" / "That's a great idea").
2 If you are at your wits' end about something, you are (happy / unhappy) about it.
3 It takes time to recover means that you (will / won't) feel better immediately.
4 Something that is a piece of cake is (easy / difficult).

B UNDERSTAND FROM CONTEXT With a partner, find these procedures in the Reading and write a definition for each one.

1 liposuction ....
2 hair restoration ....
3 a face-lift ....
4 a chemical peel ....

C CONFIRM CONTENT AND APPLY INFORMATION Complete the chart with information from the article. Then, with a partner, give your own advice for each person.

	Problem	Dr. Weiss's advice	Your advice
Josephine			
Calvin			
Dawson			

DIGITAL MORE ERCISES

NOW YOU CAN Discuss ways to improve appearance

A FRAME YOUR IDEAS Take the opinion survey about ways to improve appearance.

How far would you go to improve your appearance?

Would you try ...	definitely	maybe	probably not	absolutely not!
diet?				
exercise?				
massage?				
hair restoration?				
cosmetics and makeup?				
facials?				
face-lifts?				
liposuction?				
chemical peels?				

B NOTEPADDING Choose one method you would try and one method you would not try. On the notepad, write advantages and disadvantages.

Method	Advantage(s)	Disadvantage(s)
I would try diet.	free, safe	It's hard to do!

Method	Advantage(s)	Disadvantage(s)

C DISCUSSION What's the best way to improve your appearance? What ways would you NOT try? Explain. Use your notepad for support.

Text-mining (optional)
Find and underline three words or phrases in the Reading that were new to you. Use them in your Discussion.
For example: "surgical procedures."

GOAL Define the meaning of beauty

BEFORE YOU LISTEN

DIGITAL FLASH CARDS

A ▶ 3:13 **VOCABULARY • *Discussing beauty*** Read and listen. Then listen again and repeat.

physical features skin, hair, body shape and size, eyes, nose, mouth, etc.

beauty the physical features most people of a particular culture consider good-looking

attractive having a beautiful or pleasing physical or facial appearance

unattractive the opposite of *attractive*

youth appearing young; the opposite of looking old

health the general condition of one's body and how healthy one is

B **EXPLORE YOUR IDEAS** Write a statement or two describing, in your opinion, the characteristics of an attractive man or woman.

An attractive woman has long hair and dark eyes.

C **PAIR WORK** Use your statements to talk about the physical features you consider attractive for men and women. Use the Vocabulary.

" In my opinion, attractive people have . . . "

LISTENING COMPREHENSION

A ▶ 3:14 **LISTEN TO RECOGNIZE SOMEONE'S POINT OF VIEW** Listen to the interview. Check all of the statements that summarize Maya Prasad's and Ricardo Figueroa's ideas about beauty.

Maya Prasad

- ☐ I'm very lucky to be so beautiful.
- ☐ All the contestants were beautiful. I was just lucky.
- ☐ Physical beauty only lasts a short time.
- ☐ Love makes people beautiful.

Ricardo Figueroa

- ☐ Physical beauty is not important at all.
- ☐ Both physical beauty and inner beauty are important.
- ☐ Only inner beauty is important.
- ☐ Prasad represents an almost perfect combination of inner and outer beauty.

B ▶ 3:15 **LISTEN TO TAKE NOTES** Listen and take notes about what Figueroa says about each of the qualities below. Then compare your notes with the class.

warmth:

patience:

goodness and kindness:

C DISCUSSION Talk about one or more of the questions.

1. In what ways do you agree or disagree with Prasad's and Figueroa's ideas about beauty?
2. Do you think the Miss Universal Beauty contest sounds better than the usual beauty contest? Why or why not?
3. Do you think there should be beauty contests for men as well as for women? Why or why not? What in your opinion is the difference between a woman's beauty and a man's beauty?
4. How do you explain these words in the song Prasad talks about: "Do you love me because I'm beautiful, or am I beautiful because you love me"?

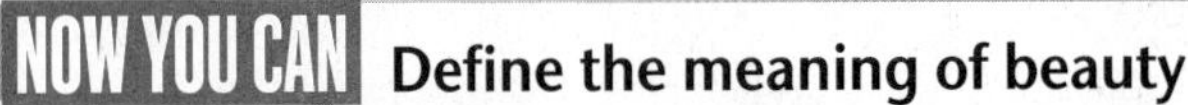

NOW YOU CAN Define the meaning of beauty

A NOTEPADDING Look at the four photos. What qualities of beauty do you find in each person? Write notes.

1 Outer beauty	Inner beauty
She has beautiful skin.	*She looks warm and friendly.*

1 Outer beauty

Inner beauty

2 Outer beauty

Inner beauty

3 Outer beauty

Inner beauty

4 Outer beauty

Inner beauty

B PAIR WORK Discuss the qualities of beauty you found in the people in the pictures. Compare your opinions. Use your notepads for support.

C DISCUSSION Define the meaning of beauty.

> "I think beauty is hard to describe. It's a combination of things. I consider my grandmother really beautiful because . . ."

A 3:16 Listen to the conversations. Infer what kind of product the people are discussing. Complete each statement.

1 Hawaii Bronzer is a brand of ....
2 Swan is a brand of ....
3 Truly You is a brand of ....
4 Mountain Fresh is a brand of ....
5 Silk 'n Satin is a brand of ....
6 Fresh as a Flower is a brand of ....

B Complete each statement or question.

1 There aren't (many / much) customers in the store right now.
2 Do they sell (any / many) sunscreen at the hotel gift shop? I forgot to pack some.
3 Your sister doesn't want (some / any) body lotion.
4 She doesn't wear (much / some) makeup. She doesn't need to—she has beautiful skin.
5 My son uses (any / a lot of) shaving cream.
6 There's (anyone / someone) on the phone for you. Do you want me to take a message?
7 There are (any / a lot of) salons in this neighborhood.

C Complete each statement about services at a salon or spa.

1 There's nothing like a professional .... when you're sick and tired of your beard.
2 If your hair is too long, get a ....
3 In the summer, before you wear sandals for the first time, your feet will look great if you get a ....
4 When your hands are a mess, you can get a ....
5 When your muscles are sore from too much work or exercise, a .... can help.

D Complete each conversation with the correct procedure.

1 A: I look so old! Look at my neck and my eyes.
B: Why don't you get (a massage / a facelift)?

2 A: My back and shoulders are sore from too much exercise.
B: They say (a chemical peel / a massage) can really help.

3 A: Look at this! I'm getting bald!
B: Have you thought about (liposuction / hair restoration)?

WRITING

Re-read the letters on page 56. Choose one letter and write a response, using your own opinion and making your own suggestions. Explain what you think is OK or appropriate for men and women.

WRITING BOOSTER p. 147
- Writing a formal letter
- Guidance for this writing exercise

For additional language practice . . .
TOP NOTCH POP • Lyrics p. 153
"Piece of Cake"
DIGITAL SONG
DIGITAL KARAOKE

DIGITAL GAMES

ORAL REVIEW

CONTEST Look at the picture for a minute, and then close your books. With a partner, try to remember all the products and services in the picture. The pair who remembers the most products and services wins.

PAIR WORK

1 Create a conversation between the client and the clerk at the front desk of the salon. Start like this:

Hi. I have a 2:30 appointment for . . .

2 Create a conversation for the man and woman waiting for salon services. For example:

What are you here for?

NOW I CAN

- ☐ Ask for something in a store.
- ☐ Make an appointment at a salon or spa.
- ☐ Discuss ways to improve appearance.
- ☐ Define the meaning of beauty.

COMMUNICATION GOALS

1 Talk about food passions.
2 Make an excuse to decline food.
3 Discuss lifestyle changes.
4 Describe local dishes.

UNIT 6 Eating Well

PREVIEW

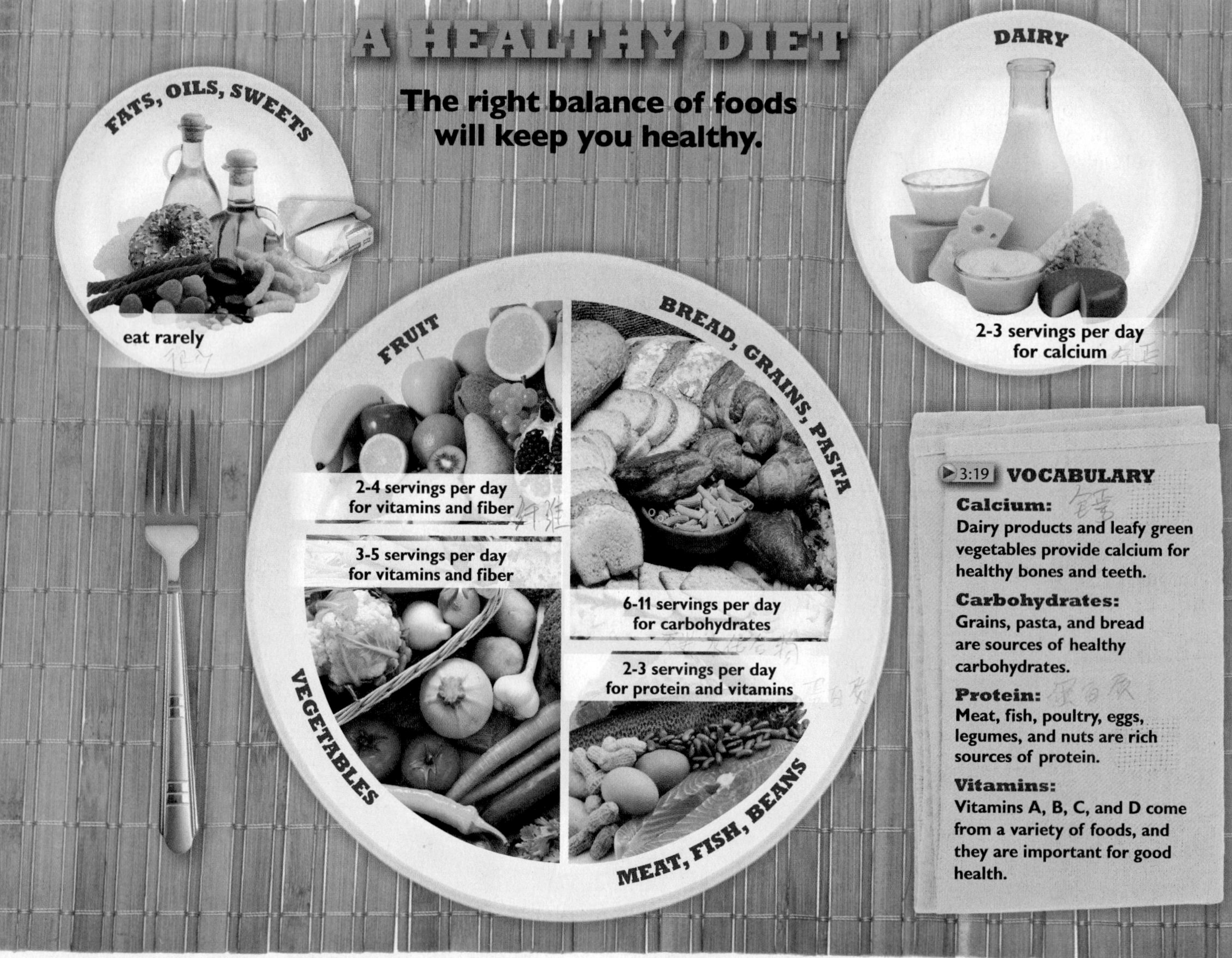

A HEALTHY DIET
The right balance of foods will keep you healthy.
FATS, OILS, SWEETS
eat rarely
DAIRY
2-3 servings per day for calcium
FRUIT
2-4 servings per day for vitamins and fiber
BREAD, GRAINS, PASTA
6-11 servings per day for carbohydrates
VEGETABLES
3-5 servings per day for vitamins and fiber
MEAT, FISH, BEANS
2-3 servings per day for protein and vitamins
3:19 VOCABULARY
Calcium:
Dairy products and leafy green vegetables provide calcium for healthy bones and teeth.
Carbohydrates:
Grains, pasta, and bread are sources of healthy carbohydrates.
Protein:
Meat, fish, poultry, eggs, legumes, and nuts are rich sources of protein.
Vitamins:
Vitamins A, B, C, and D come from a variety of foods, and they are important for good health.

A Look at the suggestions above for eating a healthy diet. Do you think this diet is healthy? Why or why not?

B Complete the chart about the foods you eat each day. Compare charts with a partner.

C **DISCUSSION** How are the Healthy Diet suggestions different from your chart? Which do you think is a healthier diet? Explain.

2–3 servings a day
3–5 servings a day
More than 5 servings a day

D ▶3:20 **PHOTO STORY** Read and listen to people talking about food choices.

Rita: Didn't you tell me you were avoiding sweets?

Joy: I couldn't resist! I had a craving for chocolate.

Rita: Well, I have to admit it looks pretty good. How many calories are in that thing anyway?

Joy: I have no idea. Want to try some?

Rita: Thanks. But I think I'd better pass. I'm avoiding carbs.*

Joy: You? I don't believe it. You never used to turn down chocolate!

Rita: I know. But I'm watching my weight now.

Joy: Come on! It's really good.

Rita: OK. Maybe just a bite.

Joy: Hey, you only live once!

*carbs (informal) = carbohydrates

E **FOCUS ON LANGUAGE** Find an underlined sentence or phrase in the Photo Story with the same meaning as each of the following.

1 I don't know. ....

2 I should say no. ....

3 I couldn't stop myself. ....

4 I'm trying not to get heavier. ....

5 I really wanted . . . .

6 I agree . . . .

7 say no to ....

8 I'll try a little. ....

SPEAKING

Read the descriptions of diets. Would you ever try any of them? Why or why not?

“I don't believe in the Atkins Diet. A lot of meat, eggs, and cheese doesn't sound like the right balance of foods for good health.”

The Mushroom Diet

For weight loss.

Replace lunch or dinner every day—for two weeks—with a mushroom dish.

The Vegan Diet

For better health and prevention of disease.

Avoid all animal products, including dairy and eggs. Eat lots of grains, beans, vegetables, and fruits.

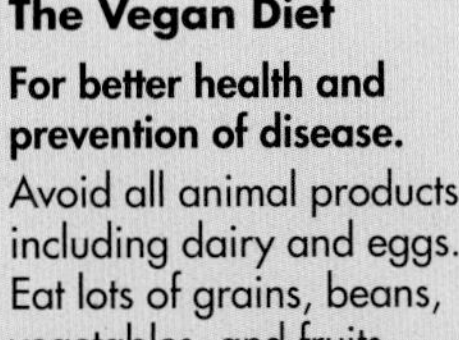

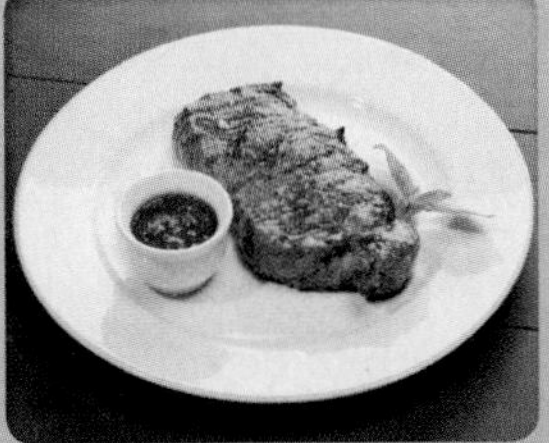

The Atkins Diet

For weight loss.

Eat high-protein foods such as meat, eggs, and cheese. Avoid foods that are high in carbohydrates, such as potatoes, bread, grains, and sugar.

The Juice Fast

For better health and prevention of disease.

Instead of food, drink four to six glasses of fresh vegetable and fruit juices for anywhere from three days to three weeks. Get plenty of rest and avoid exercise during the fast.

LESSON 1

GOAL Talk about food passions

DIGITAL FLASH CARDS

VOCABULARY *Food passions*

A ▶3:21 Read and listen. Then listen again and repeat.

I'm **crazy about** seafood.
I'm **a big** meat **eater**.
I'm **a big** coffee **drinker**.
I'm **a** chocolate **addict**.
I'm **a** pizza **lover**.
I **can't stand** fish.
I'm **not crazy about** chocolate.
I **don't care for** steak.
I'm **not much of a** pizza **eater**.
I'm **not much of a** coffee **drinker**.

B ▶3:22 **LISTEN TO ACTIVATE VOCABULARY** Circle the correct words to complete each statement about the speakers' food passions.

1 She (is crazy about / doesn't care for) sushi.
2 He (loves / can't stand) asparagus.
3 She (is a mango lover / doesn't care for mangoes).
4 He (is a big pasta eater / isn't crazy about pasta).
5 She (is an ice cream addict / can't stand ice cream).

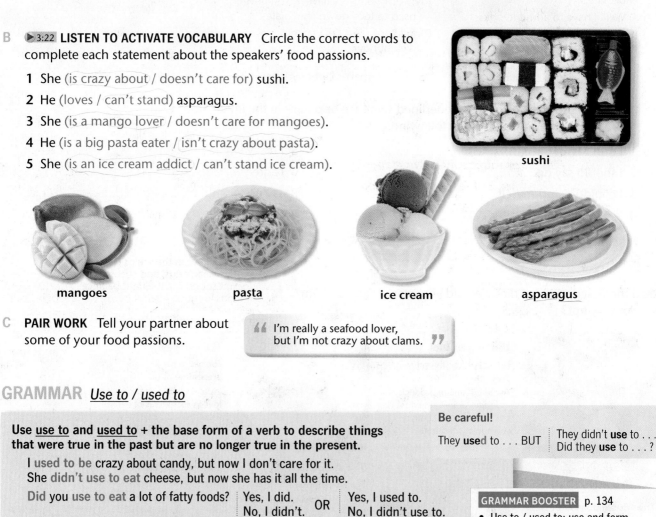

sushi

mangoes

pasta

ice cream

asparagus

C **PAIR WORK** Tell your partner about some of your food passions.

"I'm really a seafood lover, but I'm not crazy about clams."

GRAMMAR Use to / used to

Use use to and used to + the base form of a verb to describe things that were true in the past but are no longer true in the present.

I **used to be** crazy about candy, but now I don't care for it.
She **didn't use to eat** cheese, but now she has it all the time.

Did you **use to eat** a lot of fatty foods?	Yes, I did. No, I didn't.	OR	Yes, I used to. No, I didn't use to.

What **did** you **use to have** for breakfast? (Eggs and sausage. But not anymore.)
Why **did** you **use to eat** so much? (Because I didn't use to worry about my health.)

Be careful!

They **used** to . . . BUT | They didn't **use** to . . . / Did they **use** to . . . ?

GRAMMAR BOOSTER p. 134
- Use to / used to: use and form, common errors
- Be used to vs. get used to
- Repeated actions in the past: would + base form, common errors

GRAMMAR PRACTICE Use the context to help you complete each sentence with <u>used to</u> or <u>didn't use to</u>. Then write two sentences about yourself.

1 Gary .... go out to eat a lot, but now he eats at home more often.

2 Nina .... eat a lot of pasta, but now she does.

3 Vinnie .... drink a lot of coffee, but now he's a coffee addict.

4 Anton .... eat a lot of vegetables, but now he doesn't.

5 Cate .... hate seafood, but now she's crazy about fish.

6 Ted .... eat a lot of fatty foods, but now he avoids them.

7 Burt .... drink a lot of water, but now he has several glasses a day.

8 May .... like salad, but now she has salads several times a week.

9 (used to) I ....
....

10 (didn't use to) I ....
....

DIGITAL VIDEO COACH

PRONUNCIATION *Sound reduction: used to*

▶3:23 Notice how the pronunciation of <u>to</u> in <u>used to</u> changes to /tə/ in natural speech. Read and listen. Then listen again and repeat. Practice the sentences on your own.

1 I used to be a big meat eater.

2 Jack used to like sweets.

3 Sally used to be crazy about fries.

4 They didn't use to like seafood.

CONVERSATION MODEL

A ▶3:24 Read and listen to two people talking about their food passions.

A: Are you a big coffee drinker?

B: Definitely. I'm crazy about coffee. What about you?

A: I used to drink it a lot. But recently I've cut back.

B: Well, I couldn't live without it.

B ▶3:25 **RHYTHM AND INTONATION** Listen again and repeat. Then practice the Conversation Model with a partner.

NOW YOU CAN Talk about food passions

A **NOTEPADDING** Complete the notepad with foods you like and dislike.

My food passions

Foods I'm crazy about	Foods I can't stand

B **CONVERSATION ACTIVATOR** With a partner, change the Conversation Model, exchanging information about your food passions. Talk about what you used to and didn't use to eat or drink. Use your notepad and the Vocabulary from page 64.

A: Are you a big .... ?
B: .... What about you?
A: ....

DON'T STOP!

- Ask about more foods and drinks.

C **CHANGE PARTNERS** Talk about other food passions.

LESSON 2 **GOAL** Make an excuse to decline food

CONVERSATION MODEL

A ▶3:26 Read and listen to a dinner guest make an excuse to decline food.

A: Please help yourself.
B: Everything looks great! But I'll pass on the chicken.
A: Don't you eat chicken?
B: Actually, no. I'm a vegetarian.
A: I'm sorry. I didn't know that.
B: It's not a problem. I'll have something else.

B ▶3:27 **RHYTHM AND INTONATION** Listen again and repeat. Then practice the Conversation Model with a partner.

▶3:28 **Variations**
It's not a problem.
Don't worry.
I'm fine.

DIGITAL FLASH CARDS

VOCABULARY *Excuses for not eating something*

A ▶3:29 Read and listen. Then listen again and repeat.

Coffee **doesn't agree with me.**

I'm **on a diet.** / I'm **trying to lose weight**.

I don't eat beef. It's **against my religion.**

I'm **allergic to** chocolate.

I'm **avoiding** sugar.

I **don't care for** broccoli.

B ▶3:30 **LISTEN TO ACTIVATE VOCABULARY** Listen to each conversation. Write the letter to complete each statement. Then listen again to check your work.

.... **1** Cindy . . .	**a** is a vegetarian.
.... **2** Frankie . . .	**b** is avoiding fatty, salty foods.
.... **3** Marie . . .	**c** is trying to lose weight.
.... **4** Susan . . .	**d** is allergic to something.
.... **5** George . . .	**e** doesn't care for seafood.

C **PAIR WORK** Talk about foods or drinks you avoid. Explain why.

"I usually don't eat fried foods. I'm trying to lose weight."

GRAMMAR *Negative yes / no questions*

Use negative yes / no questions . . .

- **to confirm information you think is true.**
  Isn't Jane a vegetarian? (Yes, she is.)
  Didn't he go on a diet last week? (Yes. He's trying the Atkins Diet.)
- **when you want someone to agree with you.**
  Don't you love Italian food? (Yes, it's delicious!)
  Wasn't that a terrible dinner? (Actually, no. I thought it was good.)
- **to express surprise.**
  Aren't you going to have cake? (I'm sorry, but I'm on a diet.)
  Hasn't he tried the chicken? (No. He's a vegetarian.)

GRAMMAR BOOSTER p. 135

- Negative yes / no questions: short answers

GRAMMAR PRACTICE Complete each negative yes / no question.

1 A: .... you allergic to tomatoes?
B: Me? No. You're thinking of my brother.

2 A: .... that lunch yesterday delicious?
B: It was fantastic!

3 A: .... we already have steak this week?
B: Yes, we did.

4 A: .... your husband been on a diet?
B: Yes. But it's driving him crazy.

5 A: .... asparagus disgusting?
B: Actually, I like it.

6 A: .... you like your pasta?
B: Actually, it was a little too spicy for me.

DIGITAL MORE EXERCISES

NOW YOU CAN Make an excuse to decline food

A NOTEPADDING Look at the photos. On a separate sheet of paper, use the Vocabulary to write an excuse to decline each food.

B CONVERSATION ACTIVATOR With a partner, change the Conversation Model to role-play a dinner conversation. Use the photos to offer foods. Use your notepad to make excuses to decline that food. Then change roles. OPTION: Role-play a dinner conversation with more than one classmate.

A: Please help yourself.
B: Everything looks .... ! But I'll pass on the ....
A: Don't you eat .... ?
B: Actually, ...
A: I'm sorry. I didn't know that.
B: .... I'll have ....

DON'T STOP!

- Offer drinks and other foods.
- Talk about food passions.

RECYCLE THIS LANGUAGE.

be crazy about __	can't stand __
be a big __ eater / drinker	be not crazy about __
be a(n) __ addict / lover	not care for __

C CHANGE PARTNERS Practice the conversation again.

octopus

shellfish

tofu

steak

broccoli

beets

chocolate

LESSON 3 GOAL Discuss lifestyle changes

BEFORE YOU READ

EXPLORE YOUR IDEAS Do you think people's eating habits are better or worse than they used to be? Explain with examples.

READING ▶ 3:31

How Can It Be?

Americans gain weight . . . while the French stay thin

Have you ever wondered why Americans struggle with watching their weight, while the French, who consume all that rich food—the bread, the cheese, the wine, and the heavy sauces—continue to stay thin? Now a report from Cornell University suggests a possible answer. A study of almost 300 participants from France and the U.S. provides clues about how lifestyle and decisions about eating may affect weight. Researchers concluded that the French tend to stop eating when they feel full. However, Americans tend to stop when their plate is completely empty, or they have reached the end of their favorite TV show.

According to Dr. Joseph Mercola, who writes extensively about health issues, the French see eating as an important part of their lifestyle. They enjoy food and, therefore, spend a fairly long time at the table. In contrast, Americans see eating as something to do quickly as they squeeze meals between the other activities of the day. Mercola believes Americans have lost the ability to sense when they are actually full. So they keep eating long after the French would have stopped. In addition, he argues that, by tradition, the French tend to shop daily, walking to small shops and farmers' markets where they have a choice of fresh fruits, vegetables, and eggs as well as high-quality meats and cheeses for each meal. In contrast, Americans tend to drive their cars to huge supermarkets to buy canned and frozen foods for the whole week.

Despite all these differences, new reports show that recent lifestyle changes may be affecting French eating habits. Today, the rate of obesity—or extreme overweight—among adults is only 6%. However, as American fast-food restaurants gain acceptance, and the young turn their backs on older traditions, the obesity rate among French children has reached 17%—and is growing.

OMG!

A UNDERSTAND FROM CONTEXT Use the context of the article to help you choose the same meaning as each underlined word or phrase.

1 Have you ever wondered why Americans struggle with watching their weight . . .
a have an easy time b have a difficult time c don't care about

2 . . . while the French, who consume all that rich food, ...
a fatty, high-calorie food b low-fat, low-calorie food c expensive food

3 . . . continue to stay thin?
a worry about their weight b not become overweight c gain weight

4 Researchers concluded that the French tend to stop eating when they feel full.
a like they can't eat any more b worried about their weight c hungry

5 . . . the French see eating as an important part of their lifestyle.
a personal care and appearance b culture or daily routine c meals

B SUMMARIZE According to the article, why do the French stay thin while Americans gain weight? Write a four-sentence summary of the Reading. Then share your summary with the class.

Compared to Americans, the French stay thin because . . .

C COMPARE AND CONTRAST In your country, do people generally stay thin or do they struggle with watching their weight? Are lifestyles in your country closer to those of France or the U.S., as described in the article?

“I think people here are more like people in France. They like to eat, but they don't gain weight easily.”

NOW YOU CAN Discuss lifestyle changes

A FRAME YOUR IDEAS Complete the lifestyle self-assessment.

1 Have you ever changed the way you eat in order to lose weight? ○ yes ○ no

If so, what have you done?

- ○ ate less food
- ○ cut back on desserts
- ○ avoided fatty foods
- ○ other (explain) ________

Were you successful? ○ yes ○ no
Why or why not? Explain. ________

2 Have you ever changed the way you eat in order to avoid illness? ○ yes ○ no

If so, what changes have you made?

- ○ stopped eating fast foods
- ○ started eating whole grains
- ○ started eating more vegetables
- ○ other (explain) ________

Were you successful? ○ yes ○ no
Why or why not? Explain. ________

3 Have you ever tried to lead a more active lifestyle? ○ yes ○ no

If so, what have you done?

- ○ started working out in a gym
- ○ started running or walking
- ○ started playing sports
- ○ other (explain) ________

Were you successful? ○ yes ○ no
Why or why not? Explain. ________

B CLASS SURVEY On the board, summarize your class's lifestyles.

How many students . . .

- want to make some lifestyle changes?
- have gone on a diet to lose weight?
- have changed their diet to improve their health?
- have been successful with a diet?
- lead an active lifestyle?

C DISCUSSION How do you think your classmates compare to most people in your country? Are they generally healthier or less healthy? What do you think people need to do to have a healthy lifestyle?

“I think my classmates are healthier than most people in this country. Too many people eat fast foods. They need to eat healthier food and exercise more.”

Text-mining (optional)
Find and underline three words or phrases in the Reading that were new to you. Use them in your Discussion.
For example: "gain weight."

GOAL Describe local dishes

BEFORE YOU LISTEN

DIGITAL FLASH CARDS **A** ▶3:32 **VOCABULARY • *Food descriptions*** Read and listen. Then listen again and repeat.

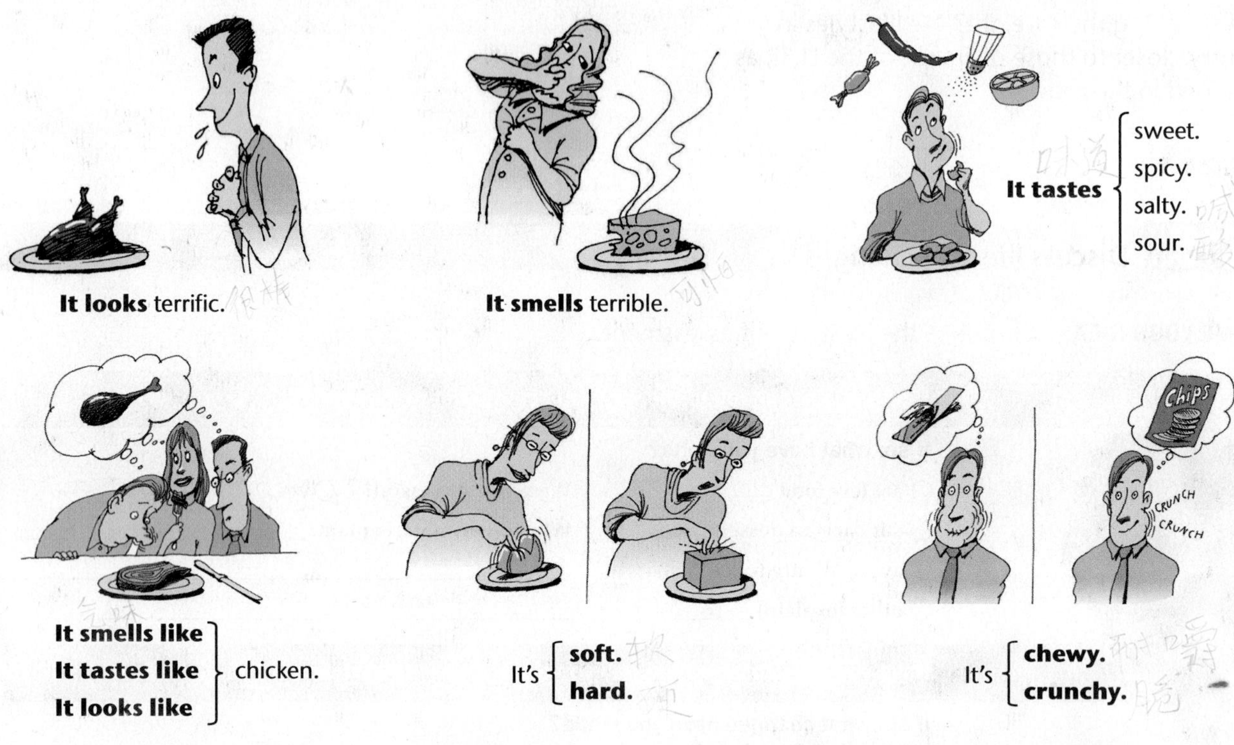

It looks terrific.

It smells terrible.

It tastes { sweet. / spicy. / salty. / sour. }

It smells like / **It tastes like** / **It looks like** } chicken.

It's { **soft.** / **hard.** }

It's { **chewy.** / **crunchy.** }

B **PAIR WORK** Use the Vocabulary to describe foods you know.

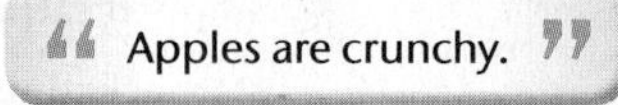

LISTENING COMPREHENSION

A ▶3:33 **LISTEN FOR DETAILS** First, listen to the descriptions of foods from around the world and write the letter of each food. Then listen again and choose the Vocabulary that completes each description.

.... **1** It's (crunchy / chewy / hard), and it tastes (salty / sweet / sour).

.... **2** It tastes (salty / sweet / spicy), and it's (soft / hard / crunchy).

.... **3** It's (soft / chewy / crunchy), and it tastes (salty / sweet / spicy).

.... **4** It tastes (salty / sweet / spicy). Some think it (tastes / smells / looks) awful.

.... **5** It (smells / tastes / looks) great, and it (smells / tastes / looks) awful.

.... **6** They're (crunchy / chewy / hard), and they taste (salty / sweet / spicy).

f **kim chee** / Korea — cabbage

e **caviar** / Russia

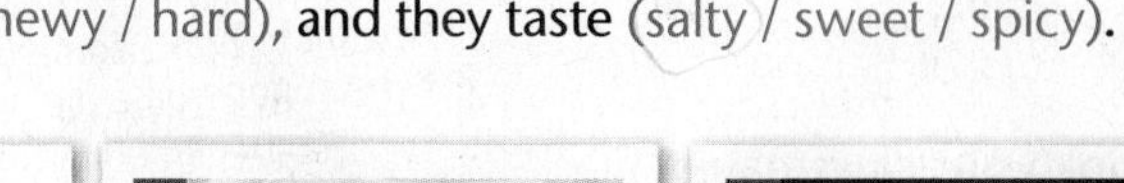

a **chapulines** / Mexico — grasshopper

b **cho dofu** / China

c **mochi** / Japan

d **Jell-O**® / United States

B ▶3:34 **LISTEN TO PERSONALIZE** Listen again. After each food, discuss with a partner whether you would like to try that food. Explain why or why not.

NOW YOU CAN Describe local dishes

A **FRAME YOUR IDEAS** Choose three local dishes that you would recommend to a visitor to your country. Write notes about each.

Name of dish:
Rain doughnuts
Description:
soft and sweet
What's in it?
flour, eggs, milk

1
Name of dish:
Description:
What's in it?

2
Name of dish:
Description:
What's in it?

3
Name of dish:
Description:
What's in it?

"rain doughnuts" / Brazil

B **PAIR WORK** Role-play a conversation in which one of you is a visitor to your country. Introduce and describe your dishes to the "visitor." Use the Vocabulary. For example:

"Have you tried rain doughnuts?"

"No, I haven't. What are they like?"

"Well, they're soft. And they taste sweet . . ."

RECYCLE THIS LANGUAGE.

Ask about the dish	Comment on the dish	
What's in [it / them]?	It sounds / they sound [great].	I'm allergic to __.
Is it / Are they [spicy / sweet]?	I'm crazy about __.	I'm avoiding __.
How do you make [it / them]?	I'm a big __ eater.	__ [don't / doesn't] agree with me.
Is it / Are they [popular]?	I'm a(n) __ [addict / lover].	__ [is / are] against my religion.
Does it / Do they taste [salty]?	I [used to / didn't use to] eat __.	I'm not much of a __ [eater].
	I don't care for __.	I'm [on a diet / trying to lose weight].

REVIEW

A ▶3:35 Listen to the conversation in a restaurant. Cross out the foods that the speakers don't mention.

beef and broccoli	chicken	clams	noodles	pasta
pizza	salmon	scallops	shrimp	steak

B ▶3:36 Now listen again and complete the statements.

The man doesn't care for ....

He would rather eat ....

C Complete the negative <u>yes</u> / <u>no</u> question for each situation.

1 The weather today is sunny and beautiful. You turn to your friend and say: "................. the weather fantastic?"

2 You've just finished dinner. It was a terrible meal. As you leave, you say to your friend: "................. that meal awful?"

3 You're sightseeing in China. From your tour bus window you see a long wall in the distance. You say to the person sitting next to you: "................. that the Great Wall?"

4 You're surprised to see your friend eating breakfast at 11:30. You say: "................. you .... breakfast yet?"

5 You see a woman on the street. You're pretty sure it's Norah Jones, the singer. You go up to her and ask: "................. you Norah Jones?"

D Write five sentences about things you used to or didn't use to do or think when you were younger. For example:

I didn't use to like coffee when I was younger.

E Write short descriptions of the following foods.

apples	bananas	carrots	grapefruit
ice cream	onions	squid	steak

Carrots are orange, and they're sweet and crunchy.

For additional language practice . . .
TOP NOTCH POP • Lyrics p. 154
"A Perfect Dish"
DIGITAL SONG
DIGITAL KARAOKE

WRITING

Write a paragraph on the following topic: Do you think people are eating healthier or less healthy foods than they used to? Give examples to support your opinion.

I think people are eating a lot of unhealthy foods today. People used to eat a lot of fresh foods. However, lately . . .

WRITING BOOSTER p. 148
- Connecting ideas: subordinating conjunctions
- Guidance for this writing exercise

DIGITAL GAMES

International Buffet
Today's Selections

Pad Thai • Thailand

Ingredients: rice noodles, tofu, peanuts, fish sauce, sugar, lime juice, vegetable oil, garlic, shrimp, eggs, hot peppers

Bi Bim Bop • Korea

Ingredients: rice, beef, soy sauce, sesame oil, garlic, black pepper, salt, eggs, lettuce, rice wine, hot peppers

Chicken Mole • Mexico

Ingredients: chicken, salt, vegetable oil, onions, garlic, tomatoes, chocolate, hot peppers

Potato Soup • Colombia

Ingredients: chicken, three kinds of potatoes, corn, avocados

Tabouleh Salad • Lebanon

Ingredients: parsley, mint, onions, tomatoes, salt, black pepper, cracked wheat, lemon juice, olive oil

Pot Stickers • China

Ingredients: flour, cabbage, pork, green onions, sesame oil, salt

Stuffed Rocoto Peppers • Peru

Ingredients: onions, garlic, ground beef, hard-boiled eggs, raisins, cheese, rocoto peppers, vegetable oil

ORAL REVIEW

CHALLENGE Choose a dish and study the photo and the ingredients for one minute. Then close your book. Describe the dish.

PAIR WORK

1 Create a conversation for the man and woman in which they look at the foods and talk about their food passions. For example:
Have you tried Pad Thai? It's terrific!

2 Create a conversation in which the man or the woman suggests and offers foods. The other makes excuses. Start like this:
A: Would you like some __?
B: Actually, __.

3 Choose a dish and create a conversation between someone from that country and a visitor. For example:
Have you ever tried __?

NOW I CAN

- ☐ Talk about food passions.
- ☐ Make an excuse to decline food.
- ☐ Discuss lifestyle changes.
- ☐ Describe local dishes.

COMMUNICATION GOALS

1 Get to know a new friend.
2 Cheer someone up.
3 Discuss personality and its origin.
4 Examine the impact of birth order.

UNIT 7 About Personality

PREVIEW

The **Psychology** of Color

According to research, colors have a powerful effect on us. Take the test and then see if your answers are confirmed by the research. You may be surprised! (Check your answers below.)

Color test

1) What color is the most attention-getting?

○ black ○ yellow ○ red ○ other

2) What color is most likely to make people feel angry?

○ black ○ yellow ○ pink ○ other

3) What color is best for a hospital room?

○ pink ○ white ○ green ○ other

4) What color often makes people feel tired?

○ green ○ blue ○ pink ○ other

5) What is the least appealing color for food?

○ black ○ yellow ○ blue ○ other

Answers

1) Experts say red attracts the most attention. Using red for traffic lights and warning lights makes them more noticeable.

2) Studies have shown that being in a yellow room makes it more likely for adults to lose their tempers and for babies to cry.

3) Green is the easiest color on the eye, and it causes people to relax. Painting a hospital room green helps patients get the rest they need.

4) Research has shown that looking at pink can cause people to feel tired. Some sports teams have painted the dressing room of the opposing team pink to reduce the players' energy.

5) Researchers in marketing have found that using blue in processed foods is unappealing. They believe that this is because blue is rare in nature. Painting a restaurant red, on the other hand, increases the appetite. Many restaurants are painted red.

Questionnaire

What are your color preferences?

Look at the colors below.

YELLOW-GREEN
EMERALD GREEN
BRIGHT ORANGE
DARK GRAY
LIGHT BLUE
TOMATO RED
LILAC

Which color do you find the most appealing? ______

Which color do you most associate with happiness? ______

Which color do you most associate with being sad? ______

A CLASS SURVEY How many classmates answered the questions on the test correctly? Which color on the questionnaire was the most appealing to your classmates?

B DISCUSSION In your opinion, what makes people like some colors and dislike others?

"I think people like colors that remind them of things they like."

"I agree. I love blue. It reminds me of the sky. I love being outdoors."

C ▶4:02 **PHOTO STORY** Read and listen to a couple talking about what color to repaint their living room.

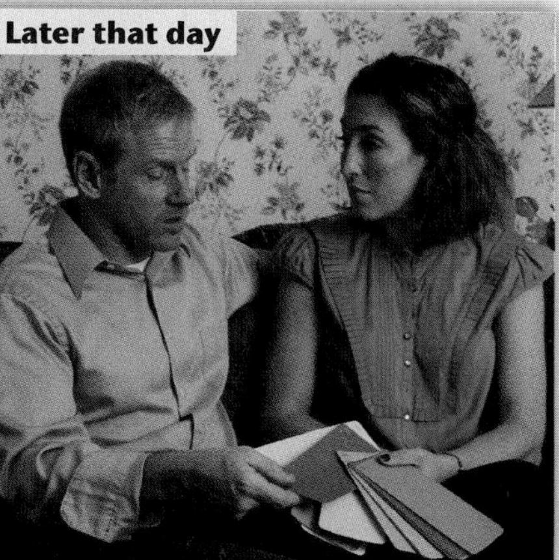

Chelsea: You know what? I'm getting a little tired of looking at this wallpaper.

Chad: Well, maybe it's time for a change. What would you think about getting the room painted? I never loved that wallpaper, anyway.

Chelsea: Actually, I don't think either of us did. We only got it because we couldn't agree on a paint color.

Chad: Oh, yeah. Now I remember. You wanted pink, and I said it was too feminine.

Chelsea: Actually, I never thought it was pink. To me it was a soft rose.

Chad: Well, what would you say to a nice blue?

Chelsea: Blue? *Way* too masculine.

Chad: *What?!*

Chelsea: I'm just pulling your leg, silly! Blue would be great.

Chad: This one's nice—very relaxing.

Chelsea: True, but I'm not sure the furniture would go with it.

Chad: Good point. I'd hate to have to get all new stuff . . . You know, maybe we're on the wrong track.

Chelsea: What do you mean?

Chad: All of a sudden, I'm thinking white. It's classic, and . . .

Chelsea: And it goes with everything!

D **PARAPHRASE** Restate the expressions from the Photo Story in your own way.

1 "I'm just pulling your leg."

2 "I'm not sure the furniture would go with it."

3 "Good point."

4 "Maybe we're on the wrong track."

E **THINK AND EXPLAIN** All the statements are false. Explain how you know they are false.

1 Chelsea still likes the wallpaper.

> Chelsea says, 'I'm getting a little tired of looking at this wallpaper.'

2 Chelsea didn't want a rose-colored living room.

3 Chelsea truly thinks that blue is too masculine.

4 Chelsea thinks the blue Chad likes would go nicely with the furniture.

5 Chad would like to buy new furniture.

6 It's Chelsea's idea to paint the living room white.

7 They agree the furniture wouldn't go with white.

SPEAKING

Choose colors for rooms. Use the Color Test for ideas. Compare charts and reasons with a partner.

Room	Color	Your reason
a bedroom for a married couple		
a bedroom for a teenaged girl		
a bedroom for a 10-year-old boy		
a kitchen		
a family living room		

LESSON 1 GOAL Get to know a new friend

GRAMMAR *Gerunds and infinitives*

Gerunds and infinitives come from verb forms but function as nouns in a sentence, often as direct objects.

Gerund = an -ing form of a verb	Infinitive = to + a base form
She enjoys **painting**.	He wants **to paint** the kitchen yellow.

Use a gerund after the following verbs and expressions: avoid, discuss, dislike, don't mind, enjoy, feel like, practice, quit, suggest

Use an infinitive after the following verbs and expressions: agree, be sure, choose, decide, expect, hope, learn, need, plan, seem, want, wish, would like

Other verbs and expressions can be followed by either a gerund or an infinitive: begin, can't stand, continue, hate, like, love, prefer, start

Remember: There are two other -ing forms:
She is **painting**. (present participle)
The trip was **relaxing**. (participial adjective)

GRAMMAR BOOSTER p. 136
- Gerunds and infinitives: usage within sentences

A GRAMMAR PRACTICE Complete the suggestions for ways to make new friends, using the verbs plus gerund or infinitive direct objects.

FIVE WAYS TO MAKE NEW FRIENDS

Everyone .... (1 want / make) friends. We .... (2 suggest / follow) these principles:

1. .... (3 decide / be) friendly to everyone you meet. Take advantage of every opportunity.

2. Even if you .... (4 not feel like / socialize), ... (5 learn / show) interest in at least one new person every day. .... (6 not expect) every new acquaintance .... (7 become) a real friend, but if you .... (8 would like / meet) new friends, this is a good way to start.

3. .... (9 be sure / ask) new acquaintances questions about themselves. People .... (10 enjoy / talk) about themselves.

4. .... (11 avoid / talk) too much about yourself. .... (12 practice / ask) people questions about their interests and opinions before you .... (13 begin / tell) them about your own.

5. If you .... (14 decide / get together) later, ... (15 plan / do) something that you both like. If your new friend has different interests from yours, say you .... (16 not mind / try) something new.

B FIND THE GRAMMAR Underline all the gerunds and infinitives in the "Answers" section on page 74.

DIGITAL VIDEO COACH

PRONUNCIATION *Reduction of to in infinitives*

4:03 Notice how an unstressed to reduces to /tə/ in natural speech. Read and listen. Then listen again and repeat.

1 I decided to repaint the bedroom a happier color.

2 We plan to see the World Cup Finals.

3 She doesn't like to hear people talking on cell phones.

4 I know you'd like to choose a more cheerful color.

CONVERSATION MODEL

A ▶4:04 Read and listen to a conversation about likes and dislikes.

A: So tell me something about yourself.

B: What would you like to know?

A: Well, for example, what do you like doing in your free time?

B: Let's see. Most of all, I enjoy playing tennis. I think it's relaxing. What about you?

A: Well, I find tennis a little boring. But I do love going to the movies.

B: So do I. We should go to the movies together sometime, then.

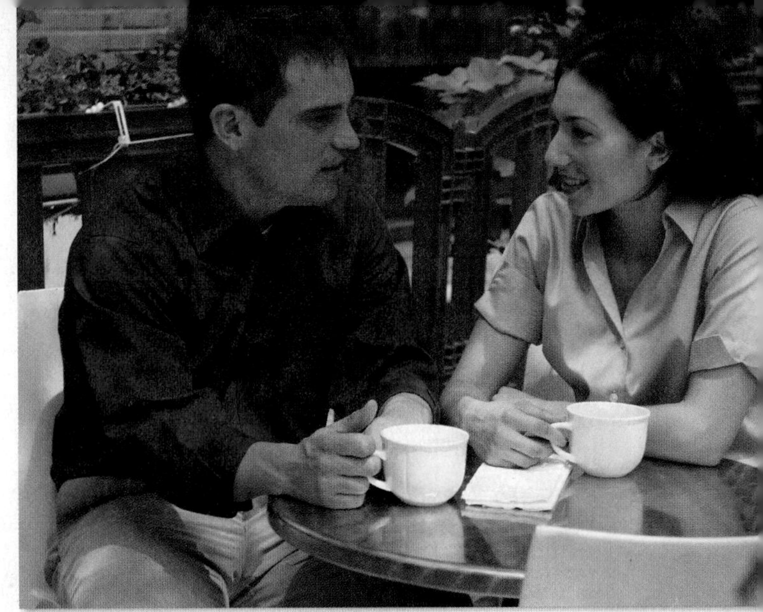

B ▶4:05 **RHYTHM AND INTONATION** Listen again and repeat. Then practice the Conversation Model with a partner.

NOW YOU CAN Get to know a new friend

A **NOTEPADDING** List your likes and dislikes in gerund form.

Likes	Dislikes
cooking	skiing

Likes	Dislikes

DIGITAL VIDEO B **CONVERSATION ACTIVATOR** With a partner, personalize the Conversation Model, using your likes and dislikes in gerund form from your notepad. Change the time or occasion.

A: So tell me something about yourself.
B: What would you like to know?
A: Well, for example, what do you like doing .... ?
B: Let's see. Most of all, I enjoy .... I think it's .... What about you?
A: Well, ...
B: ....

Other times and occasions
- in your free time
- on weekends
- on vacations
- with your friends / family
- for lunch / dinner

DON'T STOP!

Ask about your partner's plans for this weekend or for a vacation. Use the following verbs and your own infinitives:

need want
plan would like

For example:
"What do you **plan to do** this weekend?"

RECYCLE THIS LANGUAGE.

Positive adjectives	Negative adjectives
awesome	boring
fantastic	awful
wonderful	horrible
great	terrible
terrific	disgusting
relaxing	frightening
interesting	scary
exciting	silly
thrilling	weird
fascinating	

C **CHANGE PARTNERS** Talk about other likes and dislikes.

LESSON 2 **GOAL** Cheer someone up

CONVERSATION MODEL

A ▶4:06 Read and listen to someone trying to cheer a friend up.

A: You look down. What's up?

B: Oh, nothing serious. I'm just tired of the same old grind. But thanks for asking.

A: I know what you mean. I'm tired of working, too. How about going to a movie? That always helps me.

B: Great idea. Let's go this afternoon!

▶4:08 **More adjectives**
down
sad
unhappy
upset
depressed

B ▶4:07 **RHYTHM AND INTONATION** Listen again and repeat. Then practice the Conversation Model with a partner.

GRAMMAR *Gerunds as objects of prepositions*

A gerund can function as an object of a preposition.

	preposition	object
I'm afraid	of	flying.
She's bored	with	cooking.
She objects	to	discussing her feelings.

Be careful! Don't use an infinitive as the object of a preposition.

Don't say: Let's go to a movie instead of ~~to watch~~ TV.

Expressions followed by gerunds

Adjective + preposition

angry about	afraid of
excited about	sick / tired of
depressed about	bored with
happy / sad about	crazy about

Verb + preposition

complain about	apologize for
talk about	believe in
worry about	object to
think about	

With How about or What about
How about [going to a movie]?
What about [leaving work early]?

GRAMMAR BOOSTER p. 136
• Negative gerunds

A **GRAMMAR PRACTICE** Complete the descriptions with prepositions and gerunds.

Ted

Ted is an extrovert. Like most extroverts, he's direct. And he's honest; he believes .... (1 tell) the truth to everyone.

At his job, he works with other people and he never complains .... (2 work) long hours. He works hard and doesn't worry .... (3 have to) work on weekends or holidays.

He has a few fears, though. Most of all, he's afraid .... (4 fly).

Nicole

I was born in Rome. What about you?

Ted's wife, Nicole, on the other hand, is an introvert. But she doesn't object .... (5 talk) about herself from time to time.

Right now, she's bored .... (6 be) a student, and she's sick and tired .... (7 write) so many long reports and .... (8 take) exams every few weeks! She's angry .... (9 have to) spend so much time in front of a computer.

However, unlike Ted, she's not at all afraid .... (10 fly)! She's excited .... (11 go) on vacation.

B **PAIR WORK** Answer the questions about yourself, using gerunds. Then share the information with a partner.

Right now, what are you . . .	
happy about?	
excited about?	
bored with?	
sick and tired of?	

"Right now, I'm happy about getting engaged!"

DIGITAL MORE EXERCISES

NOW YOU CAN Cheer someone up

A **NOTEPADDING** Make a list of things that you are tired of. Write them as gerunds.

What are you tired of?

studying so hard

DIGITAL VIDEO

B **CONVERSATION ACTIVATOR** With a partner, role-play cheering someone up. Use your notepad for ideas. Then change roles.

A: You look .... What's up?
B: Oh, nothing serious. I'm just tired of .... But thanks for asking.
A: I know what you mean. ....
B: ....

DON'T STOP!

Make more suggestions, using gerunds and infinitives.

RECYCLE THIS LANGUAGE.

Be sure [to get enough sleep].
You should think about [quitting your job].
What about [going out for a nice dinner]?
How about [getting a massage]?
If you [avoid drinking a lot of coffee], you [will sleep better].
That always helps me.
That's a good idea.
Don't expect [to feel better right away].

C **CHANGE PARTNERS** Cheer your new partner up.

GOAL **Discuss personality and its origin**

BEFORE YOU READ

EXPLORE YOUR IDEAS In what way does a parent's behavior affect a child's development?

READING ▶4:09

Personality: from Nature or Nurture?

What is personality? Many people define personality as a person's usual manner or style of behavior. These patterns of behavior tend to be predictable throughout a person's lifetime. Some people are introverts; others are extroverts. Some people have easygoing personalities: they are usually cheerful and calm and able to cope with life's difficulties without much trouble. Their emotions are usually under control: they don't get extremely angry about little things. Others, at the other end of the personality spectrum, are more emotional, experiencing higher highs and lower lows. Most people's personalities, however, don't fall at the extreme ends but rather fall somewhere in between.

Where do we get our personality? For hundreds of years, psychologists and ordinary people have never stopped debating this fascinating question. Some people think personality develops as a result of the environment—the combination of influences that we learn from, such as our families, our culture, our friends, and our education. The people who believe this theory believe that all babies are born without a personality and that it's the environment that determines, or forms, each child's personality. This school of thought is called the "nurture school."

At the other end of the continuum we find people who believe that personality is determined by "nature," or the characteristics we receive, or "inherit," from our parents biologically, through their genes. These people believe that our personality is not determined by the environment, but rather by genetics, and that each baby is born with a personality.

The "nature-nurture controversy" The nature-nurture controversy is very old. Experimental psychologists have tried to discover which of these two factors, genetics or the environment, is more important in forming our personality. However, it's very difficult, if not impossible, to conduct research on real people with real lives. There's just no way to put people in a laboratory and watch them develop. For this reason, there's no scientific way to settle the nature-nurture controversy. Recently, however, most researchers have come to believe that both the environment AND the genes—nurture and nature—work together and are both important.

Even though the experts have largely discarded the idea that personality development is so black and white, the nature-nurture controversy remains a popular discussion among friends. It seems that everyone has an opinion.

A UNDERSTAND VOCABULARY FROM CONTEXT Match the words and phrases in the two columns.

.... 1 genes	a a person's usual pattern of behavior
.... 2 environment	b what we feel, such as anger, love, and happiness
.... 3 emotions	c the source of traits we inherit from our parents
.... 4 the "nature school" (of thought)	d the world around us
.... 5 the "nurture school" (of thought)	e the belief that learning determines personality
.... 6 personality	f the belief that genetics determines personality

B MAKE PERSONAL COMPARISONS How is your personality similar to or different from those of your parents? If you have children, how are your children similar to or different from you? Use language from the Reading.

NOW YOU CAN Discuss personality and its origin

A **FRAME YOUR IDEAS** Complete the survey to find out if you are an introvert or an extrovert.

ARE YOU AN EXTROVERT OR AN INTROVERT?

Instructions: From each pair of personality traits, check one that sounds like your personality. At the end, add up your selections for each column. Then decide for yourself: Are you an introvert or an extrovert?

	Extroverts tend to:	Introverts tend to:
1.	❍ enjoy being in a group.	❍ enjoy being alone.
2.	❍ need to interact with others.	❍ avoid interacting unnecessarily.
3.	❍ be active.	❍ be quiet.
4.	❍ be interested in events.	❍ be interested in feelings.
5.	❍ talk without thinking.	❍ think without talking.
6.	❍ be easy to understand.	❍ be hard to understand.
7.	❍ know many people a little.	❍ know few people, but well.
8.	❍ talk.	❍ listen.
9.	❍ seek excitement.	❍ seek peace.
10.	❍ express their opinions openly.	❍ keep their ideas to themselves.

Total extrovert selections ☐ Total introvert selections ☐

❍ **I'm an extrovert.** ❍ **I'm an introvert.** ❍ **I'm a mixture of both!**

B **PAIR WORK** Discuss the personality traits you checked. For each, provide a real example from your life to explain your choices.

I'm pretty active. I like to go out almost every night, to the movies or to play sports.

I tend to stay home most nights. It gives me time to think.

C **DISCUSSION** Where do you think your personality came from, nurture or nature? Did your personality traits come from your parents' genes, or did you learn to be the way you are? Explain with examples using gerunds and infinitives.

RECYCLE THIS LANGUAGE.

[never] complain about ___.
[sometimes] worry about ___.
[usually] apologize for ___.
get [angry / excited / happy / sad] about ___.
be sick and tired of ___.
be bored with ___.
be afraid of ___.
be crazy about ___.
object to ___.
believe in ___.
not care for ___.
prefer ___.
avoid ___.
not mind ___.
tend to ___.

Text-mining (optional)
Find and underline three words or phrases in the Reading that were new to you. Use them in your Discussion.
For example: "easygoing."

LESSON 4 **GOAL** Examine the impact of birth order

BEFORE YOU LISTEN

EXPLORE YOUR IDEAS Do you think the first child in a family has different personality traits from those of siblings who are born later? Explain your answer.

LISTENING COMPREHENSION

A ▶4:10 **LISTEN FOR MAIN IDEAS** Read the statements. Then listen to all three parts of the discussion. Choose the statement that best expresses the main idea of the discussion.

- ☐ First-born children are often too critical of themselves.
- ☐ Children in the same family usually have personalities that are determined by order of birth.
- ☐ Children usually have personalities that are determined by genes.

B ▶4:11 **LISTEN FOR SPECIFIC INFORMATION** Read the exercise. Then listen to each part of the discussion again separately. Complete the exercise as you listen.

Part 1: Check True or False for each statement.	**True**	**False**
1 Brian is usually dissatisfied with himself.	☐	☐
2 Brian obeys rules.	☐	☐
3 Brian does most things well.	☐	☐
4 Brian's mother thinks her husband pushed Brian to be successful.	☐	☐
5 Brian never liked being with adults when he was growing up.	☐	☐

Part 2: Complete each statement by circling the correct information.

1 Annie is (the middle child / the "baby").

2 Annie had (a lot of / only a little) time with her parents before her younger sister was born.

3 Annie is jealous of (Brian / Brian and Lucy).

4 Annie (breaks / obeys) rules.

5 Annie is (rebellious and / rebellious but not) popular.

Part 3: Circle the answer to each question.

1 How old was Annie when Lucy was born?
a 13 years
b 13 months

2 What does Lucy like most?
a making other people laugh
b laughing at other people

3 What did Lucy do to the dining room wall?
a She painted it.
b She washed it.

4 Why does Lucy drive her older siblings crazy?
a She pays too much attention to them.
b Others pay too much attention to her.

C **CLASSIFY INFORMATION** Check the most common birth position for each personality, according to the discussion. Listen again if necessary.

Personality traits	First child	Middle child	Youngest child
Breaks rules	☐	☐	☐
Feels less important than siblings	☐	☐	☐
Grows up fast	☐	☐	☐
Grows up slowly	☐	☐	☐
Has a lot of friends	☐	☐	☐
Is creative	☐	☐	☐
Is rebellious	☐	☐	☐
Is self-critical	☐	☐	☐
Plays by the rules	☐	☐	☐
Shows off	☐	☐	☐

NOW YOU CAN Examine the impact of birth order

A **FRAME YOUR IDEAS** Complete the checklist for yourself.

1 What's your birth position in your family?

- ❍ I'm the first child or the only child in the family.
- ❍ I'm a middle child—neither the first nor the last.
- ❍ I'm the "baby"—the youngest child in the family.

2 What are your personality traits? (Check all that are true.)

- ❍ I'm self-critical. I always feel I should do better.
- ❍ I'm a rebel.
- ❍ I'm popular. I have a lot of friends.
- ❍ I feel less important than my older or younger siblings.
- ❍ I love to clown around and make people laugh.
- ❍ I can be lovable one minute and a rebel the next.
- ❍ I'm creative.
- ❍ I often feel jealous of my siblings.

B **GROUP WORK** Form three groups of students, according to your birth positions. Compare your checklists with other members of your group. Do you share the same personality traits? Report your findings to the class.

Group 1: first or only children
Group 2: middle children
Group 3: youngest children

"Almost everyone in our group checked 'I'm self-critical!'"

C **DISCUSSION** Talk about how birth order can affect the development of a person's personality.

Ideas

- genetics / nature
- the environment / nurture
- introverts and extroverts
- parents' behavior

A ▶4:12 Listen to the conversations. Then circle a word or phrase to complete each statement.

1 Andy is feeling (down / happy).
2 Mollie is (an extrovert / an introvert).
3 Greg is (an extrovert / an introvert).
4 Millie thinks (genetics / the environment) is the most important factor in personality development.
5 Vera thinks (genetics / the environment) is the most important factor in personality development.

B Complete the paragraph with the correct prepositions.

Extroverts don't worry ....(1) talking in public. They believe ....(2) being honest, and they get bored ....(3) being alone. They may talk ....(4) staying home and reading a book, but when they do, they complain ....(5) having no one to talk to. They object ....(6) being by themselves.

C Complete each personal statement with a gerund or infinitive phrase.

1 When I want to stay healthy, I avoid ....
2 I really enjoy .... on Saturdays and Sundays.
3 I wish other people would quit .... in the movies.
4 Two things I can't stand are .... and ....
5 On weekends, I dislike ....
6 If the weather is bad, I don't mind ....
7 Tomorrow I would really like ....
8 If I want to do well in this class, I need ....
9 Tomorrow I plan ....
10 I think most people are afraid of ....
11 I think people are usually excited about ....
12 Too many people complain about ....
13 My family worries most about ....

D Complete each statement. Circle the best answer.

1 John is such (an extrovert / an introvert). He doesn't like to talk about himself a lot.
2 Our usual pattern of behavior is our (personality / environment).
3 Another word for characteristics is (nurture / traits).
4 Many people believe that (self-criticism / birth order) affects personality development.
5 The nature-nurture controversy is an argument about the origin of the (environment / personality).

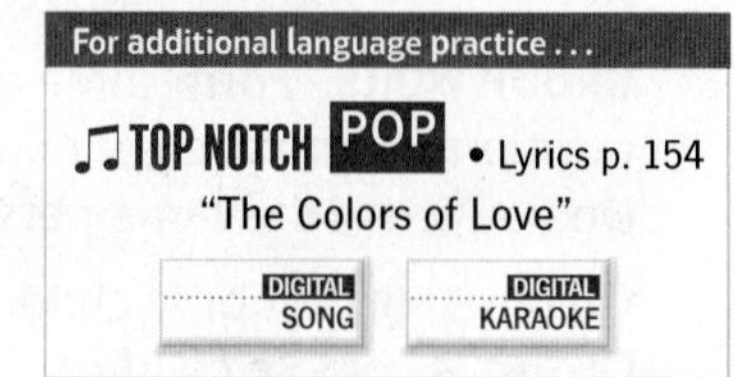

For additional language practice . . .
TOP NOTCH POP • Lyrics p. 154
"The Colors of Love"
DIGITAL SONG
DIGITAL KARAOKE

WRITING

Write at least two paragraphs about the personality of someone you know well. Use vocabulary and ideas from Lessons 3 and 4.

WRITING BOOSTER p. 149
- Parallel structure
- Guidance for this writing exercise

ORAL REVIEW

PAIR WORK

1 Create a conversation for photo 1 in which the girl on the left cheers up her friend. Use gerunds and infinities.

2 Role-play a discussion between the two people in photo 2. They discuss the birth order of their siblings and their personalities.

GROUP WORK Choose one person to be the professor in photo 3. Help that person create a lecture about personality development. Then the other classmates listen to the lecture and ask questions.

So, who is the youngest in your family?
2

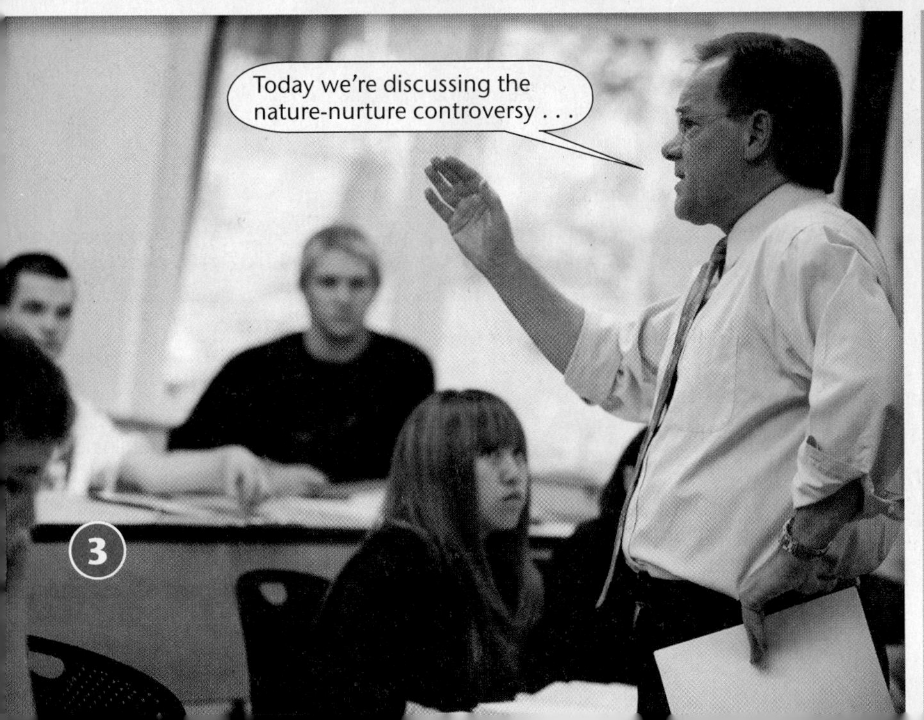

Today we're discussing the nature-nurture controversy . . .
3

✓ NOW I CAN

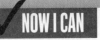

- ☐ Get to know a new friend.
- ☐ Cheer someone up.
- ☐ Discuss personality and its origin.
- ☐ Examine the impact of birth order.

COMMUNICATION GOALS

1 Recommend a museum.
2 Ask about and describe objects.
3 Talk about artistic talent.
4 Discuss your favorite artists.

UNIT 8 The Arts

PREVIEW

ART Exhibit

Drawing

Jewelry

Fashion

Sculpture

Pottery

BARKER STREET GALLERY OCT. 12–NOV. 24

Painting

Photography

A 4:15 **VOCABULARY • *Kinds of art*** Read and listen. Then listen again and repeat.

B **DISCUSSION** What kinds of art do you like? Which pieces of art in the Preview do you like? Why? Use some of the adjectives.

"I'm not really into paintings, but I think this one's beautiful."

"I like jewelry, but I don't think the necklace is very interesting."

Adjectives to describe art

beautiful	awful	feminine
exciting	boring	masculine
fascinating	weird	unusual
relaxing	silly	practical
thought-provoking	depressing	interesting

ENGLISH FOR TODAY'S WORLD
Understand English speakers from different language backgrounds.
Teo = Spanish speaker

C ▶4:16 **PHOTO STORY** Read and listen to a conversation at an art show.

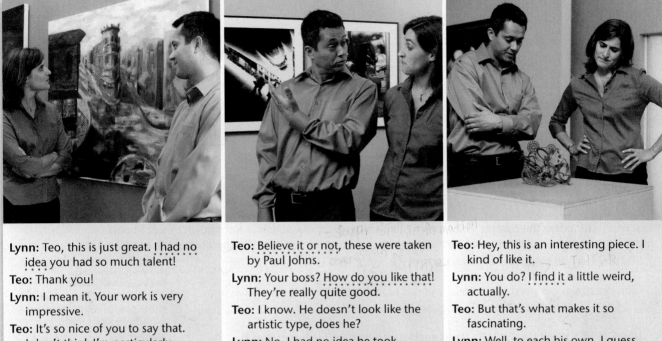

Lynn: Teo, this is just great. I had no idea you had so much talent!
Teo: Thank you!
Lynn: I mean it. Your work is very impressive.
Teo: It's so nice of you to say that. I don't think I'm particularly talented. I just love to paint.

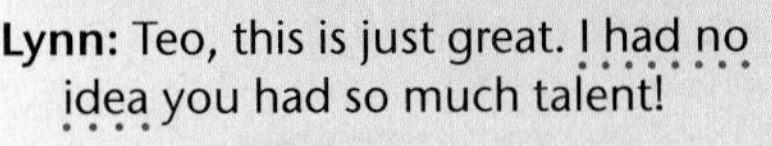

Teo: Believe it or not, these were taken by Paul Johns.
Lynn: Your boss? How do you like that! They're really quite good.
Teo: I know. He doesn't look like the artistic type, does he?
Lynn: No. I had no idea he took photos. I guess you can't always judge a book by its cover.

Teo: Hey, this is an interesting piece. I kind of like it.
Lynn: You do? I find it a little weird, actually.
Teo: But that's what makes it so fascinating.
Lynn: Well, to each his own. I guess I'm just not really into abstract art.

D **ACTIVATE VOCABULARY** Circle the three kinds of art Lynn and Teo discuss:

painting	fashion	sculpture	photography	drawing	jewelry

E **FOCUS ON LANGUAGE** With a partner, discuss and find an underlined expression in the Photo Story to match each of the phrases.

1 I didn't know . . .
2 I don't really like . . .
3 Everyone has a different opinion.
4 I have some information that may surprise you.
5 I'm really surprised!
6 You can't really know someone just by looking at him or her.
7 In my opinion, it's . . .

SPEAKING

What kinds of art do you prefer? Explain why.

"I prefer more realistic art. I'm just not into abstract paintings."

"I'm into fashion. I like clothes that are really modern."

Art can be **realistic** . . .

or **abstract**.

It can be **traditional** . . .

or **modern**.

LESSON 1

GOAL Recommend a museum

GRAMMAR *The passive voice*

Most sentences are in the active voice: the subject of a sentence performs the action of the verb. In the passive voice, the receiver of the action is the subject of the sentence.

Active voice: Architect Frank Gehry **designed** the Guggenheim Museum in Bilbao, Spain.

Passive voice: The Guggenheim Museum in Bilbao, Spain, **was designed** by architect Frank Gehry.

Form the passive voice with a form of be and the past participle of a verb.

These vases **are made** in Korea.
The museum **was built** in the 1990's.
The *Mona Lisa* **has been shown** at the Louvre Museum since 1797.

It is common to use the passive voice when the performer of the action is not known or not important. Use a by phrase in a passive voice sentence when it is important to identify the performer of an action.

Pottery is made ~~by people~~ in many parts of the world. (not important)
This bowl was found ~~by someone~~ in Costa Rica. (not important)
This dress was designed **by Donatella Versace**. (important)

GRAMMAR BOOSTER p. 137

- Transitive and intransitive verbs
- The passive voice: other tenses

A UNDERSTAND THE GRAMMAR Read each passive voice sentence and decide if the by phrase is necessary. If it isn't necessary, cross it out.

1 The glass pyramids were added to the Louvre Museum in Paris by workers in 1989.
2 The sculpture *The Thinker* was created by French artist Auguste Rodin.
3 Antoni Gaudí designed and built some of the most famous buildings in Spain. His plans for the Casa Milà in Barcelona were completed by him in 1912.
4 The melody of "Ode to Joy" is known by people all over the world. It was written by German composer Ludwig van Beethoven.
5 China's famous Terracotta Army figures in Xi'an were discovered by farmers in 1974.

B GRAMMAR PRACTICE Change each sentence from the active to the passive voice. Use a by phrase.

1 Leonardo da Vinci painted the *Mona Lisa* in the sixteenth century.

....

2 Brazilian photographer Sebastião Salgado took that photograph in 2007.

....

3 Mexican filmmaker Alfonso Cuarón directed the 2013 3D film *Gravity*.

....

4 Japanese master printmaker Katsushika Hokusai made that print over a century ago.

....

5 Korean fashion designer Sang A Im-Propp created these beautiful handbags.

....

6 Weavers have produced beautiful Persian rugs for several thousand years.

....

DIGITAL MORE EXERCISES

CONVERSATION MODEL

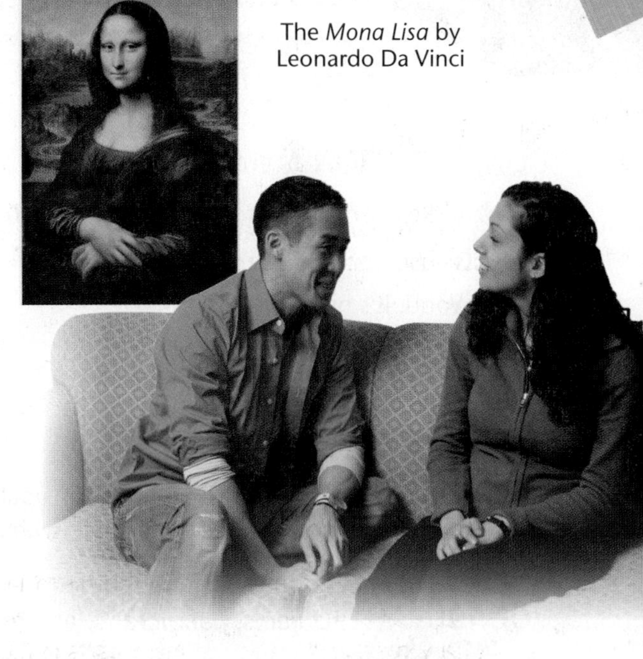
The *Mona Lisa* by Leonardo Da Vinci

A ▶4:17 Read and listen to someone recommend a museum.

A: Be sure not to miss the Louvre while you're in Paris.

B: Really? Why's that?

A: Well, for one thing, that famous painting, the *Mona Lisa*, is kept there.

B: No kidding! I've always wanted to see the *Mona Lisa*!

A: Well, they have a great collection of paintings. You'll love it.

B: Thanks for the suggestion!

B ▶4:18 **RHYTHM AND INTONATION** Listen again and repeat. Then practice the Conversation Model with a partner.

DIGITAL VIDEO COACH

PRONUNCIATION *Emphatic stress*

A ▶4:19 Notice how stress is emphasized to show enthusiasm. Read and listen. Then listen again and repeat.

1 No **KIDD**ing! **2** That's fan**TA**stic! **3** That's **PER**fect! **4** How **IN**teresting!

B Now practice saying the following statements with emphatic stress.

1 That's ter**RI**fic! **2** That's **WON**derful! **3** How ex**CI**ting! **4** How **NICE**!

NOW YOU CAN Recommend a museum

DIGITAL VIDEO

CONVERSATION ACTIVATOR With a partner, change the Conversation Model to recommend a museum. Use the information in the pictures or museums you know. Use the passive voice and emphatic stress. Then change roles.

A: Be sure not to miss .... while you're in ....
B: Really? Why's that?
A: Well, for one thing, ... is kept there.
B: .... ! I've always wanted to see ....
A: Well, they have a .... collection of .... You'll love it.
B: Thanks for the suggestion!

DON'T STOP!

- Recommend other things to see or do.

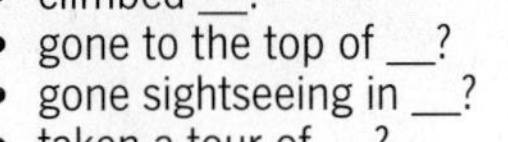

RECYCLE THIS LANGUAGE.

Have you ever . . .
- tried __?
- climbed __?
- gone to the top of __?
- gone sightseeing in __?
- taken a tour of __?

THE GOLD MUSEUM - BOGOTÁ

Famous for its large collection of jewelry and sculpture

El Dorado's Raft (gold and emeralds)

THE NATIONAL PALACE MUSEUM
TAIPEI
Known for its huge collection of traditional Chinese painting, pottery, and sculpture

The Chinese Cabbage sculpture (jade)

THE MUSEUM OF MODERN ART
NEW YORK CITY
A fantastic collection of modern painting, drawing, sculpture, and photography

Starry Night by Vincent van Gogh

LESSON 2 **GOAL** Ask about and describe objects

CONVERSATION MODEL

A ▶4:20 Read and listen to someone asking about an object.

A: Excuse me. What's this figure made of?
B: Wood. It's handmade.
A: Really? Where was it made?
B: Mexico. What do you think of it?
A: It's fantastic!

B ▶4:21 **RHYTHM AND INTONATION** Listen again and repeat. Then practice the Conversation Model with a partner.

DIGITAL FLASH CARDS

VOCABULARY *Objects, handicrafts, and materials*

A ▶4:22 Read and listen. Then listen again and repeat.

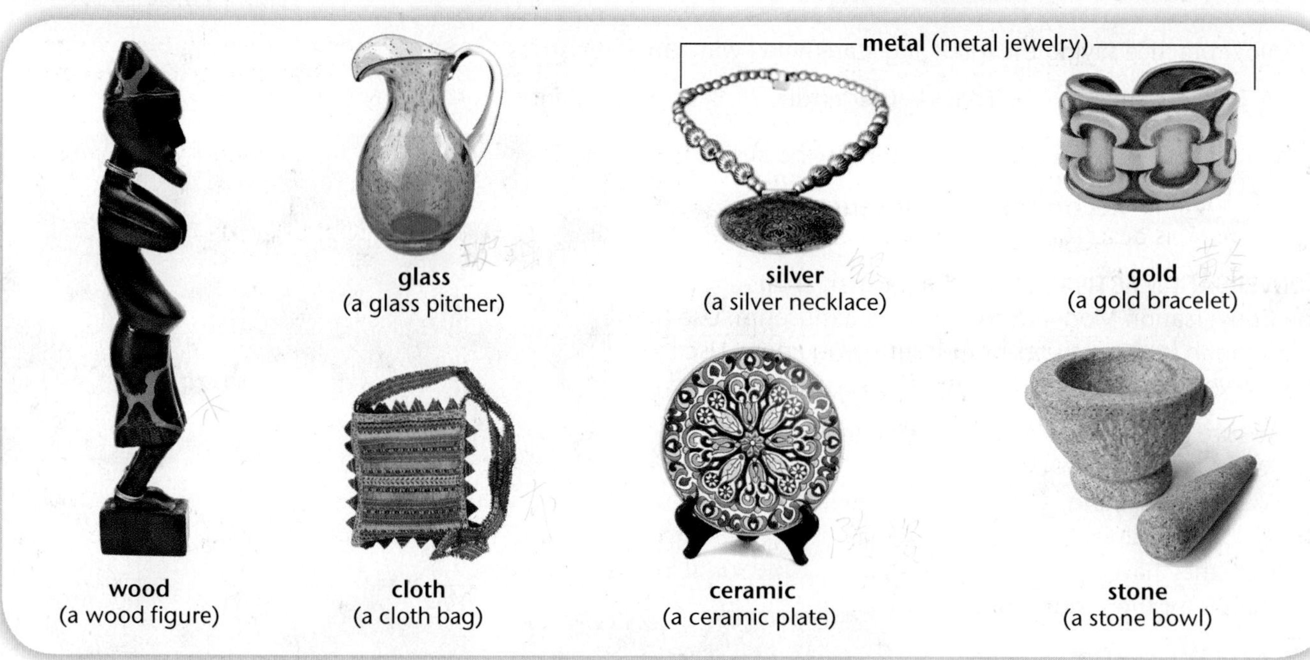

metal (metal jewelry)

wood (a wood figure)

glass (a glass pitcher)

silver (a silver necklace)

gold (a gold bracelet)

cloth (a cloth bag)

ceramic (a ceramic plate)

stone (a stone bowl)

B **PAIR WORK** Tell your partner about some of your favorite objects in your home.

"On my vacation last year, I bought a large stone bowl. It's in my kitchen, and I use it for serving."

GRAMMAR *The passive voice: questions*

Was this stone figure **carved** by hand?	Yes, it was. / No, it wasn't.
Were these wood bracelets **made** in Thailand?	Yes, they were. / No, they weren't.
What **is** this **made** of?	It's made of wood.
What **is** this ceramic bowl **used** for?	It's used for preparing food.
When **was** this picture **painted**?	It was painted in the 1980s.
Where **were** these cloth figures **made**?	In Brazil.
How **were** those handbags **manufactured**?	By machine.

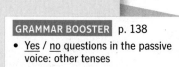

GRAMMAR BOOSTER p. 138
• Yes / no questions in the passive voice: other tenses

A GRAMMAR PRACTICE Complete the questions in the interview. Use a question word and the passive voice.

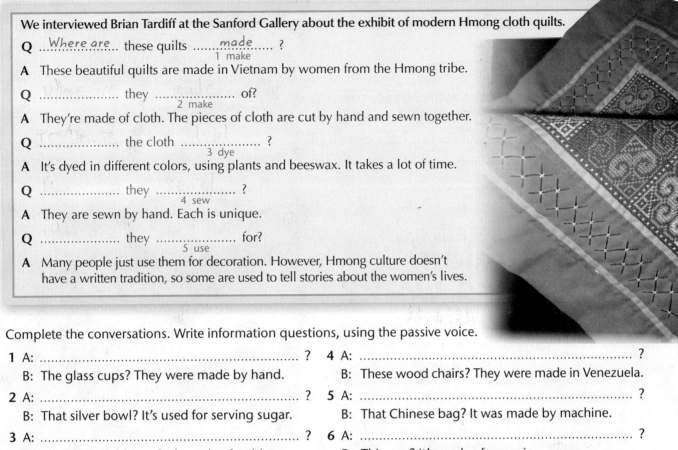

We interviewed Brian Tardiff at the Sanford Gallery about the exhibit of modern Hmong cloth quilts.

Q ...Where are... these quilts ....made.... ? (1 make)

A These beautiful quilts are made in Vietnam by women from the Hmong tribe.

Q .... they .... of? (2 make)

A They're made of cloth. The pieces of cloth are cut by hand and sewn together.

Q .... the cloth .... ? (3 dye)

A It's dyed in different colors, using plants and beeswax. It takes a lot of time.

Q .... they .... ? (4 sew)

A They are sewn by hand. Each is unique.

Q .... they .... for? (5 use)

A Many people just use them for decoration. However, Hmong culture doesn't have a written tradition, so some are used to tell stories about the women's lives.

B Complete the conversations. Write information questions, using the passive voice.

1 A: .... ?
B: The glass cups? They were made by hand.

2 A: .... ?
B: That silver bowl? It's used for serving sugar.

3 A: .... ?
B: This beautiful figure? It's made of gold.

4 A: .... ?
B: These wood chairs? They were made in Venezuela.

5 A: .... ?
B: That Chinese bag? It was made by machine.

6 A: .... ?
B: This cup? It's made of ceramic.

DIGITAL MORE EXERCISES

NOW YOU CAN Ask about and describe objects

DIGITAL VIDEO

A CONVERSATION ACTIVATOR With a partner, change the Conversation Model to ask about and describe one of the objects. Use the Vocabulary. Then change roles.

A: Excuse me. What .... made of?
B: ....
A: .... Where .... made?
B: .... What do you think of .... ?
A: ....

DON'T STOP!

- Ask about other objects.
- Ask other passive voice questions.

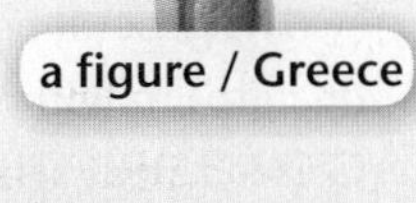

a figure / Greece

a vase / China

a plate / Italy

dolls / Russia

cups / Thailand

B CHANGE PARTNERS Practice the conversation again about other objects.

C DISCUSSION Describe an object in your own home. Ask your classmates questions about the objects they describe.

"In my living room, I have a small figure. It's made of wood. It's a piece of traditional art. I bought it on my vacation last year."

RECYCLE THIS LANGUAGE.

fantastic	cool
awesome	interesting
terrific	beautiful

LESSON 3 **GOAL** Talk about artistic talent

BEFORE YOU READ

WARM-UP Do you do anything artistic? Do you paint, draw, or do handicrafts? Why or why not?

"I paint sometimes. I find it relaxing."

"Actually, I'm not interested in art. I don't really think I have any ability."

READING ▶4:23

Is it talent or hard work?

When children are asked to draw or paint a picture, they are happy to oblige. And they are willing to talk about and show their creation to anyone they meet. But when adults are asked to do the same thing, they typically get nervous and refuse to even try, claiming that they have no talent.

Most adults see themselves as lacking the "artistic gene." However, when you look at drawings made by artists when they were children, their work doesn't differ much from the scribbles and stick figures all children draw when they are young. When Don Lipski, who makes a successful living as a professional artist, looks back at drawings that he made as a child, he doesn't find any early evidence of his own artistic talent. "I was always making things . . . doodling and putting things together. I didn't think of myself as a creative person. I was just doing what all kids do."

The general belief is that artistic talent is something one is born with: a person either has talent or does not. Clearly, great artists like Michelangelo or Picasso had natural talent and possessed more artistic ability than the average person. However, one factor that isn't often considered is the role that years of training, practice, and hard work have played in the creation of great pieces of art. In addition, most artists are successful because they are passionate about their art—they love what they do. Their passion motivates them to continue to create—and improve their ability—day after day. While natural talent may be an advantage, hard work appears to be a necessary part of the creative process.

All young children scribble, doodle, and draw stick figures.

In *Drawing on the Right Side of the Brain*, author Betty Edwards argues that while few people are born with natural artistic talent, all of us have the potential to improve our artistic ability. We just have to be willing to keep working at it. She claims that anyone can learn to use the right side of the brain, the side that governs visual skills like drawing and painting. In other words, artistic ability can be learned.

A **RECOGNIZE THE MAIN IDEA** Choose the main idea of the article.

a Artistic skill can be taught.

b Children are better artists than adults.

c To draw well, you have to be born with artistic talent.

d Few people are born with artistic talent.

B IDENTIFY SUPPORTING DETAILS Read each statement. Check True or False, according to the article. Support your choice with details from the article.

		True	False
1	Young children generally don't worry if they are talented or not.	☑	☐
2	Most adults think they are not talented.	☑	☐
3	It's easy to see which children are going to be artists when you look at their drawings.	☐	☑
4	There isn't much difference between famous artists and other people.	☐	☑
5	Talent is all one needs to create great artistic work.	☐	☑
6	People who don't have natural talent can improve their artistic skill.	☑	☐

C PARAPHRASE Read the paragraph in the article about *Drawing on the Right Side of the Brain* again. In your own words, restate Betty Edwards's theory about artistic ability.

According to Betty Edwards, . . .

DIGITAL MORE ERCISES

NOW YOU CAN Talk about artistic talent

A FRAME YOUR IDEAS Complete the survey. Then compare responses with a partner.

Who's Got Talent?

1. Do any of your family members or friends have artistic talent? ○ yes ○ no

   Relationship to you: ____________

   In which of the arts? ____________

   Where do you think this talent comes from?

   ____

2. Do you think you have natural artistic talent?
   ○ yes ○ no ○ not sure

3. Do other people think you're talented?
   ○ yes ○ no ○ not sure

4. How would you rate your own artistic talent on a scale of 1 to 5?

1	2	3	4	5
POOR		AVERAGE		EXCELLENT

5. In which of the arts do you think you may have talent? Explain.

   example
   ✓ music *I sing and play several musical instruments.*

   ○ music ____________
   ○ drawing / painting ____________
   ○ handicrafts ____________
   ○ acting ____________
   ○ dancing ____________
   ○ photography ____________
   ○ other ____________

B DISCUSSION Do you think people are born with artistic talent? Or is it developed through years of training, practice, and hard work?

Text-mining (optional)
Find and underline three words or phrases in the Reading that were new to you. Use them in your Discussion.
For example: "have talent."

GOAL Discuss your favorite artists

BEFORE YOU LISTEN

DIGITAL FLASH CARDS

A ▶4:24 **VOCABULARY • *Passive participial phrases*** Read and listen. Then listen again and repeat.

be inspired by He **is inspired by** nature. He tries to capture nature's beauty in his photographs.

be influenced by She **was influenced by** Stella McCartney's work. You can see similarities between McCartney's fashion designs and her own.

be fascinated by He **has** always **been fascinated by** the life of Vincent van Gogh. He thinks the artist was extremely fascinating.

be moved by You **will be moved by** Charlie Chaplin's films. Even though they are funny, their themes of life and love really touch your heart.

Stella McCartney
fashion designer

Vincent van Gogh
painter

Charles Chaplin
actor, filmmaker

B **PAIR WORK** Tell your partner what inspires, influences, interests, fascinates, and moves you. Use passive participial phrases.

"I'm inspired by my parents. They work really hard."

LISTENING COMPREHENSION

A ▶4:25 **UNDERSTAND FROM CONTEXT** Listen to the interviews. Complete each statement with the name of the artist.

1 Burt Hildegard is fascinated by the work of ....
2 Susan Wallach is influenced by the work of ....
3 Katherine Wolf is inspired by the work of ....
4 Nick Jenkins is moved by the work of ....

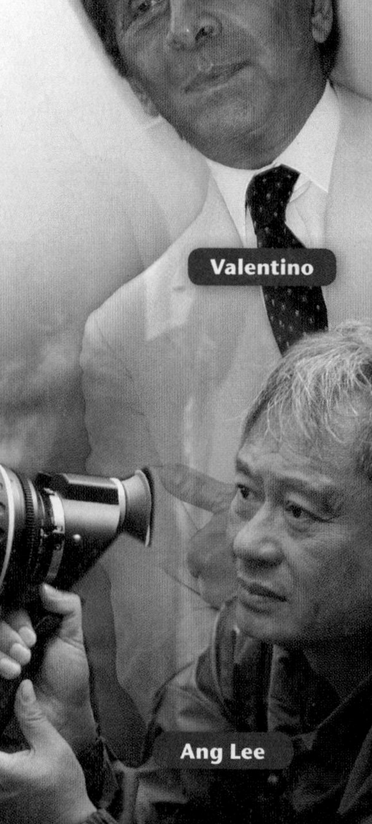

Valentino

Ang Lee

Frida Kahlo

Henri Cartier-Bresson

B ▶4:26 **LISTEN TO TAKE NOTES** Listen again to each interview and write some of the details you hear about each artist. Compare notes with a partner.

1 Ang Lee	2 Henri Cartier-Bresson	3 Valentino	4 Frida Kahlo
explores culture	took black-and-white photos	is Italian	was sick as a child

C **DISCUSSION** Which of the artists described in the Listening do you find the most fascinating? Use your notes to explain why.

NOW YOU CAN Discuss your favorite artists

A **FRAME YOUR IDEAS** Complete the questionnaire. Then compare answers with a partner.

Which qualities attract you to an artist?
Check all that apply.

His or her work . . .

- ◯ is realistic / traditional.
- ◯ is abstract / modern.
- ◯ is easy to understand.
- ◯ makes you think.
- ◯ touches your heart.
- ◯ makes you laugh.
- ◯ other: ___________

He or she . . .

- ◯ is a rebel.
- ◯ is creative.
- ◯ tries new things.
- ◯ has his or her own style.
- ◯ inspires people.
- ◯ other: ___________

Types of artists
a painter
a writer
a sculptor
a filmmaker / director
a fashion designer
an architect
a photographer
an actor
a singer
a dancer

Types of art
drawing
painting
sculpture
photography
jewelry
pottery
fashion
handicrafts

B **NOTEPADDING** On your notepad, write about some of your favorite artists.

	Artist's name	Type of artist	Why I like this artist
1			
2			
3			

C **GROUP WORK** Discuss your favorite artists. Tell your class why you like them. Ask your classmates questions about the artists they describe.

I'm a real fan of the Mexican painters Frida Kahlo and Diego Rivera. I'm fascinated by their lives.

Donatella Versace is my favorite designer. Her fashions are so creative!

One of my favorite Japanese artists is Naoki Urasawa. His drawings in the comic book *Yawara!* are really exciting.

REVIEW

A ▶4:27 Listen and write the letter of the piece of art each person is talking about. Then listen again and circle the best way to complete each statement.

a  **b**  **c** 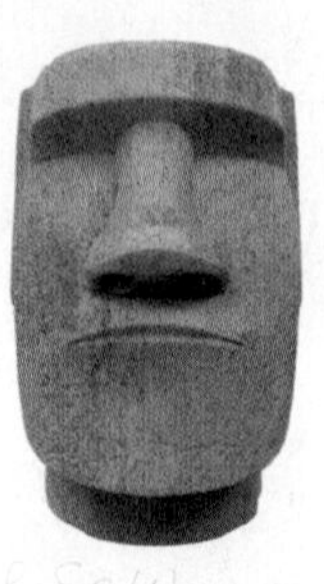 **d**  **e** 

.... **1** She thinks it's (beautiful / ugly / abstract).

.... **2** He thinks it's (traditional / ugly / fascinating). She thinks it's (fantastic / OK / abstract).

.... **3** She thinks it's (OK / awful / great). He thinks it's too (abstract / dark / traditional).

B On a separate sheet of paper, change each sentence from active to passive voice.

1 César Pelli designed the Petronas Twin Towers in Kuala Lumpur.
2 The great Iranian filmmaker Majid Majidi directed *Children of Heaven* in 1998.
3 Henri Matisse made the print *Icarus* in 1947.
4 Annie Leibovitz took that photograph of John Lennon in 1980.
5 The Japanese artist Hokusai produced *The Great Wave of Kanagawa* in the early 1830s.

C List materials under each category. Answers may vary.

Materials that are expensive	Materials that weigh a lot	Materials that break easily
gold		

D Complete the statements.

1 The art of designing clothes is called ....
2 One type of .... is a figure carved from wood or stone.
3 Two types of metal often used to make jewelry are .... and ....
4 Art in a conservative style from the past is called .... art.
5 A piece of art made with a pen or pencil is called a ....

For additional language practice . . .
TOP NOTCH POP
• Lyrics p. 154
"To Each His Own"
DIGITAL SONG
DIGITAL KARAOKE

WRITING

Choose a favorite object that decorates your home. Describe it in a paragraph.

WRITING BOOSTER p. 150
- Providing supporting details
- Guidance for this writing exercise

Ideas
- a painting or drawing
- a photo or poster
- a piece of furniture
- a figure or sculpture
- a plate, bowl, or vase
- (your own idea) ___

ORAL REVIEW

CONTEST Look at the page for one minute and close your books. Using the passive voice, who can describe the most objects and art?

The horse figure is made of __. The statue of David is kept in the __.

PAIR WORK

1 Create a conversation for the man and woman. Recommend a museum. Start like this:

Be sure not to miss the __ while you're in __.

2 Create a conversation for the customer and the store clerk. Ask about the objects. Start like this:

Excuse me. What's this __ made of?

DISCUSSION Talk about the pieces of art in the photos. Say what you like or don't like about each one.

THE GREAT MUSEUMS OF EUROPE

The Accademia Gallery

FLORENCE, ITALY

The world's largest collection of statues by Michelangelo!

David by Michelangelo

Musée d'Orsay

PARIS, FRANCE

Home of the best collection of 19th-century French art, including famous painters such as Monet, Degas, and Renoir

Apples and Oranges by Paul Cézanne

China

India

Peru

Sweden

NOW I CAN

- ☐ Recommend a museum.
- ☐ Ask about and describe objects.
- ☐ Talk about artistic talent.
- ☐ Discuss my favorite artists.

COMMUNICATION GOALS

1 Troubleshoot a problem.
2 Compare product features.
3 Describe how you use the Internet.
4 Discuss the impact of the Internet.

UNIT 9 Living in Cyberspace

PREVIEW

Our Community Friends Search Home

FRANK CARUSO

- Edit
- Search
- Messages
- My photo albums
- Videos
- Groups
- Upload

Frank Caruso Hey, I'm in Rome now! How do you like my new profile pic? That's the Colosseum behind me. This place is awesome!

Kathy Chu Wow! You take good selfies, Frank! You look like you're having fun! Hey, didn't you just post a message from Tokyo two days ago?

Frank Caruso I did. But I've always wanted to see Italy, so someone suggested visiting my airline's web page to look for specials. I got a great deal on a return ticket with a stop here. I'm heading back home to Boston on Friday. Did you all catch the Japan photos I posted?

Nardo Madureira No. What album are they in?

Frank Caruso Actually, they're not here. They're on that new photo-sharing site, GlobalPhoto. Log on and add me to your friends. Or I can send you a link. Click on it to go right to the pics.

Kathy Chu Well, I just looked and they're very cool. Can't wait to see the ones from Italy. I hope they're as nice as the ones from Japan! Nice chatting with you guys! Ciao!

A **PAIR WORK** Read the posts on the social network website. Are you on any similar sites? Do you post regularly? Why or why not?

B **DISCUSSION** Discuss these questions.

1 What photo-sharing services do you know about online? Do you store your photos on any of these sites? What are the advantages and disadvantages of photo-sharing services?

2 Have you ever posted photos while you were traveling? Do you know anyone who has?

C ▶5:02 **PHOTO STORY** Read and listen to a conversation in an office.

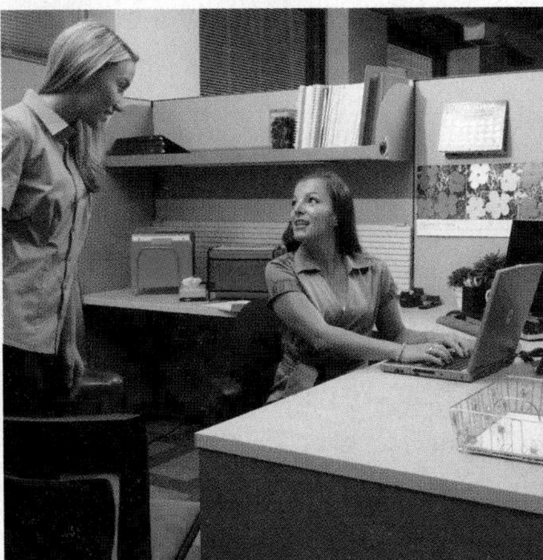

Amy: What are you doing here at this hour? I wasn't sure I'd find you.

Dee: Oh hi, Amy. I'm just fooling around online. I guess I forgot about the time!

Amy: Am I interrupting you?

Dee: Not at all. Paul and I are just instant messaging.

Amy: Sorry to bother you. But I'm a little worried about something.

Dee: What's wrong?

Amy: I just got this e-mail from someone I don't know, and I clicked on the attachment to see what it was. My computer totally crashed. Everything froze, and no matter what I do, nothing happens.

Dee: Actually, you should never open an attachment if you don't know the sender. It could be malware or carry a virus.

Amy: I know. I don't know what I was thinking! It just happened so fast.

Dee: Look. First, try shutting down and restarting, OK? Sometimes that takes care of it.

Amy: You think that would work?

Dee: It couldn't hurt. Listen, Paul's still there. Let me send a quick response, OK? I'll just be a second.

Amy: No problem. I'll go and try restarting to see if that does the trick.

D **FOCUS ON LANGUAGE** Look at the five expressions from the Photo Story. Write the letter of the meaning of each expression. (Two expressions have the same meaning.)

.... **1** just fooling around
.... **2** takes care of it
.... **3** couldn't hurt
.... **4** I'll just be a second
.... **5** does the trick

a won't take a long time
b not doing anything serious
c is worth trying
d fixes the problem

SPEAKING

Do you know how to solve computer problems? Complete the chart. Then compare answers with a partner and discuss some possible solutions.

Do you know what to do if . . .			
	Yes	No	Not sure
1 you think you have a virus?	☐	☐	☐
2 your printer won't print?	☐	☐	☐
3 you click on a link and nothing happens?	☐	☐	☐
4 your computer is really slow?	☐	☐	☐
5 your computer crashes?	☐	☐	☐
6 you forget your password?	☐	☐	☐

Some computer solutions
- try restarting
- check if it's turned on
- buy a new computer
- [your own idea]

LESSON 1

GOAL Troubleshoot a problem

CONVERSATION MODEL

A ▶5:03 Read and listen to people troubleshooting a computer problem.

A: Eugene, could you take a look at this?

B: Sure. What's the problem?

A: Well, I clicked on the toolbar to save a file, and the computer crashed.

B: Why don't you try restarting? That sometimes works.

A: OK. I'll give that a try.

B ▶5:04 **RHYTHM AND INTONATION** Listen again and repeat. Then practice the Conversation Model with a partner.

▶5:05 **Ways to reassure someone**
That sometimes works.
That sometimes helps.
That sometimes does the trick.

DIGITAL FLASH CARDS

VOCABULARY *The computer screen, components, and commands*

A ▶5:06 Read and listen. Then listen again and repeat.

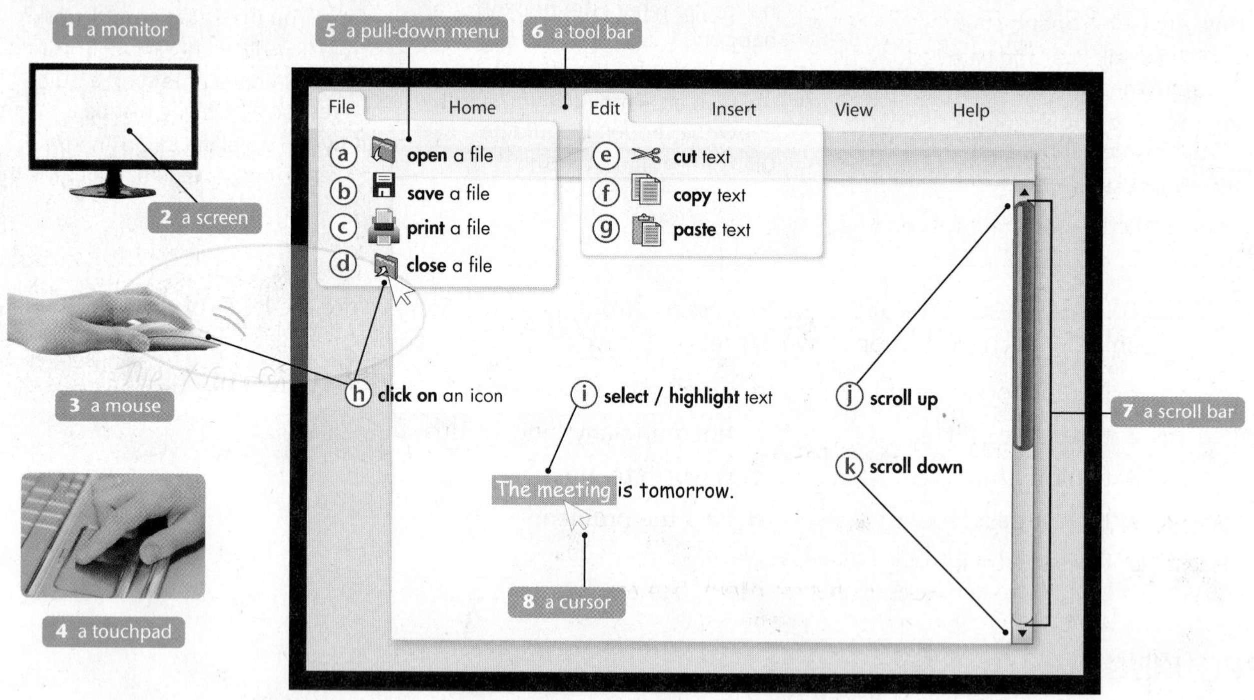

B ▶5:07 **LISTEN TO ACTIVATE VOCABULARY** Listen. Check the computer command each person needs.

	open	save	print	cut	copy	paste	scroll up	scroll down
1 He needs to click on . . .	☐	☐	☐	☐	☐	☐	☐	☐
2 She needs to click on . . .	☐	☐	☐	☐	☐	☐	☐	☐
3 He needs to click on . . .	☐	☐	☐	☐	☐	☐	☐	☐
4 She needs to click on . . .	☐	☐	☐	☐	☐	☐	☐	☐
5 He needs to click on . . .	☐	☐	☐	☐	☐	☐	☐	☐
6 She needs to click on . . .	☐	☐	☐	☐	☐	☐	☐	☐

GRAMMAR *The infinitive of purpose*

GRAMMAR BOOSTER p. 139

- Expressing purpose with in order to and for

An infinitive can be used to express a purpose.

I scrolled down **to read** the text. (= because I wanted to read the text)
Put the cursor on the toolbar **to choose** a file. (= if you want to choose a file)

Answering a Why question with an infinitive of purpose is similar to answering with Because.

Why did you click on that icon? **To save** the file before I close it. (= Because I want to save it.)
Why did you highlight that word? **To select** it so I can copy it. (= Because I want to copy it.)

A **FIND THE GRAMMAR** Look at the Conversation Model on page 100. Find an infinitive of purpose. Restate the sentence, using because.

B **PAIR WORK** Look at Cathy's to-do list. Ask and answer questions, using infinitives of purpose.

"Why is Cathy going shopping?"

"To get something for dinner."

TO DO TODAY

- go shopping – get something for dinner
- call Dad – wish him Happy Birthday!
- meet Brandy – talk about next weekend
- talk to Mark – ask for help with scanner
- e-mail Hillary – send her my new photos
- drop off car at service station – fix windshield wipers
- visit Katonah Museum – see new art exhibit
- call salon – make appointment for manicure

C **GRAMMAR PRACTICE** Complete each sentence in your own way. Use infinitives of purpose.

1 Don't forget to click on the save icon ....
2 You can click on the print icon ....
3 Put the cursor on the pull-down menu ....
4 I bought a new scanner ....
5 I e-mailed my friend ....
6 I connected to the Internet ....

NOW YOU CAN Troubleshoot a problem

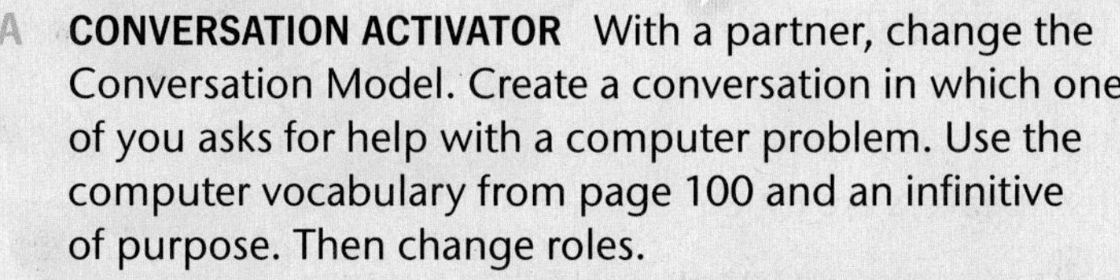

A **CONVERSATION ACTIVATOR** With a partner, change the Conversation Model. Create a conversation in which one of you asks for help with a computer problem. Use the computer vocabulary from page 100 and an infinitive of purpose. Then change roles.

A: .... , could you take a look at this?
B: Sure. .... ?
A: Well, I clicked on .... to .... , and ....
B: Why don't you try .... ? That ....
A: .... I'll give that a try.

DON'T STOP!

- Discuss other problems.
- Offer other suggestions.

RECYCLE THIS LANGUAGE.

- The computer crashes.
- The screen freezes.
- The printer won't print.
- The file won't [open / close / print].
- The [mouse] doesn't work.
- Nothing happens.
- (your own idea) __

B **CHANGE PARTNERS** Practice the conversation again with other problems.

LESSON 2 **GOAL** Compare product features

GRAMMAR *Comparisons with as . . . as*

To express similarity

Use as . . . as with an adjective to indicate how two things are equal or the same. Use the adverb just for emphasis.

The new speakers are as good as the old ones.
The iFriend tablet is just as nice as the F40.

Use the adverb almost in affirmative statements to indicate that two things are very similar but not exactly the same.

The Zeta B is almost as fast as the Panasox.

To express difference

Use not as . . . as to indicate how two things are different. Use not quite when the difference is very small. Use not nearly to indicate that there's a big difference.

Our new printer isn't as noisy as the old one.
The G4 isn't quite as expensive as the Z90.
The Panasox isn't nearly as affordable as the Zeta B.

You can use shortened statements with as when the meaning is clear.

The old monitor was great. But the new one is just as good. (= just as good as the old one)
Have you seen Carl's new laptop? My laptop isn't as nice. (= as nice as his laptop)

GRAMMAR BOOSTER p. 139

- As . . . as to compare adverbs
- Comparatives and superlatives: review
- Comparison with adverbs

A GRAMMAR PRACTICE Read each statement about a product. Write a sentence with as . . . as and the cue to compare the products.

1 The new Shine keyboard is popular. The one from Digitek is popular, too.
(just) ....

2 The XCue joystick is easy to use. The JRock joystick is also easy to use.
(just) ....

3 The C50 monitor is large. The C30 monitor is a little larger than the C50.
(almost) ....

4 Comtec's new mini-tablet is very small. Sango's new mini-tablet is also very small.
(just) ....

5 The CCV speakers are very powerful. The Soundtec speakers are much more powerful.
(not / nearly) ....

6 The Icon monitors are very inexpensive. The Sentinel monitors are a little more expensive.
(not / quite) ....

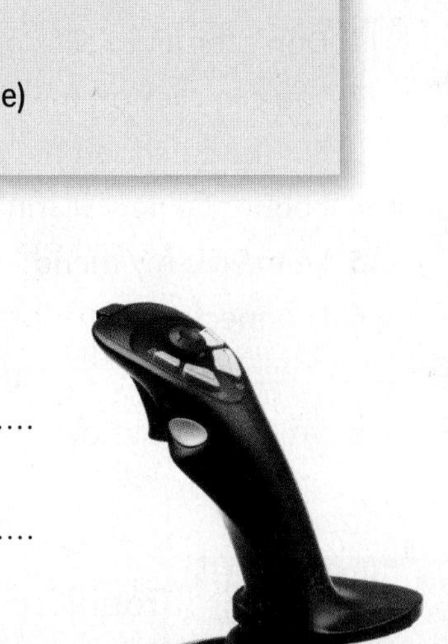
a joystick

B On a separate sheet of paper, write five statements comparing things you are familiar with. Use as . . . as.

In my opinion, the Mardino sports car isn't nearly as good as the Strega.

Ideas for comparisons

- cars
- electronic products
- stores
- restaurants
- (your own idea) ___

MORE EXERCISES

DIGITAL VIDEO COACH

PRONUNCIATION *Stress in as . . . as phrases*

A ▶5:08 Read and listen. Then listen again and repeat.

1 The new printer is as slow as the old one.

2 My old smart phone is just as small as the new one.

3 The X12 mouse isn't nearly as nice as the X30.

4 The M200 keyboard isn't quite as cheap as the Z6.

B Read the statements you wrote in Exercise B on page 102 aloud, paying attention to stress.

CONVERSATION MODEL

A ▶5:09 Listen to someone compare product features.

A: I'm thinking about getting a new game controller.

B: Oh, yeah? What kind?

A: Everyone says I should get a Macro.

B: Well, I've heard that the Panatel is as good as the Macro, but it costs a lot less.

A: Really? I'll check it out.

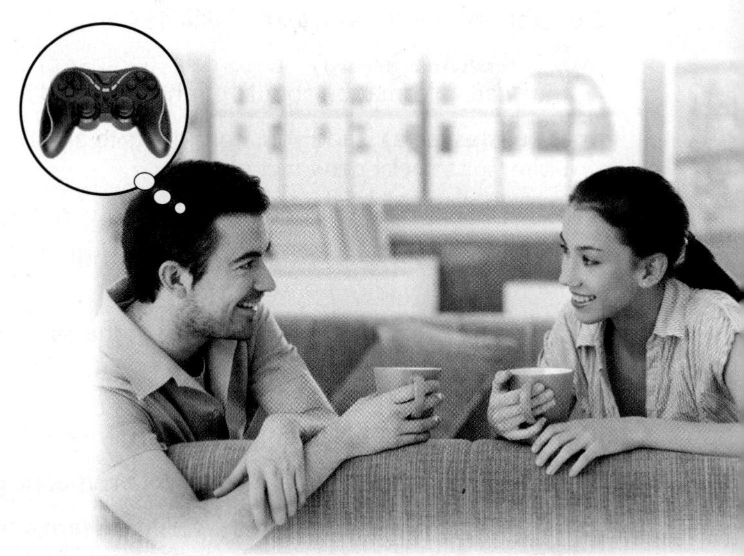

B ▶5:10 **RHYTHM AND INTONATION** Listen again and repeat. Then practice the Conversation Model with a partner.

NOW YOU CAN Compare product features

DIGITAL VIDEO

A **CONVERSATION ACTIVATOR** With a partner, change the Conversation Model, using the magazine ratings to compare features of different products. Use as . . . as. Then change roles.

A: I'm thinking about getting a new ....

B: .... ? What kind?

A: Everyone says I should get ....

B: Well, I've heard that ....

A: Really? ....

DON'T STOP!

- Ask about other features.

RECYCLE THIS LANGUAGE.

Which ...

is more popular?	is newer?
is easier / harder to use?	is quieter / noisier?
is lighter / heavier?	is slower / faster?
is larger / smaller?	has more features?
is less / more expensive?	looks nicer?
costs less / more?	gets better reviews?

Buyer's Friend *Magazine*

Our recommendations!

eMax Wireless Mouse	very good	US $25
eMax X15 Wireless Keyboard	very comfortable	US $30
eMax Y80 Webcam	easy to use	US $52
eMax Z40 Monitor	15 inches / 38 centimeters	US $250

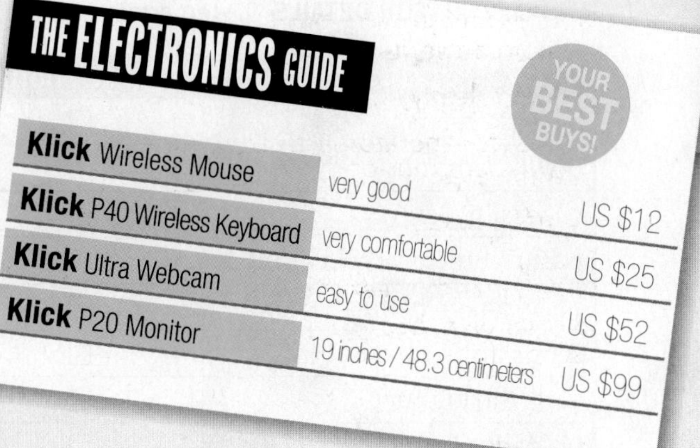

THE ELECTRONICS GUIDE YOUR BEST BUYS!

Klick Wireless Mouse	very good	US $12
Klick P40 Wireless Keyboard	very comfortable	US $25
Klick Ultra Webcam	easy to use	US $52
Klick P20 Monitor	19 inches / 48.3 centimeters	US $99

B **CHANGE PARTNERS** Now practice the conversation again, using other products and features.

LESSON 3 **GOAL** Describe how you use the Internet

BEFORE YOU LISTEN

DIGITAL FLASH CARDS ▶ 5:11 **VOCABULARY • *Internet activities*** Read and listen. Then listen again and repeat.

visit a website go to a specific address on the Internet and read its content

surf the Internet visit a lot of different websites for information that interests you

join (an online group) become a member of an Internet group to meet friends and share information about your hobbies and interests

post (a message) add your comments to an online discussion on a message board, a blog, or a social networking site

attach (a file) place a document or photo into an e-mail

upload (a file) move a document, music file, or picture from a personal computer, phone, or MP3 player onto the Internet

share (a link) send an e-mail or post a message with the address of an interesting website you want someone to visit

download an application download a useful program that you can use to play games, get information, or perform tasks

send an instant message "chat" with someone online in real time by typing messages

look up information go to a website to learn about something

Remember also:
- download (a file)
- stream a video
- check e-mail

LISTENING COMPREHENSION

A ▶ 5:12 **LISTEN FOR THE MAIN IDEA** Listen to people describe how they use the Internet. Write a checkmark next to the person who seems to enjoy the Internet the least. Explain your answer.

☐ 1 George Thomas

☐ 2 Sonia Castro

☐ 3 Robert Kuan

☐ 4 Nadia Montasser

B ▶ 5:13 **LISTEN FOR DETAILS** Listen again and check the activities each person does.

	George Thomas	Sonia Castro	Robert Kuan	Nadia Montasser
buys products	☐	☐	☐	☑
downloads music	☐	☐	☐	☑
checks the latest news	☐	☐	☐	☐
participates in online groups	☐	☐	☐	☐
plays online games	☐	☐	☐	☐
sends instant messages	☐	☐	☐	☐
surfs the Internet	☐	☐	☐	☐
uploads photos	☐	☐	☐	☐
uses a computer at work	☐	☐	☐	☐

NOW YOU CAN Describe how you use the Internet

A **FRAME YOUR IDEAS** Complete the survey about your own Internet use.

New Tab

Internet User Survey

1. I usually spend ___ hours a week online.

- ○ 0 – 10
- ○ 11 – 20
- ○ 21 – 30
- ○ 31 – 40
- ○ 41 – 50
- ○ over 50

2. I use . . .

- ○ a desktop
- ○ a laptop
- ○ a smart phone
- ○ a tablet
- ○ (none of these)

3. I use the Internet . . .

- ○ for work
- ○ for study
- ○ for fun
- ○ I never use the Internet.

4. I use the Internet . . .

- ○ to search for new websites
- ○ to upload photos
- ○ to download photos
- ○ to design websites
- ○ to look up information
- ○ to create art
- ○ to shop for things
- ○ to take classes
- ○ to send instant messages
- ○ to keep in touch with friends
- ○ to keep in touch with family
- ○ to meet new people
- ○ to watch movies
- ○ to look at my bank accounts
- ○ to sell things
- ○ to practice English
- ○ to download music
- ○ to upload videos
- ○ to download videos
- ○ to send and receive e-mail
- ○ to play games
- ○ to pay bills
- ○ to read or watch the news
- ○ to just fool around
- ○ other: ....

5. Check the statements that are true about you.

- ○ People consider me to be a technology expert. They come to me for help.
- ○ You could say I'm an Internet addict. I'm always online.
- ○ Compared to most people, I spend a lot of time on the Internet.
- ○ I spend just as much time on the Internet as most people.
- ○ I don't spend nearly as much time on the Internet as most people.
- ○ I'm really not comfortable using the Internet.

B **GROUP WORK** Walk around your classroom and ask your classmates about their Internet use. Ask questions to get more information and take notes.

Ideas for questions
Why . . . ? When . . . ?
Where . . . ? How . . . ?

Find someone who. . .	Name	Notes
is an Internet expert.		
is an Internet addict.		
isn't comfortable using the Internet.		
uses the Internet to meet people.		
uses the Internet to avoid people.		

C **DISCUSSION** Tell your class what you found out about your classmates and how they use the Internet.

"May spends a lot of time online. She uses her tablet to meet new people and keep in touch with friends. Gary spends a lot of time online with his smart phone. He uploads photos and . . . "

LESSON 4 **GOAL** Discuss the impact of the Internet

BEFORE YOU READ

1 What kinds of problems have you had on the Internet?

2 What kinds of Internet problems have you heard about on the news?

READING ▶ 5:14

Identity Thieves Steal 40 Million Credit Card Numbers

Eleven hackers around the world were accused of stealing more than 40 million credit card numbers on the Internet. They included three people from the U.S. who are accused of hacking into the wireless networks of popular online stores.

Once inside these networks, they searched for customers' credit card numbers, passwords, and personal information so they could pretend to be those customers. When the identity theft was completed, credit card numbers and other details were then sold on the Internet, allowing criminals to withdraw thousands of dollars at a time from ATMs.

Computer Viruses Are Getting Harder to Prevent

"We're losing the battle against computer viruses," says David Farber, professor of computer science at Carnegie Mellon University. These viruses, which can enter computer systems through junk e-mail from hackers, have reached epidemic proportions, slowing down computers—and sometimes causing whole office computer systems to crash—in both large and small companies. In one year alone, they were reported to have caused $13 billion USD in damage.

Companies have been trying for years to protect themselves with anti-virus programs, but criminals are creating newer, improved viruses faster than these programs can keep up with.

Cyberbullying Leads to Teenager's Death

Megan Taylor Meier, age 13, joined an online social networking group where she became online friends with a 16-year-old boy named Josh. Megan and Josh never communicated by phone or in person, but she enjoyed exchanging messages with him in the group.

Over time, Josh changed. He began to bully her daily—criticizing her personality and telling her what a bad person she was. Some of their communications were posted so everyone could see them. Josh's last message to her said, "The world would be a better place without you." A short time later, Megan committed suicide.

After her death, it was discovered that there was no "Josh." The messages came from the mother of one of Megan's classmates. The mother had been angry with Megan because she believed Megan had said some untrue things about her daughter.

A UNDERSTAND FROM CONTEXT Use the context of the articles to help you to complete each definition.

.... **1** A hacker is . . .	**a** a software program that causes problems in computers.
.... **2** A computer virus is . . .	**b** a software program that tries to stop the spread of viruses.
.... **3** A criminal is . . .	**c** a person who enters computer systems without permission.
.... **4** Junk e-mail is . . .	**d** a person who steals other people's personal information.
.... **5** An anti-virus program is . . .	**e** an advertisement you didn't request.
.... **6** A cyberbully is . . .	**f** a person who breaks the law; for example, by stealing money.
.... **7** An identity thief is . . .	**g** a person who sends cruel and negative messages to another person online.

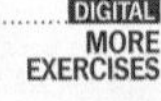
DIGITAL MORE EXERCISES

B RELATE TO PERSONAL EXPERIENCE What news stories have you heard about the Internet? Do you ever worry about using the Internet? Why or why not?

NOW YOU CAN Discuss the impact of the Internet

A NOTEPADDING With a partner, discuss each statement. Write at least one good change and one bad change for each.

1 The Internet has changed the way people find information.

Good changes:

Bad changes:

2 The Internet has changed the way people work in offices.

Good changes:

Bad changes:

3 The Internet has changed the way people shop.

Good changes:

Bad changes:

4 The Internet has changed the way people communicate.

Good changes:

Bad changes:

B DISCUSSION Do you think that computers and the Internet have brought more benefits or more problems? Support your opinions with examples.

Text-mining (optional)
Find and underline three words or phrases in the Reading that were new to you. Use them in your Discussion.
For example: "exchanging messages."

In my opinion, there are more benefits than problems. For example, it's easy to look up information, and it's really fast.

I think the Internet is OK, but there are really too many problems. First of all, you have to be very careful if you shop online with a credit card.

REVIEW

A ▶5:15 Listen to the conversations. Circle T for true and F for false. Then listen again and infer how to complete each statement.

1 She recommends the C40.	T	F
2 She recommends the Hip web camera.	T	F
3 He recommends the new Sender tablet.	T	F
4 He recommends the Play Zone 3.	T	F

1 The C40's monitor is .... the X8's.
a the same size as **b** larger than **c** smaller than

2 The Hip web camera is .... the Pentac web camera.
a the same price as **b** cheaper than **c** more expensive than

3 Sender's new model is .... Sender's old model.
a the same as **b** nicer than **c** worse than

4 Play Zone 3 is .... Play Zone 2.
a as cool as **b** less cool than **c** more cool than

B Answer each question in your own words, using infinitives of purpose.

1 Why do people join social networking sites? ....
2 Why do people send instant messages? ....
3 Why do people surf the Internet? ....
4 Why do people shop online? ....
5 Why are you studying English? ....

C Complete each statement.

1 .... on an icon on the screen to select it.
2 If you want to print a document, click on the print icon on the ....
3 To read more text on your monitor's .... , use the scroll .... to scroll down.
4 Click on File on the toolbar so you can choose an icon from the .... menu.
5 When you're finished working on a document, don't forget to .... it before you close the file.

D Unscramble the letters of the words in the box to complete each sentence.

chatated	clorls	doalwond	esmou	rekcha	rusvi

1 Last year, a .... got into the company's computer systems and stole important information.
2 Use the .... to click on a file and open it.
3 It isn't difficult to .... songs from the Internet.
4 Use the .... bar to see more text on the screen.
5 Her computer isn't working now because she downloaded a .... from a piece of junk e-mail.
6 I .... the photos to the e-mail I sent this morning.

For additional language practice . . .

TOP NOTCH POP
• Lyrics p. 154
"Life in Cyberspace"
DIGITAL SONG
DIGITAL KARAOKE

WRITING

Write two paragraphs about the benefits and the problems of the Internet. Use your notepads from page 107 for support.

WRITING BOOSTER p. 151
• Organizing ideas
• Guidance for this writing exercise

ORAL REVIEW

CONTEST Look at the photos for one minute. Then close your books. Who can name all the computer parts and activities in the photos? For example:

There's a printer and . . . OR
He's trying to print photos . . .

PAIR WORK

1 Create a conversation for the man and the woman. They are troubleshooting a problem. Start like this:
Could you take a look at this?

2 Create a conversation for the two men. One is asking for a product recommendation. Start like this:
I'm thinking about getting a new . . .

3 Create a conversation for the two women on the phone. One is asking the other about what she is doing on the computer. Start like this:
Am I interrupting you?

1

2

3

NOW I CAN

- ☐ Troubleshoot a problem.
- ☐ Compare product features.
- ☐ Describe how I use the Internet.
- ☐ Discuss the impact of the Internet.

COMMUNICATION GOALS

1 Discuss ethical choices.
2 Return someone else's property.
3 Express personal values.
4 Discuss acts of kindness and honesty.

UNIT 10 Ethics and Values

PREVIEW

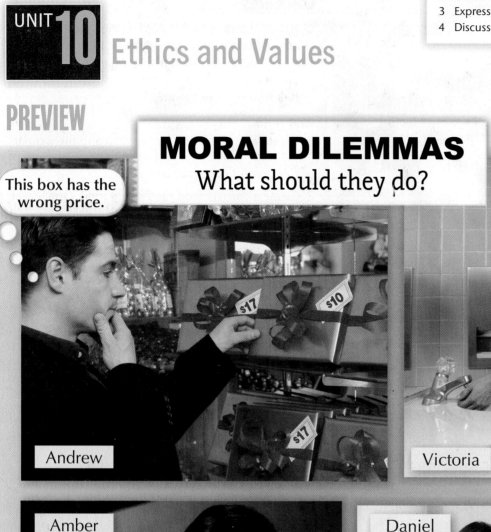

A **GROUP WORK** Have you ever been faced with a moral dilemma similar to the ones in the pictures? Tell your classmates what happened.

B ▶5:18 **PHOTO STORY** Read and listen to a conversation about a moral dilemma.

Matt: I can't believe it! I just picked this up to look at it and the thing broke in two. And with these ridiculous prices, it's going to cost me an arm and a leg.

Noah: Oh, forget it. I'll bet it was already broken.

Matt: You're probably right.

Noah: Just put it back on the shelf. The place is empty. No one saw. Let's just split.

Matt: I couldn't do that.

Noah: Why not? You said it yourself. The prices are ridiculous.

Matt: Well, put yourself in the owner's shoes. Suppose the plate were yours? How would you feel if someone broke it and didn't tell you?

Noah: Well I'm *not* the owner. And, anyway, for him it would be just a drop in the bucket. To *you* it's a lot of money.

Matt: Maybe so. But if I ran out without telling him, I couldn't face myself.

C **FOCUS ON LANGUAGE** Match each idiom from the Photo Story with its meaning.

1 an arm and a leg
2 split
3 put yourself in someone's shoes
4 a drop in the bucket
5 I couldn't face myself.

a a small amount of money
b I would feel bad about it.
c a lot of money
d imagine another person's point of view
e leave

D **THINK AND EXPLAIN** Answer the following questions. Support your answers with quotations from the Photo Story.

1 Does Noah think Matt broke the plate?
2 Why does Noah think it would be easy to leave without saying anything?
3 What does Matt want to do about the plate?

SPEAKING

A **SURVEY** Look at "Moral Dilemmas" and the Photo Story again. Do you agree with the statements below? Circle yes or no, and then give a reason for your answers.

1 Andrew should buy the chocolate with the lower price.	yes / no	
2 Victoria should keep the watch.	yes / no	
3 Amber should tell the waiter there's a mistake.	yes / no	
4 Daniel should send the second jacket back.	yes / no	
5 Matt should tell the store owner what happened.	yes / no	

B **GROUP WORK** Form small groups. Compare your answers and explain your reasons.

GOAL Discuss ethical choices

GRAMMAR *The unreal conditional*

> **Remember:** Conditional sentences express the results of actions or conditions. The real conditional expresses the results of real conditions—conditions that exist.
> If I don't use English in class, I won't learn to speak it.

Meaning

Unreal conditional sentences describe the results of unreal conditions—conditions that don't exist.

unreal action or condition	result (if it were true)
If I found a wallet in the street,	I'd try to return it. (unreal: I haven't found one.)

> **Contraction**
> would → 'd

Formation

In the if clause, use the simple past tense. For the verb be, always use were.
In the result clause, use would + a base form.

unreal action or condition	result (if it were true)
If I had to make a hard decision,	I would try to do the right thing
If she knew how to speak French,	she'd help them.
If you broke something in a store,	would you pay for it?
If you were Matt,	what would you do?
If I were you,	I wouldn't do that.
If you weren't my friend,	I wouldn't tell you what happened.

> **Be careful!**
> Don't use would in the if clause.
> If I knew his name, I would tell you.
> NOT If I ~~would know~~ his name . . .

Note: In real and unreal conditional sentences, the clauses can occur in either order. Use a comma if the if clause comes first.

If I knew, I would tell you. OR I would tell you if I knew.

> GRAMMAR BOOSTER p. 140
> Expressing ethics and obligation: expansion
> - should, ought to, had better
> - have to, must, be supposed to

A UNDERSTAND THE GRAMMAR Check the conditional sentences that describe an unreal condition.

- ☐ **1** If we ate in a restaurant, I would pay the bill.
- ☐ **2** I'll pay the bill if we eat in a restaurant.
- ☐ **3** If you get a haircut, you'll look younger.
- ☐ **4** His wife would worry if he came home really late.
- ☐ **5** If I were you, I'd tell him the truth.
- ☐ **6** If I have problem with my office computer, I always ask my co-worker Jim to help.
- ☐ **7** If they sent me the wrong pants, I would return them.

B GRAMMAR PRACTICE Complete each unreal conditional sentence with the correct forms of the verbs.

1 If they .... (put) the wrong price on the coat, ... you .... (buy) it without telling the clerk?

2 I'm sure you .... (say) something if the restaurant check .... (be) wrong.

3 If I .... (find) an expensive piece of jewelry in a public bathroom and .... (can not) find the owner, I .... (not keep) it.

4 If you .... (be) friends with someone who did something wrong, ... you .... (say) something to him or her?

5 If you .... (have) two tickets, ... you .... (give) one to a friend?

6 What .... (happen) if it .... (snow) here tomorrow?

7 They .... (go) to India if they .... (have) the money.

8 If you .... (receive) two jackets instead of the one you ordered, ... you .... (send) one of them back?

9 If they .... (be) here, I .... (tell) them what happened.

DIGITAL MORE EXERCISES

CONVERSATION MODEL

A ▶5:19 Read and listen to people discussing an ethical choice.

A: Look at this. They didn't charge us for the desserts.
B: Really? I think we'd better tell the waiter.
A: You think so?
B: Absolutely. If we didn't tell him, it would be wrong.

B ▶5:20 **RHYTHM AND INTONATION** Listen again and repeat. Then practice the Conversation Model with a partner.

▶5:21 **Express an ethical obligation**

We'd better tell	the waiter.
We should tell	
We ought to tell	

PRONUNCIATION *Blending of d + y in would you*

A ▶5:22 Notice how the /d/ and /y/ sounds blend to /ʤ/ in questions with "would you." Read and listen. Then listen again and repeat.

1 What would you do if the waiter didn't charge you for the dessert?
2 What would you do if you found a wallet on the street?
3 Who would you call if you were sick?
4 Where would you go if you wanted a great meal?

B **PAIR WORK** Complete the following questions. Ask a partner the questions, using blending with would you. Then answer your partner's questions.

1 What would you do if .... ?
2 Where would you go if .... ?
3 When would you eat if .... ?

NOW YOU CAN Discuss ethical choices

A **CONVERSATION ACTIVATOR** With a partner, change the Conversation Model. Discuss ethical choices, using the situations in the pictures. Then change roles.

A: Look .... They ....
B: .... ? I think .... 'd better ....
A: You think so?
B: Absolutely. If .... , ...

DON'T STOP!
- Say more.

RECYCLE THIS LANGUAGE.
I couldn't face myself.
Put yourself in [his / her / their] shoes.
If you don't tell the [clerk], [she'll have to pay for it].
If [he didn't charge us], [we would tell him].

▶5:23 **Situations that require an ethical choice**

They didn't charge us for the cake.
They undercharged me.
They gave me too much change.
They gave me more than I ordered.

B **DISCUSSION** Tell your classmates about an ethical choice you had to make in the past.

LESSON 2 **GOAL** Return someone else's property

CONVERSATION MODEL

A ▶5:24 Read and listen to a conversation about returning property.

A: Excuse me. I think you forgot something.

B: I did?

A: Isn't this jacket hers?

B: Oh, you're right. It is. That's nice of you.

A: Don't mention it.

▶5:26 **Acknowledging thanks**
Don't mention it.
My pleasure.
You're welcome.
Not at all.

B ▶5:25 **RHYTHM AND INTONATION** Listen again and repeat. Then practice the Conversation Model with a partner.

GRAMMAR *Possessive pronouns / Whose*

Possessive pronouns can replace nouns and noun phrases. They answer questions with Whose and clarify answers to questions with Which.

A: Whose coat is that? B: It's mine. (= It's my coat.)
A: Which is her cup? B: This one is hers.

subject pronouns	possessive adjectives	possessive pronouns	
I	my	mine	That's my jacket. / It's mine.
you	your	yours	Your dinner was great. / Yours was great.
he	his	his	Are these his keys? / Are these his?
she	her	hers	She drives her car to work. / She drives hers to work.
we	our	ours	These are our shoes. / These are ours.
they	their	theirs	They finished their assignment. / They finished theirs.

Be careful!
- Don't use a possessive adjective in place of a possessive pronoun.
  Is this **yours**? NOT Is this ~~your~~?
- Don't use a noun after a possessive pronoun.
  These shoes are **mine**. NOT These are ~~mine shoes~~.

GRAMMAR BOOSTER p. 141
- Possessive nouns: review and expansion
- Pronouns: summary

A **GRAMMAR PRACTICE** Replace the noun phrases with possessive pronouns.

1. Those gloves are ~~my gloves~~. mine
2. That is ~~her coat~~.
3. The books on that table are ~~Mr. Davison's~~.
4. Their car and ~~our car~~ are parked on the same street.
5. Are those my tickets or ~~her tickets~~?
6. The white house is ~~my mother's house~~.
7. Is this painting ~~your painting~~ or ~~her brother's painting~~?
8. The newspaper under the chair is ~~his daughter's paper~~.
9. Is this DVD ~~your DVD~~ or ~~your friends'~~?
10. Are these ~~your son's shoes~~?

B GRAMMAR PRACTICE Complete the conversations. Circle the correct adjectives and pronouns.

1 A: Whose umbrella is this, (he / his) or (her / hers)?
B: I'm not sure. Ask them if it's (their / theirs).

2 A: Who is more conservative about clothes? Your parents or your husband's parents?
B: (He / His), I think. (My / Mine) parents are pretty liberal.

3 A: Is this (ours / our) suitcase?
B: No, I already got (our / ours) suitcase, so this one can't be (our / ours).

4 A: I found this necklace near Carrie's desk. Is it (her / hers)?
B: No, it's (my / mine) necklace. I'm so happy someone found it!

5 A: Is that (their / theirs) car?
B: No, (their / theirs) is the black one over there.

6 A: Where should we meet? At (your / yours) house or (my / mine)?
B: Neither. Let's meet at (my / mine) office.

C ▶5:27 **LISTEN TO ACTIVATE GRAMMAR** Listen to the conversations and complete each statement with a possessive pronoun.

1 The bag is ....
2 The phone is .... , but the keys belong to Brad's wife. They're ....
3 The coat isn't ....
4 The concert tickets aren't ....

DIGITAL MORE RCISES

NOW YOU CAN Return someone else's property

DIGITAL VIDEO

A CONVERSATION ACTIVATOR With a partner, change the Conversation Model to role-play returning the items in the pictures. Then change roles.

A: Excuse me. I think you forgot something.
B: I did?
A: .... yours?
B: Oh, you're right. .... That's nice of you.
A: ....

B GROUP WORK First, collect personal items from your classmates. Then role-play returning someone else's property. Walk around the room to find the owners. Use possessive pronouns.

C EXTENSION Place all your classmates' personal items on a table. Ask about each item. Identify the owner, using possessive pronouns.

"Whose phone is this?"

"It's his."

GOAL Express personal values

BEFORE YOU LISTEN

EXPLORE YOUR IDEAS Which actions would be OK, and which wouldn't be OK for the following people: you? your parents? your grandparents? your own teenaged child?

"It wouldn't be OK if my grandmother pierced her nose. Face piercing is for young people. She's too old."

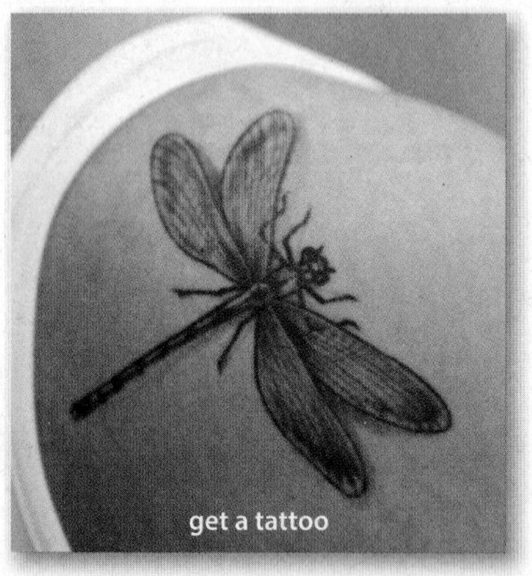
get a tattoo

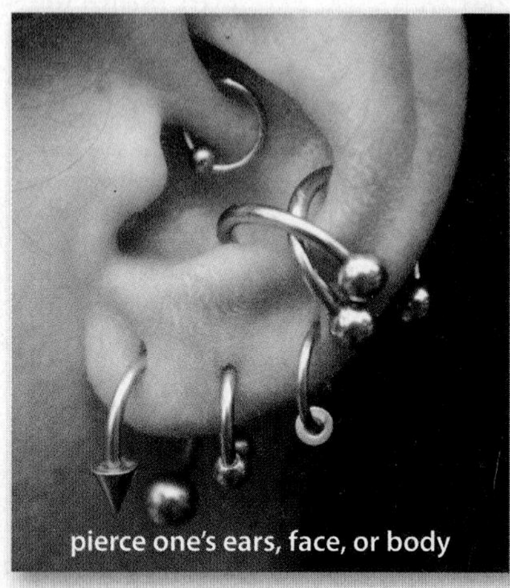
pierce one's ears, face, or body

dye one's hair a wild color

LISTENING COMPREHENSION

A ▶5:28 **LISTEN FOR MAIN IDEAS** Listen to each conversation. Then circle the correct word or phrase to complete each statement.

1 a Beth thinks it's (OK / not OK) to wear an earring to the office.
  b Beth (convinces / doesn't convince) Luke.

2 a Celia's husband thinks it's (OK / wrong) for a woman to have a tattoo.
  b Celia's husband thinks it's (OK / wrong) for a man to have a tattoo.

3 a The first man is (happy / not happy) that his daughter is going to law school.
  b He wants his daughter to (stay home / work).

4 a Kate's dad is (worried / not worried) about what people think of Kate.
  b Kate is (worried / not worried) about what people think of her.

B **UNDERSTAND VOCABULARY FROM CONTEXT** Read the following quotations from the conversations. Then choose the meaning of each underlined word or phrase. Listen again if necessary.

1 "But lots of people are <u>old-fashioned</u>, and they don't think men should wear earrings."
  a preferring the way things were in the past
  b preferring the way things are now

2 "What a <u>double standard</u>!"
  a having the same rules for everyone
  b having different rules for different people

3 "That's a little <u>sexist</u>, if you ask me!"
  a not treating men and women in the same way
  b treating men and women in the same way

4 "But <u>modesty</u> is very important for girls."
  a wearing clothes that cover one's body
  b wearing clothes that show one's body

C **APPLY NEW VOCABULARY** Write an example for each word or phrase from your own experience. Compare examples with a partner.

> “I think an example of old-fashioned is not letting teenagers go out on dates.”

old-fashioned	
a double standard	
sexist	
modesty	

D **PAIR WORK** Discuss the picture. Use the following words and phrases in your discussion: old-fashioned, sexist, double standard, modesty.

> “He's measuring the woman's swimsuit. If she were a man, he wouldn't measure it. That's a double standard.”

Man measuring the length of a woman's swimsuit (U.S., 1920s)

NOW YOU CAN Express personal values

A **IDEA FRAMING** Complete the Values Self-Test. Then compare answers with a partner. Do you have the same values?

Values Self-Test

Check the boxes that best describe your values. Include a specific example.

1. ❑ I'm modern in my attitudes about modesty.
   ❑ I'm old-fashioned in my attitudes about modesty.
   Explain. ______________________
2. ❑ I think tattoos and body piercing are OK for men.
   ❑ I think tattoos and body piercing are OK for women.
   Explain. ______________________
3. ❑ I think it's OK to have a double standard for different people.
   ❑ I think the rules should be the same for everyone.
   Explain. ______________________
4. ❑ Some people might say I'm sexist.
   ❑ Nobody would say I'm sexist.
   Explain. ______________________

B **NOTEPADDING** Answer each question and explain your opinion, using examples.

Is it sometimes OK to have a double standard for men and women?

Can people be sexist when they talk about men, or only about women?

Are old-fashioned ideas usually better or worse than modern ideas?

C **GROUP WORK** Now discuss each question, expressing your personal values. Expect people to disagree with you!

RECYCLE THIS LANGUAGE.

Agreement and disagreement	Likes and dislikes	Adjectives
I agree.	I like __.	liberal
I disagree.	I dislike __.	conservative
It depends.	I hate __.	strict
	I can't stand __.	modest
	I don't mind __.	
	__ drives me crazy!	

GOAL Discuss acts of kindness and honesty

BEFORE YOU READ

PREDICT Look at the headlines of the three news stories. In what way do you think the stories will be similar?

READING ▶5:29

Homeless Man Returns Wallet with $900

Posted on: Monday, 17 April

SANTA ANA, Calif. - A homeless man searching through trash bins for recyclable cans found a missing wallet and returned it to its owner. Kim Bogue, who works in the city, realized that her wallet was missing last week and doubted she'd ever get back the $900 and credit cards inside. "I prayed that night and asked God to help me," said Bogue, who was saving the money for a trip to her native Thailand.

Days later, a homeless man found the wallet wrapped in a plastic bag in the trash, where Bogue had accidentally thrown it away with her lunch. He gave it to Sherry Wesley, who works in a nearby building. "He came to me with the wad of money and said, 'This probably belongs to someone that you work with. Can you return it?'" Wesley said.

"He has a very good heart," said Bogue, who gave the man a $100 reward. "If someone else had found it, the money would have been gone."

Search

Man Risks Life to Save Another

Many people who ride a busy urban subway wonder, "What would happen if I fell off the platform and onto the tracks? What would I do?" Others wonder, "What would I do if someone else fell?"

That question was answered in a split-second decision made by "subway hero" Wesley Autrey, a fifty-year-old New York City construction worker on his way to work. Autrey jumped onto the tracks to save a fellow passenger from an oncoming New York City subway train.

The passenger, Cameron Hollopeter, 20, a film student at the New York Film Academy, had fallen between the tracks after suffering a seizure. Autrey rolled Hollopeter into a gap between the rails and covered him with his own body just as the train entered the station. Both men survived.

"I don't feel like I did something spectacular; I just saw someone who needed help," Mr. Autrey said. "I did what I felt was right."

An act of honesty by airport screener

NEW DELHI: In a display of honesty, a security agent at the Indira Gandhi International Airport handed over a small plastic bag with US $3,000 in cash to a passenger who had completely forgotten the bag after it passed through the airport screening machine.

Noticing that the bag had been left behind, Dalbir Singh made an announcement asking passengers to come forward to claim it. However, when no one claimed it, Singh inspected the baggage tag and guessed it probably belonged to a passenger en route to Mumbai. An announcement was made on the next flight to Mumbai, and the owner of the bag came forward to collect it.

Singh was given a cash reward for his honesty.

A SUMMARIZE Summarize one of the articles. Close your book and tell the story in your own words.

B INTERPRET INFORMATION Discuss each person's motives for his or her actions.

1 Why did Kim Bogue give the homeless man a reward?
2 Why did Wesley Autrey risk his life to save a stranger?
3 Why do you think Dalbir Singh returned the money to the passenger?

DIGITAL MORE EXERCISES

C RELATE TO PERSONAL EXPERIENCE Think of a story you have heard about someone who helped a stranger in need. Tell it to the class.

NOW YOU CAN Discuss acts of kindness and honesty

A **NOTEPADDING** Answer the questions about each situation.

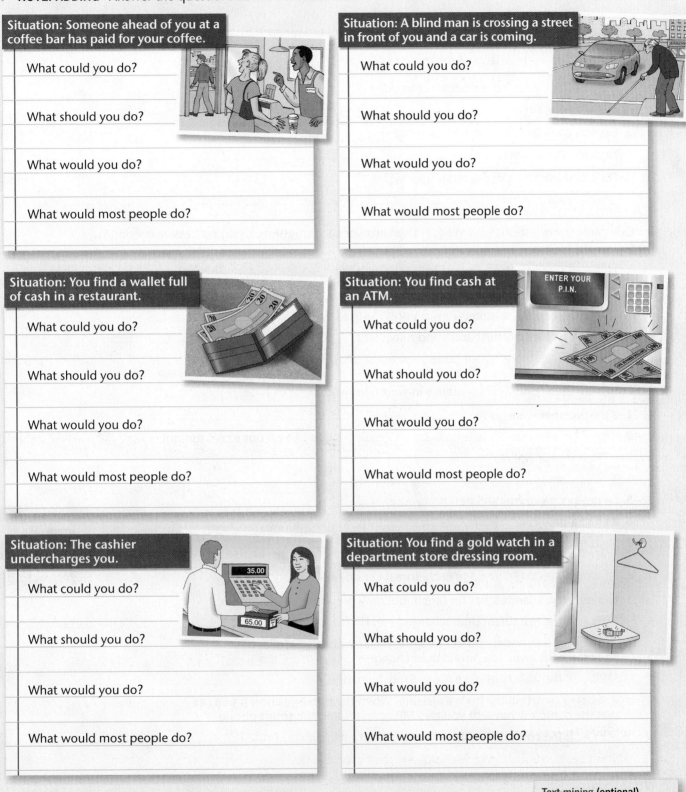

Situation: Someone ahead of you at a coffee bar has paid for your coffee.

What could you do?

What should you do?

What would you do?

What would most people do?

Situation: A blind man is crossing a street in front of you and a car is coming.

What could you do?

What should you do?

What would you do?

What would most people do?

Situation: You find a wallet full of cash in a restaurant.

What could you do?

What should you do?

What would you do?

What would most people do?

Situation: You find cash at an ATM.

What could you do?

What should you do?

What would you do?

What would most people do?

Situation: The cashier undercharges you.

What could you do?

What should you do?

What would you do?

What would most people do?

Situation: You find a gold watch in a department store dressing room.

What could you do?

What should you do?

What would you do?

What would most people do?

B **GROUP WORK** Compare your notes. Would you all do the same things in these situations? Use the unreal conditional and expressions from the Photo Story on page 111.

> "If I found cash near an ATM, I would keep it. There would be no way to find the owner."

Text-mining (optional)
Find and underline three words or phrases in the Reading that were new to you. Use them in your Group Work
For example: "a split-second decision."

A 5:30 Listen to the conversations. Check Yes or No to answer each question and explain your answers.

	Yes	No
1 Do you think John has a double standard?	☐	☐
Explain your answer:		
2 Do you think Jessica's mom is sexist?	☐	☐
Explain your answer:		
3 Do you think Alex's dad is old-fashioned?	☐	☐
Explain your answer:		

B Complete the questions with Whose. Then answer each question, using possessive pronouns. Follow the example.

1 Those shoes belong to my daughter. *Whose are* they? *They're hers.*
2 That sweater belongs to my son. .... it? ....
3 The house across the street is my parents' house. .... it? ....
4 These tickets are my husband's and mine. .... they? ....
5 The table over there is your table. .... it? ....

C Complete each conditional sentence in your own words.

1 If the weather were good, ...
2 If ...., I'd go out to eat tonight.
3 If I found your wallet, ...
4 If ...., I'd call home.
5 I'd be angry with my children if ....
6 If I had a new car, ...
7 I would choose a new career if ....

For additional language practice . . .

TOP NOTCH POP • Lyrics p. 154
"What Would You Do?"
DIGITAL SONG DIGITAL KARAOKE

D What would you do? Complete each unreal conditional sentence.

1 You order two sandwiches for lunch, but they only charge you for one.
YOU "If the restaurant undercharged me, I ...."
2 You pay for a newspaper that costs one dollar with a five-dollar bill. The merchant gives you nine dollars change.
YOU "If the merchant gave me too much change, I ...."
3 You buy a smart phone from a website. When the package arrives, you see that the company has sent you two MP3 players and the smart phone.
YOU "If the company sent me more items than I paid for, I ...."

WRITING

Write three paragraphs about Matt's dilemma in the Photo Story on page 111. In the first paragraph, summarize the situation. In the second paragraph, write about what Matt could or should do. In the third paragraph, write what you would do if you were Matt. Explain your reasons, using the unreal conditional.

WRITING BOOSTER p. 152
- Introducing conflicting ideas
- Guidance for this writing exercise

ORAL REVIEW

CONTEST Form teams. With your team, look at the two pictures for one minute. Then close your books and tell the story you saw in the pictures. The team that remembers more details wins.

PAIR WORK

1 Tell your partner what you would do if you were the woman who found the lost object. Use the unreal conditional. Start like this:
If I found . . . , I would . . .

2 Create a conversation for the people in the second picture. Use possessive pronouns. Start like this:
Excuse me. Is this your . . .

A few minutes later

NOW I CAN

- ☐ Discuss ethical choices.
- ☐ Return someone else's property.
- ☐ Express personal values.
- ☐ Discuss acts of kindness and honesty.

Reference Charts

PRONUNCIATION TABLE

Vowels

Symbol	Key Words
i	beat, feed
ɪ	bit, did
eɪ	date, paid
ɛ	bet, bed
æ	bat, bad
ɑ	box, odd, father
ɔ	bought, dog
oʊ	boat, road
ʊ	book, good
u	boot, food, flu
ʌ	but, mud, mother
ə	banana, among
ɚ	shirt, murder
aɪ	bite, cry, buy, eye
aʊ	about, how
ɔɪ	voice, boy
ɪr	deer
ɛr	bare
ɑr	bar
ɔr	door
ʊr	tour

Consonants

Symbol	Key Words	Symbol	Key Words
p	pack, happy	z	zip, please, goes
b	back, rubber	ʃ	ship, machine, station,
t	tie		special, discussion
d	die	ʒ	measure, vision
k	came, key, quick	h	hot, who
g	game, guest	m	men
tʃ	church, nature, watch	n	sun, know, pneumonia
dʒ	judge, general, major	ŋ	sung, ringing
f	fan, photograph	w	wet, white
v	van	l	light, long
θ	thing, breath	r	right, wrong
ð	then, breathe	y	yes
s	sip, city, psychology		
t̬	butter, bottle		
tˀ	button		

IRREGULAR VERBS

base form	simple past	past participle	base form	simple past	past participle
be	was / were	been	leave	left	left
become	became	become	let	let	let
begin	began	begun	lose	lost	lost
break	broke	broken	make	made	made
bring	brought	brought	mean	meant	meant
build	built	built	meet	met	met
buy	bought	bought	pay	paid	paid
catch	caught	caught	put	put	put
choose	chose	chosen	quit	quit	quit
come	came	come	read /rid/	read /rɛd/	read /rɛd/
cost	cost	cost	ride	rode	ridden
cut	cut	cut	ring	rang	rung
do	did	done	rise	rose	risen
draw	drew	drawn	run	ran	run
dream	dreamed / dreamt	dreamed / dreamt	say	said	said
drink	drank	drunk	see	saw	seen
drive	drove	driven	sell	sold	sold
eat	ate	eaten	send	sent	sent
fall	fell	fallen	shake	shook	shaken
feed	fed	fed	sing	sang	sung
feel	felt	felt	sit	sat	sat
fight	fought	fought	sleep	slept	slept
find	found	found	speak	spoke	spoken
fit	fit	fit	spend	spent	spent
fly	flew	flown	stand	stood	stood
forget	forgot	forgotten	steal	stole	stolen
get	got	gotten	swim	swam	swum
give	gave	given	take	took	taken
go	went	gone	teach	taught	taught
grow	grew	grown	tell	told	told
have	had	had	think	thought	thought
hear	heard	heard	throw	threw	thrown
hit	hit	hit	understand	understood	understood
hold	held	held	wake up	woke up	woken up
hurt	hurt	hurt	wear	wore	worn
keep	kept	kept	win	won	won
know	knew	known	write	wrote	written

1 THE PRESENT OF BE

Statements

I	am	late.
You We They	are	
He She It	is	

2 THE SIMPLE PRESENT TENSE

Statements

I You We They	speak English.
He She	speaks English.

Yes / no questions

Do	I you we they	know them?
Does	he she	eat meat?

Short answers

Yes,	I you we they	do.
	he she it	does.

No,	I you we they	don't.
	he she it	doesn't.

Information questions

What do	you we they	need?
When does	he she it	start?
Who	wants needs likes	this book?

3 THE PRESENT CONTINUOUS

Statements

I	am	watching TV.
You We They	are	studying English.
He She It	is	arriving now.

Yes / no questions

Am	I	going too fast?
Are	you we they	
Is	he she it	

Short answers

Yes,	I	am.
	you	are.
	he she it	is.
	we they	are.

No,	I'm not. you aren't / you're not. he isn't / he's not. she isn't / she's not. it isn't / it's not. we aren't / we're not. they aren't / they're not.

Information questions

What	are	you we they	doing?
When	is	he she it	leaving?
Where	am	I	staying tonight?
Who	is		driving?

4 THE PAST OF BE

Statements

I He She It	was late.
We You They	were early.

(The past of be*–continued)*

Yes / no questions

Was	I he she it	on time?
Were	we you they	in the same class?

Short answers

Yes,	I he she it	was.
	we you they	were.

No,	I he she it	wasn't.
	we you they	weren't.

Information questions

Where	were	we? you? they?	
When	was	he she it	here?
Who	were	they?	
Who	was	he? she? it?	

5 THE SIMPLE PAST TENSE

Many verbs are irregular in the simple past tense. See the list of irregular verbs on page 123.

Statements

I You He She It We They	stopped working.

I You He She It We They	didn't start again.

Yes / no questions

Did	I you he she it we they	make a good dinner?

Short answers

Yes,	I you he she it we they	did.

No,	I you he she it we they	didn't.

Information questions

When did	I you he she it we they	read that?
Who		called?

6 THE FUTURE WITH BE GOING TO

Statements

I'm You're He's She's It's We're They're	going to	be here soon.

I'm You're He's She's It's We're They're	not going to	be here soon.

Yes / no questions

Are	you we they	going to want coffee?
Am	I	going to be late?
Is	he she it	going to arrive on time?

Short answers

Yes,	I	am.
	you	are.
	he she it	is.
	we they	are.

No,	I'm not. you aren't / you're not. he isn't / he's not. she isn't / she's not. it isn't / it's not. we aren't / we're not. they aren't / they're not.

Information questions

What	are	you we they	going to see?
When	is	he she it	going to shop?
Where	am	I	going to stay tomorrow?
Who	is		going to call?

Grammar Booster

The Grammar Booster is optional. It offers a variety of information and extra practice. Sometimes it further explains or expands the unit grammar and points out common errors. In other cases, it reviews and practices previously learned grammar that would be helpful when learning new grammar concepts. If you use the Grammar Booster, you will find extra exercises in the Workbook in a separate section labeled Grammar Booster. The Grammar Booster content is not tested on any *Top Notch* tests.

UNIT 1 *Lesson 1*

The present perfect: information questions

Form information questions by inverting have and the subject of the sentence.

What have you seen in Paris?
What (OR Which) countries have you visited?
Where has she gone scuba diving?
How have your parents been?
How many cities have you visited this week?
Who have you traveled with?

Note: When Who is the subject of the sentence, there is no inversion.

Who has traveled to Miami in the last two months?

On a separate sheet of paper, write information questions. Use the present perfect.

1 what dishes / she / try / in Mérida
2 who / you / invite / to the party
3 where / he / work / before
4 which movies / they / see
5 how / your children / be
6 who / climb / Grouse Mountain
7 what / they / hear / about the new school
8 how many times / she / take / that class

UNIT 1 *Lesson 2*

The present perfect: use and placement of yet and already

Remember: Use yet or already in questions.

Have you read the book yet? OR Have you already read the book?

Use already in affirmative statements. Place already before the main verb or at the end of the statement.

I've already read the book. OR I've read the book already.

Use yet in negative statements. Place yet at the end of the statement or between have and the base form.

I haven't read the book yet. OR I haven't yet read the book.

Be careful!
Don't use yet in affirmative statements. Don't use already in negative statements.

DON'T SAY Yes, I've read the book ~~yet~~. / No, I haven't ~~already~~ read the book.

Don't use ever with yet or already.

DON'T SAY Have you ~~ever~~ read the book ~~yet~~? / Have you ~~ever~~ read the book ~~already~~?

A On a separate sheet of paper, rewrite each statement or question, using already or yet.

1 (yet) Has she finished the homework?
2 (yet) They haven't seen the movie.
3 (already) We've tried fried clams several times.
4 (already) Has your father left?

B On a separate sheet of paper, rewrite each sentence, using already or yet.

1 I haven't had dinner.
2 She's been to London, Berlin, and Rome.
3 They haven't called home.
4 We've finished our class.

The present perfect: ever, never, and before

Use ever in questions. Use never in negative statements and short answers. Do not use ever in affirmative statements.

Have you ever made sushi? — Yes, I have. OR Yes, I've made sushi. NOT Yes, I've ~~ever~~ made sushi.
No, I never have. OR No, I've never made sushi.

You can also use before in negative statements with never.

I've never been to Thailand before.

In very informal speech, ever is sometimes used with never for strong emphasis. This meaning of ever is similar to "in my whole life."

I've never ever seen a Charlie Chaplin movie.

C On a separate sheet of paper, answer each question, using real information. If the answer is yes, write when this happened.

1 Have you ever gone on a cruise?
2 Have you ever tried Indian food?
3 Have you ever been to Hawaii?
4 Have you ever met a famous person?
5 Have you ever fallen in love?
6 Have you ever played golf?

UNIT 2 *Lesson 1*

The present perfect and the present perfect continuous: unfinished (or continuing) actions

Unfinished (or continuing) actions are those that began in the past, continue in the present, and may possibly continue into the future. Here are three ways to talk about unfinished actions:

1 **the present perfect with since: Use since with a stated start time in the past.**
I've lived here since 2001. (2001 is the stated start time. I still live here, so the action "continues.")

2 **the present perfect with for: Use for to describe the period of time from its start until the present.**
I've lived here for five years. (Emphasis is on the five-year period. I still live here, so the action "continues.")

3 **the present perfect continuous with for or since: Form the present perfect continuous with the present perfect of be and a present participle.**
I've been living here since 2001. OR I've been living here for five years. (In both cases, the action "continues.")

When describing unfinished or continuing actions with for and since, the present perfect and the present perfect continuous are both correct. Some people feel the present perfect continuous emphasizes the continuing time a bit more.

A Read the sentences with the present perfect. Check each sentence that describes an unfinished or continuing action.

☐ 1 The Pitts have lived in China since the late nineties.
☐ 2 Carmen has been living in Buenos Aires since last year.
☐ 3 I've visited Paris three times.
☐ 4 Ted has been visiting Paris since 2005.
☐ 5 We have eaten in that great Indian restaurant for years.
☐ 6 They've eaten in that Indian restaurant before.
☐ 7 My brother has been playing tennis for many years.
☐ 8 Min-ji has played tennis twice.

B Complete each statement with the present perfect continuous.

1 *Rio* .... (play) at the Children's Classics Cinema every Saturday since 2010.
2 Robert .... (wait) in the ticket holders' line for a pretty long time.
3 People .... (worry about) violence in movies since the sixties.
4 I'.................................... (talk about) that movie for weeks.
5 We'.................................... (come) to this classics movie theater for two years.

Spelling rules for the present participle: review

Add -ing to the base form of the verb

speak → speaking

If the base form ends in a silent -e, drop the -e and add -ing.

have → having

In verbs of one syllable, if the last three letters are a consonant-vowel-consonant (C-V-C) series, double the last consonant and then add -ing.

C V C
s i t → sitting

Be careful! Don't double the last consonant in words that end in -w, -x, or -y.

flow → flowing
fix → fixing
pay → paying

In verbs of more than one syllable that end in a consonant-vowel-consonant series, double the last consonant only if the stress is on the last syllable.

con • trol → controlling BUT or • der → ordering

C Write the present participle for these base forms.

1 find ....
2 be ....
3 lose ....
4 put ....
5 get ....
6 say ....
7 write ....
8 go ....
9 make ....
10 fix ....
11 know ....
12 speak ....
13 hear ....
14 let ....
15 come ....
16 leave ....
17 drive ....
18 meet ....
19 blow ....
20 give ....
21 run ....
22 forget ....
23 eat ....
24 pay ....
25 stand ....
26 think ....
27 buy ....
28 see ....
29 begin ....
30 tell ....
31 bring ....
32 take ....

UNIT 2 *Lesson 2*

Like, want, would like, would rather: review and expansion; common errors

Use like and want + a direct object to express likes, dislikes, and desires.

They like documentaries. We don't like science fiction.
She wants a ticket to the late show.

Use would like + a direct object to make a polite offer or a request.

A: Would you like tickets for *Casablanca*?
B: Yes, please. We'd like two tickets for the 8:00 show.

Use would like + an infinitive (to + base form) to make a polite offer or to express wants.

Would you like to stream a movie on your tablet?
Where would you like to go?
I'd like to download a movie onto my tablet.
She'd like to see a comedy.

Use would rather + a base form to express a preference for an activity.

A: Would you like to see the movie downtown or at the theater in the mall?
B: I'd rather see it at the mall.

Use than with would rather to contrast preferences.

I'd rather stream a movie than go to the theater.
They'd rather go to a Woody Allen film than a Martin Scorsese film.

Be careful!
Don't use a base form after would like.

My friends would like to meet in front of the theater. NOT My friends ~~would like meet~~ in front of the theater.

Don't use an infinitive after would rather.

We'd rather get tickets for the early show. NOT We~~'d rather to get~~ tickets for the early show.

A On a separate sheet of paper, write sentences and questions using these words and phrases.

1 They / would like / see / the Woody Allen film.
2 What time / you / would rather / meet?
3 Who / would like / order / eggs for breakfast?
4 they / rather / Would / watch TV or go out?
5 Jason / would like / have / a large container of popcorn.
6 I'd rather / rent / a sci-fi film tonight.
7 Her parents / rather / not / watch / anything too violent.
8 Who'd rather / not / see / that silly animated film?

B Correct the errors in these sentences.

1 I would rather to stay home than to go out.
2 She would like buy a ticket to tonight's show.
3 My friends would like download movies from the Internet.
4 Would they rather to see an animated film than an action film?
5 Do they rather see movies at home?
6 Who would like go to the late show tonight?
7 My husband likes two tickets to the concert.

C On a separate sheet of paper, answer each question in a complete sentence, expressing your own preference.

1 What genre of movie do you usually like?
2 What movie do you want to see this weekend?
3 What would you like to have for dinner tonight?
4 Would you rather see a comedy or a horror film?
5 Would you like to rent a DVD or go to the movies?

UNIT 3 *Lesson 1*

Will: expansion

Will and be going to

Use will or be going to for predictions about the future. The meaning is the same.

It'll rain tomorrow. = It's going to rain tomorrow.

Use be going to, NOT will, when you already have a plan for the future.

A: Are you going to come to class tomorrow?
B: No. I'm going to go to the beach instead. NOT No. ~~I'll go~~ to the beach instead.

Other uses of will

Use will, NOT be going to, to talk about the immediate future when you do not already have a plan.

Maybe I'll go to the beach this weekend. NOT Maybe ~~I'm going to go~~ to the beach this weekend.

Use will, NOT be going to, to express willingness.

I'll pay for Internet service, but I won't pay for the airport shuttle. (= I'm willing to pay for Internet service, but I'm not willing to pay for the airport shuttle.)

Can, should, and have to: future meaning

Can and should are modals and should never be used with will.

You can use can alone to express future possibility.

Tomorrow morning you can ask the hotel for a rollaway bed.
They can't go to the museum tomorrow. It's closed on Mondays.

You can use should alone to express future advice.

You should visit the Empire State Building next week. It's great.

However, you can use will with have to + a base form to express future obligation.

I'll have to leave the 2:00 meeting early.
We won't have to make a reservation at a restaurant tonight.

A On a separate sheet of paper, write five sentences about your plans for the weekend, using be going to. Then write the sentences again, using will.

B On a separate sheet of paper, write five sentences with will or won't for willingness on one of the following topics.

Topics
- kinds of exercise you're willing (or not willing) to do
- kinds of food you're willing (or not willing) to eat for breakfast
- kinds of clothes you're willing (or not willing) to wear

C Complete the sentences, using will or won't with have to.

1 .... (she / have to / call) the office before 6:00.
2 .... (they / have to / reserve) their tickets by Monday.
3 .... (we / not have to / cancel) the meeting if Mr. Carson's flight is on time.
4 .... (I / have to / leave) a message for my boss.
5 .... (you / not have to / order) room service if you arrive before 10:00 P.M.
6 .... (we / have to / take) a taxi to the airport.

UNIT 3 *Lesson 2*

The real conditional: present

Use the present real conditional to express general and scientific facts. Use the simple present tense or the present tense of be in both clauses.

If it rains, flights are late. [fact]
If you heat water to 100 degrees, it boils. [scientific fact]

In present real conditional sentences, when (or whenever) is often used instead of if.

When (or Whenever) it rains, flights are late.
When (or Whenever) you heat water to 100 degrees, it boils.

A On a separate sheet of paper, write present real conditional sentences.

1 Water (freeze) when you (lower) its temperature below zero degrees.
2 Whenever my daughter (take) her umbrella to school, she (forget) to bring it home.
3 She (go) on vacation every August if she (not have) too much work.
4 He (run) in the park if the weather (be) dry.
5 In my company, if cashiers (make) a mistake, they (repay) the money.

The real conditional: future

Use the future real conditional to express what you believe will happen in the future under certain conditions or as a result of certain actions. Use the simple present tense or the present of be in the if clause. Use a future form (will or be going to) in the result clause.

If I go to sleep too late tonight, I won't be able to get up on time. (future condition, future result)
If she comes home after 8:00, I'm not going to make dinner. (future condition, future result)

Remember: Use a comma when the if clause comes first. Don't use a comma when the if clause comes at the end of the sentence.

If I see him, I'll tell her. I'll tell her if I see him.

Be careful! Don't use a future form in the if clause.

If I see him, I'll tell her. NOT If I ~~will see~~ him, I'll tell her. NOT If I~~'m going to see~~ him, I'll tell her.

B Circle the correct form to complete each future real conditional sentence.

1 If they (like / will like) the movie, they (see / will see) it again.
2 I ('m going to talk / talk) to her if she (does / 's going to do) that again.
3 If you (buy / are going to buy) some eggs, I (make / 'll make) you an omelet tonight.
4 If they (see / will see) her tomorrow, they (drive / 'll drive) her home.
5 (Are you going to study / Do you study) Italian if they (offer / will offer) it next year?

C On a separate sheet of paper, complete each future real conditional sentence with true information. Use a comma when the if clause comes first.

1 If I live to be 100 . . .
2 My family will be angry if . . .
3 If I don't practice English every day . . .
4 If I go to my favorite restaurant next week . . .
5 I'll buy a new smart phone if . . .
6 If I need new shoes . . .

UNIT 4 Lesson 1

The past continuous: expansion

The past continuous describes an action that was continuous until (and possibly after) the moment at which another action took place. The words when or while are often used in sentences that contrast continuing and completed actions.

He **was talking** on the phone when the storm **began**. (continuous action, then completed action)
While I **was living** in Chile, I **got married**. (continuous action, then completed action)

The past continuous also describes two continuing actions occurring in the same period of time.

While she **was driving**, her husband **was reading** the newspaper.
They **were eating**, and the music **was playing**.

On a separate sheet of paper, use the prompts to write logical sentences. Use the past continuous and the simple past tense in each sentence.

1 She / take a test at school / when / she / hear the fire alarm
2 While I / talk to my mother on the phone / the TV show / start
3 Mr. Park / cook dinner / when / Mrs. Park / finish the laundry
4 Mr. Kemp / work in the garden / when / the rain / begin
5 While / Claudia / pick up / their rental car / Alex / call / their hotel
6 While / Nancy / shop at the grocery store / she / see / an old friend

UNIT 4 Lesson 2

Nouns and pronouns: review

A noun is a word that names a person, a place, or a thing. Nouns are either common or proper. A proper noun is capitalized.

common nouns: car, windshield, doctor, woman, father
proper nouns: Martin, Caracas, Carla's Restaurant

Two functions of nouns in sentences are subjects and direct objects. The subject performs the action of the verb. The object receives the action.

subject		direct object	
Carla's Restaurant	serves	**breakfast**	all day long.

A pronoun is a word that represents or replaces a noun. Pronouns also function as subjects and direct objects.

subject pronouns: I, you, he, she, it, we, they
object pronouns: me, you, him, her, it, us, them

subject		direct object	
My parents / **They**	drove	**the car** / **it**	to the airport.

First, underline the subjects and circle the objects in these sentences. Then label each noun as either "common" or "proper." Finally, put a check (✓) above each pronoun. (Note: Not every sentence contains a pronoun.)

- Italians [proper] drive fast cars. [common]

1 We love big vans.
2 The children broke the side-view mirror.
3 Ms. Workman picked up the car this morning.
4 Rand loves sports cars, and his wife loves them, too.
5 A man driving a sports car hit our minivan.
6 I returned the rental car at the airport.
7 A-1 Rental Agency called me about the reservation.

UNIT 5 Lesson 1

Some and any: review

Some and any are indefinite quantifiers. They indicate an indefinite number or amount.

There are some toothbrushes in aisle 2. (We don't know how many.)
They are buying some shaving cream. (We don't know how much.)
Could I get some nail files? (We're not asking for a specific number of nail files.)
Do they have any makeup in this store? (We're not asking specifically how much.)

Be careful to use some and any correctly with count and non-count nouns:

Some: with non-count nouns and plural count nouns in affirmative statements

We need some sunscreen (non-count noun) and some combs (plural count noun). They have some here.

Any: with non-count nouns and plural count nouns in negative statements

A: She doesn't want any shampoo (non-count noun), and he doesn't need any nail clippers (plural count noun).
B: Good! We don't have to buy any, then. I'm out of cash.

Any or some: with count and non-count nouns in questions

Do they need any toothpaste or sunscreen for the trip?
Do we need any razors or toothbrushes?

Remember: Count nouns name things you can count individually. They have singular and plural forms (1 nail file, 3 combs). Non-count nouns name things you cannot count individually. They don't have plural forms. Use containers, quantifiers, and other modifiers to make non-count nouns countable.

a bottle of shampoo / aftershave
a tube of toothpaste / lipstick
a bar of soap
a can of hairspray / deodorant / shaving cream
250 milliliters of sunscreen

A On a separate sheet of paper, change these sentences from affirmative to negative. Follow the example.

There is some shampoo in the shower. *There isn't any shampoo in the shower.*

1 There are some razors next to the sink.
2 We have some nail clippers.
3 They need some brushes for the children.
4 She's buying some mascara.
5 The manicurists need some new nail polish.
6 I want some sunscreen on my back.
7 There is some dental floss in aisle 4.
8 They need some deodorant for the trip.

B Complete each sentence with some or any.

1 I don't need .... more hand lotion.
2 There isn't .... makeup in the bag.
3 We don't see .... scissors in the whole store.
4 They need .... soap to wash their hands.
5 It's too bad that there isn't .... toothpaste.
6 I don't see .... combs or brushes on those shelves.
7 I know I had .... nail files in my bag. Now I can't find them.

Too many, too much, and enough

The word too indicates a quantity that is excessive—more than someone wants or needs. Use enough to indicate that a quantity or amount is satisfactory.

Use too many and not too many for count nouns.
There are **too many customers** waiting in line.

Use too much and not too much for non-count nouns.
There's **too much toothpaste** on the toothbrush.

Use enough and not enough for both count and non-count nouns.
There's **enough shampoo**, but there aren't **enough razors**.

C Complete each sentence with too many, too much, or enough.

1 Let's do our nails. Do we have .... nail polish for both of us?
2 This shampoo has .... perfume. It smells awful!
3 It's not a good idea to buy .... fruit. We're not going to be home for a few days.
4 This menu has .... choices. I can't make up my mind.
5 Check the bathroom shelf to see if we have .... soap. Mom and Dad are coming to visit.
6 I don't like when there are .... brands. I can't decide which one to buy.
7 There's no way to get a haircut today. .... people had the same idea!
8 They don't want to spend .... money on makeup. They're trying to save money.

Comparative quantifiers fewer and less

Use fewer for count nouns. Use less for non-count nouns.
The Cosmetique store has **fewer brands** of makeup than the Emporium.
There's **less shampoo** in this bottle than in that tube.

D Complete each sentence with fewer or less.

1 Which class has .... students—the early class or the late one?
2 The recipe calls for .... cheese than I thought.
3 It has .... ingredients, too.
4 Don't rent from Cars Plus. They have .... kinds of cars than International.
5 The Cineplus has .... movies this weekend than usual.
6 Is there .... body lotion in the small size or the economy size?

UNIT 5 *Lesson 2*

Indefinite pronouns: something, anything, everything, and nothing

Use something, nothing, or everything in affirmative statements.
There's **something** in this box.
Nothing can convince me to get a pedicure.
Everything is ready.

Use anything in negative statements.
There isn't **anything** in the fridge.

Use something, anything, or everything in yes / no questions.
Is there **something** we should talk about? Is **anything** wrong?
Do you have **everything** you need?

Nothing has the same meaning as not anything. Don't use nothing in negative statements.
There **isn't anything** in the fridge. = There's **nothing** in the fridge. NOT There ~~isn't nothing~~ in the fridge.

Choose the correct indefinite pronoun to complete each sentence.

1 I need to go to the store to buy (something / anything).
2 There is (something / anything) I can do to help.
3 There isn't (everything / anything) you can do to make yourself taller.
4 I went on the Internet to find (something / anything) about how to use sunscreen.
5 They have (something / anything) that helps you lose weight.
6 There's (anything / nothing) that can make you look young again.
7 They can't get (anything / nothing) to eat there after ten o'clock.

UNIT 6 *Lesson 1*

Use to / used to: use and form

Use to and used to express a past habitual action, but one that is no longer true today.

When I was a kid, I **didn't use to eat** vegetables. But now I do.

Remember: In yes / no questions and negative statements, use use to NOT used to.

I **used to** stay up late. Now I don't.
I **didn't use to** (NOT ~~used to~~) get up early. Now I do.
Did you **use to** (NOT ~~used to~~) go dancing more often?

Note: The simple past tense can express a past habitual action if there is a reference to a period of time in the past.

When I was a kid, I **didn't eat** peppers. I still don't today.

A On a separate sheet of paper, change each statement into a yes / no question.

I used to go running every day. *Did you use to go running every day?*

1 There used to be a large tree in front of your house.
2 Mr. and Mrs. Palmer used to go dancing every weekend.
3 Their grandmother used to put sugar in their orange juice.
4 Luke used to be very overweight.

B On a separate sheet of paper, use the prompts to write logical sentences with negative or affirmative forms of use to / used to.

1 Jason and Trish / get lots of exercise, but now they go swimming every day.
2 There / be a movie theater on Smith Street, but now there isn't.
3 No one / worry about fatty foods, but now most people do.
4 English / be an international language, but now everyone uses English to communicate around the world.
5 Women in North America / wear pants, but now it's very common for them to wear them.

Be used to / get used to

Be used to + a noun phrase means to be accustomed to something. Compare use to / used to with be used to.

I **didn't use to like** spicy food. But now I do. (used to + base form)
I**'m used to** the noise now. But at first, it really bothered me. (be used to + a noun phrase)

Get used to + a noun phrase means to become accustomed to something.

You'll **get used to** the new menu after a few days.

Be careful! With be used to, don't change used in negative statements or questions.

He **wasn't used to** the weather there. NOT He wasn't ~~use~~ to . . .
Are you **used to** life here? NOT Are you ~~use~~ to . . .

C Check the sentences in which <u>used to</u> means "accustomed to something."

☐ **1** When the school term ended, I was finally used to the new teacher.
☐ **2** In our other class, the teacher used to be very strict.
☐ **3** They used to like red meat, but now they don't.
☐ **4** Because we lived in the mountains, we weren't used to fresh seafood.
☐ **5** I'm sure she'll get used to her new apartment soon.
☐ **6** These shoes used to be comfortable, but now they're too loose.
☐ **7** I'm sure she'll get used to wearing high-heeled shoes.

D Write ✓ if the sentence is correct. Write ✗ if it is incorrect and make corrections.

☐ **1** I'll never get use to the traffic here.
☐ **2** We didn't use to take vacations very often.
☐ **3** Is he use to his new roommate yet?
☐ **4** Will she ever get use to life in the city?
☐ **5** What did you used to do on weekdays when you weren't working?

E On a separate sheet of paper, write two sentences about something you're used to and two sentences about something you're not used to.

Repeated actions in the past: <u>would</u> + base form

You can also use <u>would</u> + the base form of a verb to describe repeated past actions. In this use, <u>would</u> has the same meaning as <u>used to</u>.

When we were young, our parents **would go camping** with us. (= **used to go camping** with us.)

Be careful! With non-action verbs that don't describe repeated actions, use <u>used to</u>, not <u>would</u>.

I **used to have** a lot of clothes. NOT I ~~would have~~ a lot of clothes.
My hometown **used to be** Dakar. NOT My hometown ~~would be~~ Dakar.
I **used to be** a terrible English student. NOT I ~~would be~~ a terrible English student.
My friends and I **used to hate** baseball. NOT My friends and I ~~would hate~~ baseball.

F If it is possible, complete the sentence with <u>would</u>. If not, use a form of <u>used to</u>.

1 They .... go to the beach every Saturday in the summer.
2 I .... have a really large kitchen in my old house.
3 My husband never .... like coffee, but now he can't get enough of it.
4 Almost every evening of our vacation we .... eat at a terrific outdoor restaurant.
5 Before the microwave, people .... heat up soup on the top of the stove.
6 Sigrid .... be a tour guide, but now she's a professional chef.
7 There .... be three or four Italian restaurants in town, but now there aren't any.

UNIT 6 *Lesson 2*

Negative <u>yes</u> / <u>no</u> questions: short answers

Answer negative <u>yes</u> / <u>no</u> questions the same way as you would answer affirmative <u>yes</u> / <u>no</u> questions.

Is Jane a vegetarian? **Isn't** Jane a vegetarian?	Yes, she is. / No, she isn't.
Do they have two sons? **Don't** they **have** two sons?	Yes, they do. / No, they don't.

Answer each negative question with a short answer. (Use the information for your answer.)

1 A: Isn't Jeremy a lawyer?
B: .... He's not a lawyer.

2 A: Doesn't Bob have two brothers?
B: .... He has two younger brothers.

3 A: Haven't you been to Siberia before?
B: .... I've never been here before.

4 A: Aren't you learning English right now?
B: .... I'm studying English at the institute.

5 A: Wasn't Nancy at the movies last night?
B: .... She didn't go to the movies.

6 A: Don't Sachiko and Tomofumi have a car?
B: .... They own a minivan.

UNIT 7 Lesson 1

Gerunds and infinitives: usage within sentences

Gerunds (-ing form of a verb) and infinitives (to + base form) function as nouns within sentences.

Gerunds

Like nouns, gerunds can be subjects, subject complements, direct objects, and objects of prepositions.

Painting is my favorite leisure-time activity. (subject)
My favorite activity is painting. (subject complement; usually follows be)
I enjoy painting. (direct object)
I read a book about the history of painting. (object of the preposition of)

Infinitives

Infinitives can be subjects, subject complements, and direct objects.

To paint well is a talent. (subject)
The only thing he needs is to paint. (subject complement; usually follows be)
I want to paint. (direct object)

Underline the gerunds and circle the infinitives in these sentences. How is each used in the sentence? On the line next to each sentence, write *S* for subject, *C* for subject complement, *DO* for direct object, or *OP* for object of a preposition.

.... 1 I enjoy watching old movies every night on TV.
.... 2 Her greatest dream was to see all of her children attend college.
.... 3 What's the point of creating a nice environment at home if genetics is the only thing that counts?
.... 4 Avoiding too much pressure helps children become less critical.
.... 5 My niece plans to study personality development next semester.

UNIT 7 Lesson 2

Negative gerunds

A gerund can be made negative by using a negative word before it.

I like not going to bed too late.
They complained about never having enough time.

Complete the paragraph with affirmative and negative gerunds.

I really want to do something to improve my appearance and lose weight. I'm sick of .... (1 be) able to fit into my clothes. I know it's not enough to complain about .... (2 gain) weight—I need to do something about it! I plan to spend every afternoon .... (3 ride) my bike. Also, I want to go on a diet, but I'm afraid of .... (4 feel) hungry all the time. I worry about .... (5 have) enough energy to exercise if I'm .... (6 get) enough to eat.

UNIT 8 *Lesson 1*

The passive voice: transitive verbs and intransitive verbs

A transitive verb can have a direct object. Transitive verbs can be used in the active voice or passive voice.

active voice		passive voice
Picasso **painted** *Guernica* in 1937.	➔	*Guernica* **was painted** in 1937.

An intransitive verb cannot have a direct object. With an intransitive verb, there is no "receiver" of an action.

The painting **arrives** tomorrow.
The *Mona Lisa* **will stay** at the Louvre.
That new sculpture **looks** like a Botero.

Remember: The subject of a sentence performs the action of the verb. A direct object receives the action of the verb.

Common intransitive verbs

arrive	happen	sit
come	laugh	sleep
die	live	stand
fall	rain	stay
go	seem	walk

A Check each sentence that has an intransitive verb.

- ☑ 1 Pedro Almodóvar's new film arrives in theaters this fall.
- ☐ 2 A Canadian art collector has bought two of Michelangelo's drawings.
- ☐ 3 Someone stole Edvard Munch's painting *The Scream* in 2004.
- ☑ 4 The painter Georgia O'Keeffe lived in the southwestern part of the United States.
- ☐ 5 The Van Gogh Museum in Amsterdam sent *Sunflowers* on a world tour.
- ☑ 6 The traveling collection of ancient Roman sculpture is coming to San Diego this week.
- ☐ 7 The Metropolitan Museum of Art opened a new gallery last year.

The passive voice: form

Form the passive voice with a form of be and the past participle of a verb.

	Active voice	Passive voice
Simple present tense	Art collectors **buy** famous paintings all over the world.	Famous paintings **are bought** by art collectors all over the world.
Present continuous	The Film Center **is showing** Kurosawa's films.	Kurosawa's films **are being shown** at the Film Center.
Present perfect	Some world leaders **have bought** Yu Hung's paintings.	Yu Hung's paintings **have been bought** by some world leaders.
Simple past tense	I. M. Pei **designed** the Grand Pyramid at the Louvre.	The Grand Pyramid at the Louvre **was designed** by I. M. Pei.
Past continuous	In 2010, the museum **was selling** copies of Monet's paintings.	In 2010, copies of Monet's paintings **were being sold** by the museum.
Future with will	Ang Lee **will direct** a new film next year.	A new film **will be directed** by Ang Lee next year.
Future with be going to	The Tate Modern **is going to show** Van Gogh's drawings next month.	Van Gogh's drawings **are going to be shown** at the Tate Modern next month.

B On a separate sheet of paper, rewrite each sentence in the passive voice. Use a by phrase only if it is important to know who is performing the action.

1 Someone actually stole the *Mona Lisa* in 1911.
2 Paloma Picasso designed these pieces of silver jewelry.
3 Someone will repair the sculpture when it gets old.
4 People have paid millions of U.S. dollars for some of Van Gogh's paintings.
5 They are showing some new paintings at the Smith Gallery this week.
6 The Malcolm Museum is going to exhibit ten sculptures by Asian artists.
7 Frida Kahlo was painting these pieces while she was sick in bed.
8 People built great pyramids throughout Central America during the height of the Mayan civilization.

C On a separate sheet of paper, rewrite the sentences in Exercise A that have a transitive verb, changing the active voice to the passive voice.

UNIT 8 *Lesson 2*

The passive voice: yes / no questions

To form yes / no questions in the passive voice, move the first auxiliary verb before the subject.

Simple present tense	Are famous paintings ~~are~~ bought by art collectors?
Present continuous	Are Kurosawa's films ~~are~~ being shown at the Film Center?
Present perfect	Have Yu Hung's paintings ~~have~~ been bought by some world leaders?
Simple past tense	Was the Grand Pyramid at the Louvre ~~was~~ designed by I. M. Pei?
Past continuous	Were copies of Monet's paintings ~~were~~ being sold by the museum?
Future with will	Will a new film ~~will~~ be directed by Ang Lee next year?
Future with be going to	Is a collection of Van Gogh's drawings ~~is~~ going to be shown next month?

On a separate sheet of paper, rewrite the sentences as yes / no questions in the passive voice.

1 That new film about families is being directed by Gillian Armstrong.
2 One of da Vinci's most famous drawings has been sold by a German art collector.
3 A rare ceramic figure from the National Palace Museum in Taipei will be sent to the Metropolitan Museum of Art in New York.
4 A new exhibit is going to be opened at the Photography Gallery this week.
5 Some new paintings have been bought by the Prado Museum for their permanent collection.
6 *Las Meninas* can be seen at the Prado Museum in Madrid.
7 The *Jupiter* Symphony was written by Mozart.
8 Some of Michelangelo's work was being shown around the world in the 1960s.

UNIT 9 *Lesson 1*

Other ways to express a purpose

In order to

You can use in order to with a base form of a verb to express a purpose. The following three sentences have the same meaning.

I scrolled down in order to read the text.
I scrolled down because I wanted to read the text.
I scrolled down to read the text.

For

You can use for to express a purpose before a noun phrase or gerund phrase.

She e-mailed me for some advice.
They shop online for electronic products.
I use my smart phone for e-mailing clients.

Be careful! Don't use for before an infinitive of purpose.

DON'T SAY She e-mailed me ~~for~~ to ask a question.

A On a separate sheet of paper, rewrite the sentences with in order to.

1 She joined Facebook to meet new people.
2 Jason surfs the Internet to see what's new.
3 Alison uses online banking to pay all her bills.
4 They always print their documents first to read them carefully.
5 I never use the pull-down menu to open files.
6 He used an online telephone service to call his family.

B Complete each sentence with for or to.

1 My friend e-mailed me .... say he's getting married.
2 Jane shops online .... clothing.
3 I went online .... find a new keyboard.
4 Matt created a web page .... keeping in touch with his family and friends.
5 Sometimes I use my computer .... download movies.
6 We both log on to the Internet .... information.
7 Just click the icon .... open the file.
8 When Gina's computer crashed, her brother came over .... help her.

UNIT 9 *Lesson 2*

Comparison with adjectives: review

As . . . as

Use as . . . as to indicate how two things are equal or the same. Use not as . . . as to indicate how two things are different.

The new Jax 10 monitor is just as good as the Jax 20.
The Jax 10 monitor is not as big as the Jax 20.

Comparatives

Use comparatives to show how two things are not equal. Use than if the second item is mentioned.

My laptop is heavier than John's (is). OR My laptop is heavier.
Regular mail is less convenient than e-mail. OR Regular mail is less convenient.

Superlatives

Use superlatives to show how one thing is different from two or more other things. Remember to use the with the superlative.

The M2, LX, and Bell printers are all good. But the Bell is the best.
The Gatt 40 monitor is the least expensive one you can buy.

A Correct the error in each sentence.

1. The Orca speakers aren't as heavier as the Yaltas.
2. My old laptop didn't have as many problems than my new laptop.
3. I checked out the three top brands, and the Piston was definitely the better.
4. Maxwell's web camera is much more expensive as their digital camera.
5. Of all the monitors I looked at, the X60 is definitely larger.
6. The Jaguar is most powerful computer in the world.

Comparison with adverbs

Comparatives

My new computer **runs faster than** my old one.
The X20 **operates more quietly than** the X30.

<u>As</u> . . . <u>as</u>

My new phone **works as well as** my old one.
The Macro laptop **doesn't run as slowly as** the Pell does.

Superlatives

Of these three laptops, the MPro **starts up the most slowly**.

> **Remember: Adverbs often give information about verbs.**
> My phone works **well**. My printer prints **fast**.
>
> **Many adjectives can be changed to adverbs by adding -ly.**
> loud → **loudly** quick → **quickly** quiet → **quietly**
> poor → **poorly** bad → **badly** slow → **slowly**

B On a separate sheet of paper, rewrite each pair of sentences into a single sentence using comparatives. Then write single sentences using <u>as</u> . . . <u>as</u>.

1. My brother's smart phone downloads music quickly. My MP3 player doesn't download quickly.
2. My new computer doesn't log on slowly. My old computer logs on slowly.
3. Your old monitor works well. My new monitor doesn't work well.
4. The Rico printer prints quickly. The Grant printer doesn't print quickly.
5. The Pace scanner doesn't run quietly. The Rico scanner runs quietly.

UNIT 10 *Lesson 1*

<u>Should</u> and <u>ought to</u>; <u>had better</u>

Use <u>should</u> or <u>ought to</u> + a base form to state an opinion or give advice, especially about an ethical choice. <u>Ought to</u> has the same meaning as <u>should</u>, but <u>should</u> is slightly less formal.

You **should** (or **ought to**) **return** the wallet. You **shouldn't keep** it.

Use <u>had better</u> + a base form to state an opinion or give stronger advice. The meaning is similar to <u>should</u> and <u>ought to</u>, but <u>had better</u> expresses the idea that there is a consequence for not doing something.

You**'d better tell** the waiter that the check is wrong. If you don't, he will have to pay.
You**'d better not eat** at the Fairway Café. I got sick there the last time I did.

Remember: <u>Should</u>, <u>ought to</u>, and <u>had better</u> precede other verbs and give them a special meaning. They never change form.

> **Note:** In American English it's very uncommon to use <u>ought to</u> in negative statements or questions. Use <u>should</u> or <u>shouldn't</u> instead.

A On a separate sheet of paper, complete the statements about an ethical choice, expressing your own ideas.

1. Colleagues in an office should always ....
2. Parents of young children should not ....
3. We ought to tell the store owner when ....
4. You forgot to pay your check? You had better ....
5. We had better not .... It's too expensive.

B On a separate sheet of paper, write five suggestions to a visitor to your country, using <u>had better</u> or <u>had better not</u>.

> "You'd better not take the local train to Bradbury. It's too slow."

Have to, must, and be supposed to

Have to and must

Use have to or the modal must + a base form to express obligation when there is no other choice of action available.

Students **must take** this exam.

You **have to take** the 6:00 train if you want to arrive on time.

Use don't have to (NOT must) to express a lack of obligation.

You **don't have to pay** for the shoes if you don't like them. You can return them.

Use must not (NOT don't have to) for a strong or legal prohibition.

Passengers **must not leave** their baggage unattended in the waiting area.

Be supposed to

Use be supposed to (or not be supposed to) + a base form to express an expected, but not a required, action. The degree of obligation is weaker than with have to or must.

We**'re supposed to pay** our check at the front of the coffee shop, not at the table. (The restaurant expects diners to pay at the front.)

Hotel guests **are not supposed to use** the towels from their rooms at the pool.

> **Note:** Must is very formal and not very common in speaking. It is generally used by a person in authority (e.g., a teacher or boss) to state policy or law. Have to is much more common in both speaking and writing. The more informal have got to is also common in spoken English.
>
> Sorry. **I've got to hurry**. I'm going to be late.
>
> Don't use must not for a lack of obligation. Use don't have to or doesn't have to.

C On a separate sheet of paper, write each sentence two ways: with must and with have to.

1 Drivers / obey the speed limit.
2 Students / arrive on time for class.
3 In this beach restaurant / diners / wear shoes. If you are barefoot, don't come in.
4 You / have a reservation to eat at the Palace Restaurant.

D On a separate sheet of paper, write five sentences that describe actions your school expects from its students. Use be supposed to.

Students are supposed to come on time to class. They're not supposed to be late.

E Choose the sentence closer in meaning to each numbered statement or question.

1 Do you think the Milton Restaurant is a good place to eat?
  a Do you think I should eat at the Milton Restaurant?
  b Do you think I have to eat at the Milton Restaurant?

2 If you don't have a reservation, the restaurant won't give you a table.
  a The restaurant is supposed to give you a table.
  b You had better have a reservation.

3 They don't accept credit cards in this store. They only accept cash.
  a You have to pay with cash.
  b You ought to pay with cash.

4 Don't wear shorts in the restaurant.
  a You must not wear shorts in the restaurant.
  b You don't have to wear shorts in the restaurant.

UNIT 10 *Lesson 2*

Possessive nouns: review and expansion

Add 's (an apostrophe + s) to a name or a singular noun.

Where is Glenn's car?
This is Ms. Baker's class.
What's your daughter's married name?
I love Dickens's novels.

Add an apostrophe to plural nouns that end in s. For irregular plurals, such as women or children, add 's.

the women's room
the boys' clothes
the Jacksons' car

Add 's to the name or noun that comes last in a list of two or more.

Jean and Ralph's house

A Correct the following sentences, adding an apostrophe or an apostrophe + s to the possessive nouns.

Carmen's jacket is under the table.

1 The two girls keys are lost.
2 Mr. Stiller English is really fluent.
3 The doctor office is downstairs.
4 Sarah and Tom children are at the Taylor School.
5 That man car is parked in a no-parking zone.
6 Julia friend brother is going to get married tonight.
7 The Smiths garden is beautiful.

Pronouns: summary

Subject pronouns

Subject pronouns represent subject nouns and noun phrases. The subject pronouns are I, you, he, she, it, we, and they.

Matt didn't break the plate = He didn't break the plate.

Object pronouns

Object pronouns represent nouns (and noun phrases) that function as direct objects, indirect objects, and objects of prepositions. The object pronouns are me, you, him, her, it, us, and them.

They gave Susan the toy car for the children.
They gave it to her for them.

B On a separate sheet of paper, rewrite the sentences, replacing the underlined nouns and noun phrases with pronouns.

Matt didn't break the plate. *He didn't break it.*

1 Our children love TV.
2 Janet and I never buy food at that store.
3 Do you and I have the car this afternoon?
4 Sylvia's family laughs at her jokes.
5 My friends are speaking with Ms. Rowe today.
6 Mr. Harris is teaching the students with Mr. Cooper.
7 All the students are speaking English very well this year.
8 Does Carl need to give the paper to his teachers?
9 Martin and Larry returned the money to the woman.

Writing Booster

The Writing Booster is optional. It is intended to teach students the conventions of written English. Each unit's Writing Booster is focused both on a skill and its application to the Writing exercise from the Unit Review page.

UNIT 1 Avoiding run-on sentences

An independent clause is a sentence with a subject and a verb.

subject	verb
I	saw a photo of the mountain.
It	looked very high.

> **Remember:** A sentence begins with a capital letter and ends with a period.

In writing, don't combine independent clauses without using a coordinating conjunction, such as and or but.

Run-on sentence ✗ ~~I saw a photo of the mountain it looked very high.~~

Correct a run-on sentence by (a) using a period to separate it into two sentences, or (b) using a coordinating conjunction to combine the two independent clauses. A comma before the conjunction is optional.

✓ I saw a photo of the mountain. It looked very high.
✓ I saw a photo of the mountain, and it looked very high.

Be careful! Do not use a comma to combine independent clauses. Use a period to separate them.

Run-on sentence ✗ ~~A new student arrived yesterday, he is from Santos.~~
✓ A new student arrived yesterday. He is from Santos.

A Write ✗ if the item contains a run-on sentence. Write ✓ if the item is written correctly.

☐ **1** Ann is Canadian she doesn't speak French.
☐ **2** They're good students they work very hard.
☐ **3** My brother is a lawyer, he lives in Hong Kong.
☐ **4** Victor and Lisa came home late last night. They stayed up until 4:00 A.M.
☐ **5** Some people think cities are beautiful I don't agree.
☐ **6** I have been to three foreign countries, I have never been to the United States.
☐ **7** We haven't tried Polish food, but we have tried Hungarian food.
☐ **8** I have never been to the top of the Empire State Building in New York, I have been to the top of Taipei 101 in Taipei.
☐ **9** I visited Jeju in Korea, and it was really beautiful.

B On a separate sheet of paper, write each of the run-on sentences in Exercise A correctly.

C **Guidance for the Writing Exercise (on page 12)** After you write about your interesting experience, check carefully to see if you have written any run-on sentences. Use a period to separate the independent clauses, or use the coordinating conjunctions and or but to combine them.

A paragraph is a group of sentences that relate to a topic or a theme. When your writing contains sections about a variety of topics, it is a good idea to divide it into separate paragraphs.

When there is more than one paragraph, it is customary, though not required, to include **a topic sentence** in each paragraph that summarizes or announces the main idea of the paragraph. The other sentences in the paragraph traditionally include details or facts that support the main idea. Using topic sentences makes paragraphs clearer and easier to understand.

In the writing model to the right, there are two paragraphs, each beginning with a topic sentence (highlighted in yellow).

In the first paragraph, the topic sentence informs us that the paragraph will contain details about violence in movies "before the 1960s."

In the second paragraph, the topic sentence informs us that the paragraph will shift focus. The word "Today" lets the reader know what the focus of the paragraph will be.

Without the topic sentences, the ideas would run together and be difficult to follow.

Remember: Indent the first word of each new paragraph so readers know that a new section of the writing is beginning.

indent ⟶ [ ]Before the 1960s, most movies did not show much graphic violence. When fighting or shooting occurred on the screen, it was clean: Bang! You're dead! The victim fell to the ground and died, perhaps after speaking a few final words. The viewer never saw blood or suffering. But in the late 1960s, filmmakers such as Arthur Penn and Sam Peckinpah began making movies with more graphic violence, such as *Bonnie and Clyde* and *The Wild Bunch*. They believed that if audiences could see how truly horrible real violence was, people would be less violent in their own lives.

Today, special-effects technology has made it possible to create very realistic images of bloodshed and violence. Steven Prince, author of *Savage Cinema: Sam Peckinpah and the Rise of Ultraviolent Movies*, describes the difference between early movies and the movies of today: ". . . filmmakers can create any image that they can dream up." So, Prince believes, because of technology, movies today are more and more violent and bloody.

A Choose a topic sentence for each paragraph.

1

_______ . Some people are worried that viewing a lot of violence in movies and video games can be dangerous. They feel that it can make violence seem normal and can cause people to imitate the violent behavior, doing the same thing themselves. Other people disagree. They believe that showing violence is honest and can even be helpful.

a Many people say violence in movies can be harmful.
b People have different opinions about how violence can affect viewers.
c People imitate violent behavior they see in movies.

2

_______ . This 1967 Arthur Penn movie is about a real gang of violent bank robbers who terrorized the U.S. Southwest in the 1930s. Bonnie (Faye Dunaway) and Clyde (Warren Beatty), and their gang were believed to be responsible for thirteen deaths and many robberies before they were finally killed.

a *Bonnie and Clyde* is based on a true story.
b Arthur Penn is one of the most famous directors of the 1960s.
c There were a lot of bank robberies in the 1930s.

3

_______ . The U.S. documentary *Spellbound* visits the homes of eight finalists for the National Spelling Bee and then follows them to the finals in Washington, D.C. We get to know the kids and their families.

a Spelling bees are popular in the U.S., and there have been a number of them in Washington.
b The finals of the National Spelling Bee take place in Washington, D.C.
c Some documentaries give us an intimate view of people and their lives.

B On a separate sheet of paper, write two paragraphs of three to five sentences each with details about the following topics. Make sure you have included a topic sentence for each paragraph that summarizes or announces the main idea of the paragraph.

Paragraph 1	**Paragraph 2**
The story of a time you (or others) were late to meet someone for an event	The story of what you (or the others) did after the event

C Guidance for the Writing Exercise (on page 24) On the notepad, write notes about why some people think watching violence is harmful and why others think it isn't. Use your notes as a guide for your paragraphs about violence. Include a topic sentence for each paragraph to summarize the main ideas.

Harmful:

Not harmful:

UNIT 3 Avoiding sentence fragments with because or since

Remember: You can use the subordinating conjunctions because or since to give a reason. Because and since answer a Why question. A clause that begins with because or since is called a dependent clause. A dependent clause gives information about an independent clause.

— independent clause —	— dependent clause —
I prefer the Hotel Casablanca	because (or since) it looks very interesting.

A dependent clause with because or since can also come at the beginning of a sentence. If it comes first, use a comma.

Because it looks very interesting, I prefer the Hotel Casablanca.

In writing, a dependent clause alone is an error called a "sentence fragment." It is not a sentence because it does not express a complete idea.

Sentence fragment ✗ I prefer the Hotel Casablanca. ~~Because it looks very interesting.~~

To correct a sentence fragment with because or since, make sure it is combined with an independent clause. Or rewrite the sentence without because or since to create an independent clause.

✓ I prefer the Hotel Casablanca because it looks very interesting.

✓ I prefer the Hotel Casablanca. It looks very interesting.

A In the following paragraph, underline four sentence fragments with because or since.

> When I was a child, I had three very important dreams. Because I was young, I thought they would all come true. The first one was that I wanted to be an architect. Because I loved modern buildings. Since I wanted to help people. The second dream was to be a doctor. The last one was to be a flight attendant. Since I liked to travel. Only one of my dreams became a reality. I am an architect today. Because I really love my job. I think it was really the right choice for me.

B On a separate sheet of paper, write the paragraph again. Correct all the sentence fragments. Combine the dependent clauses with independent clauses to make complete sentences.

C Guidance for the Writing Exercise (on page 36) In your paragraph about a hotel, include at least three reasons using because or since. Then check carefully to make sure that there are no sentence fragments.

UNIT 4 And, In addition, Furthermore, and Therefore

And

And connects two or more words in a series. Use commas to separate words when there are more than two in the series. (The last comma is optional.)

I'm concerned about **aggressive and inattentive** driving. (no comma: and connects two adjectives.)

Inattentive drivers sometimes **eat and talk** on their cell phones while they are driving. (no comma: and connects two verbs with the same subject.)

Gesturing, staring, and multitasking are three things aggressive drivers often do. (A comma is necessary: and connects more than two words in a series. The comma after staring is optional.)

And can also combine two separate complete sentences into one sentence. In the new sentence, the two original sentences are called "independent clauses." The comma is common but optional.

——— complete sentence ——— —— complete sentence ——

Aggressive drivers do many dangerous things. They cause a lot of crashes.

——— independent clause ——— —— independent clause ——

Aggressive drivers do many dangerous things, **and** they cause a lot of crashes.

A Insert commas where necessary or optional in the sentences.

1 She enjoys swimming hiking and fishing.
2 I don't like SUVs and other large cars.
3 We're traveling to France Italy and Spain.
4 Marianne and Sally are coming with us.
5 I'm renting a car and I'm driving it to Chicago.
6 This agency has nice convertibles vans and sports cars.

B On a separate sheet of paper, combine each pair of sentences into one sentence consisting of two independent clauses. Use and.

1 They made a call to a car rental company. They reserved a minivan for the weekend.
2 The left front headlight is broken. It won't turn on.
3 We rented a full-size sedan with a sunroof. We opened it because the weather was beautiful.
4 I hit the car in front of me. A passenger in the back seat was hurt.
5 You can drop the car off at nine o'clock. You can pick it up in the late afternoon.

In addition, Furthermore, and Therefore

Use In addition and Furthermore to add to the ideas in a previous sentence. In addition and Furthermore are approximately equal in meaning, but Furthermore is a little more formal. You can use both in the same writing to avoid repetition.

People should pay attention to their own driving. **In addition**, they should be aware of the driving of others.

I think defensive driving makes sense. **Furthermore**, it has been proven to reduce the number of accidents.

Use therefore to introduce a result.

——————— result ———————

Ron has had a lot of accidents. **Therefore**, the rental company said he couldn't rent one of their cars.

Note: It's customary to use a comma after In addition, Furthermore, and Therefore.

C Complete the statements with In addition or Therefore.

1 The other driver was speeding. ________, she wasn't paying attention.
2 No one was hurt. ________, we didn't have to go to the hospital after the crash.
3 I was taking a business trip with a lot of equipment. ________, I rented a car with a lot of trunk space.
4 They need to rent a minivan for their trip to Montreal. ________, they have to stay in a pet-friendly hotel because they plan to bring their pet dog.

D **Guidance for the Writing Exercise (on page 48)** In your paragraph about good and bad drivers, use And, In addition, Furthermore, and Therefore. Then check your paragraph carefully to see if you have used commas correctly.

There aren't many rules for informal social communication such as e-mails, text messages, and handwritten social notes. There are, however, important rules and conventions for formal written communication, such as business letters, memos, and e-mails. For these, be sure to include the following elements:

- your address
- the recipient's name, position, and address
- the date
- a salutation
- a complimentary close
- your typewritten name and, in a letter or memo, your handwritten signature

Note: When business correspondence is an e-mail, it's not necessary to include addresses.

If you know the recipient's name, the salutation should use the following format: Dear [title + last name]. It's common in a formal letter to use a colon (:) after the name. In less formal letters, a comma is appropriate.

Dear Mr. Smith: Dear Marie,

If you don't know the recipient's name or gender, use this format:

Dear Sir or Madam: OR To whom it may concern:

Follow the layout and punctuation in the writing model to the right.

your address { 657 Boulevard East
New Compton, Fortunia
e-mail: fclasson@vmail.gr

date { December 14, 2016

Manager
The Tipton Spa
Tipton Hotel
2200 Byway Street
Sylvania, Sorrento } **recipient's address**

Dear Sir or Madam: } **salutation**

I'm writing to tell you that I was very happy with the service provided by the staff of the Tipton Spa when I was in Sylvania last week. The hair stylist gave me a wonderful haircut, and the masseur was really top notch. I particularly enjoyed the relaxing music that played over the public address system. Finally, the prices were fair, and I left the spa feeling great.

I want you to know that I am recommending the Tipton Spa to all my friends and have told them that they should visit you even if they are staying in another hotel or if they are in Sylvania for the day. In fact, I have told them that it's worth traveling to Sylvania just to visit the spa. Congratulations on such a wonderful spa.

Sincerely, } **complimentary close**
Francine Classon } **signature**
Francine Classon } **typewritten name**

Other common complimentary closes
Cordially,
Sincerely yours,
Best regards,

A Think of a business, such as a hotel, a store, a salon, a gym, or a restaurant where you have received good service. On the notepad, write notes about the business.

Name of business:

Address:

Why you are happy with the service:

B On a separate sheet of paper, write a letter of thanks to the manager of the business in Exercise A. Explain what you like about the service. Use your notes and the writing model above as a guide.

C **Guidance for the Writing Exercise (on page 60)** Look at the letter that you chose from page 56. On the notepad below, list three methods that the writer could use to improve his or her appearance. Make notes of the advantages and disadvantages of each method. Then use your notes as a guide to help you write your response letter. Be sure to include your name and address, the date, a salutation, and a complimentary close in your letter.

Method	Advantages	Disadvantages
1.		
2.		
3.		

UNIT 6 Connecting ideas: subordinating conjunctions

A subordinating conjunction connects a dependent clause to an independent clause.

independent clause	dependent clause
People are eating more fast foods today	**because** they want to save time.
I generally avoid carbohydrates	**even though** it isn't easy.

Subordinating conjunctions

because	unless
since	although
if	(even) though

A dependent clause can also come at the beginning of a sentence. Use a comma after the dependent clause when it comes first.

dependent clause	independent clause
Because people want to save time,	they are eating more fast foods today.
Even though it isn't easy,	I generally avoid carbohydrates.

Use the subordinating conjunction if to express a condition. Use unless to express a negative condition.

You will be healthy **if** you eat right and exercise regularly.
You will gain weight **unless** you eat right and exercise regularly. (= if you don't)

Use the subordinating conjunctions although, even though, or though to express a contradiction.

Although / **Even though** / **Though** they knew fatty foods were unhealthy, people ate them anyway.

Remember: Use because or since to give a reason.

A Choose the best subordinating conjunction to complete each sentence.

1 (Though / If / Unless) I learn to speak English well, I will be very happy.
2 (Even though / Because / If) she is an artist, she is interested in science.
3 Studying English is important (although / because / unless) it can help you do more.
4 (Unless / Although / Since) English grammar isn't easy, I like studying it.
5 They have to go on a diet (because / unless / though) they're overweight.
6 He cut back on desserts and sodas (even though / if / because) he didn't want to.
7 (Even though / Because / Unless) my grandmother is 80 years old, she is in very good health.
8 (Unless / Because / Though) I think I'm going to get sick, I don't want to change my eating habits.
9 She won't eat red meat (because / unless / although) she has to.
10 (Unless / Even though / Since) she's a vegetarian, she sometimes eats fish.

B Read each sentence. Then, on a separate sheet of paper, write and connect a clause to the sentence, using the subordinating conjunction.

1 Most people don't want to change their eating habits. (even though)
2 Children become overweight. (if)
3 Obesity will continue to be a global problem. (unless)
4 Eating too much fast food is bad for you. (because)
5 Most people continue to eat unhealthy foods. (although)

1 Most people don't want to change their eating habits even though they have health problems.

C **Guidance for the Writing Exercise (on page 72)** Using four different subordinating conjunctions, write four sentences: two about eating habits in the past and two about eating habits in the present. Use your sentences in your paragraph about eating habits.

UNIT 7 Parallel structure

When writing a series of words or phrases in a sentence, be sure that all items in the series are in the same grammatical form. This feature of good writing is called "parallel structure."

Lucy is creative. She likes **painting**, **playing** the piano, and **dancing**. (all items in the series are gerunds)

Be careful! Don't combine gerunds and infinitives in the same series.
Don't write: Lucy is creative. She likes painting, ~~to play~~ the piano, and dancing.

In a series of infinitives, it is correct to use to before each item in the series or to use to only before the first item.

✗ I decided to study medicine, get married, and ~~to~~ have children before my thirtieth birthday.
✓ I decided **to study** medicine, **to get** married, and **to have** children before my thirtieth birthday.
✓ I decided **to study** medicine, **get** married, and **have** children before my thirtieth birthday.

Remember: When a sentence includes a series of more than two words or phrases, separate them with commas. Use and before the last item in the series. The comma before and is optional.

no comma (two items)	**commas (three items)**

Jake and May have three favorite activities: **painting, singing, and dancing.**

A Correct the errors in parallel structure in the sentences.

1 I have begun studying psychology and to learn about personality development.
2 They avoid arguing about the nature-nurture controversy and to disagree about which is more important.
3 The Bersons love to run, to swim, and lift weights.
4 She's both responsible and social. She prefers to study early in the evening and going out afterwards.
5 Introverts hate to talk about their feelings and being with a lot of people.
6 Marjorie is a classic extrovert. She likes to be very active, knowing a lot of people, and to seek excitement.
7 To be quiet, be hard to know, and to seek peace are traits typical of the introvert's personality.
8 Psychologists of the nineteenth century continued believing in the importance of genetics and to write about it in books and articles.

B **Guidance for the Writing Exercise (on page 84)** On a separate sheet of paper, write sentences to answer some or all the following questions about the person you chose. If appropriate, use verbs and phrases from the box on the right. Be careful to use parallel structure. Use the sentences in your paragraphs about the person.

- Who is the person?
- What is his or her relation to you?
- Who are the people in his or her family?
- How many siblings does he or she have?
- What kind of personality does he or she have?
- What are his or her likes and dislikes?
- Are there some things he or she is excited about, bored with, angry about, or worried about right now?

- Are there some things he or she is excited about, bored with, angry about, or worried about right now?

Words to describe likes / dislikes	
avoids	hopes
hates	would like
can't stand	is happy about
doesn't mind	is excited about
enjoys	is bored with
expects	is sick and tired of

UNIT 8 Supporting details

Remember: A good paragraph has a topic sentence that clearly states what the main idea of the paragraph is.

In addition, a paragraph should have **supporting details**—that is, information that provides support for, and is clearly tied to, the topic sentence.

Be careful! If a detail doesn't support the topic sentence or isn't tied to it clearly, then it may not belong in the paragraph.

In the writing model to the right, the topic sentence of the paragraph is highlighted in yellow. The sentences that follow are details. Two of the sentences are crossed out because they do not support the topic sentence and should not be included in the paragraph. These two sentences do not provide information about the chair and do not indicate why the writer likes the chair. The remaining sentences are supporting details—they all support the topic sentence and are clearly tied to it. They provide more information about the chair and they explain why the writer likes the chair.

In my living room, my favorite possession is an old wooden chair. My parents gave it to me when I left home. ~~A wooden chair can be very expensive if it is an antique.~~ It has lots of memories for me because it was in my parents' bedroom when I was growing up. ~~It's important to take very good care of wooden furniture.~~ The chair is very comfortable, and I used to sit in it a lot as a child.

A Read each topic sentence. Circle the detail that does not support the topic sentence.

1 Many French artists in the nineteenth century were influenced by Japanese art and printmaking.
- a Today, the work of Hokusai, Japan's most famous printmaker, is popular in Western countries.
- b Looking at the work of the French impressionists, it is clear that they chose to imitate the Japanese artistic styles of the time.
- c A number of French artists had collections of Japanese art.

2 I love my poster of Álvaro Saborío, the Costa Rican soccer player, but my wife hates it.
- a I think Saborío is a great player.
- b My wife doesn't think I should keep it in our bedroom.
- c The number on Saborío's uniform is 15.

3 Rodin's statue, *The Thinker*, is probably one of the most famous sculptures in the world.
- a This metal sculpture of a man deep in thought is recognized all over the world.
- b Rodin was born on November 12, 1840.
- c The image of *The Thinker* can be seen in popular art and advertisements.

4 On a side table in my dining room, I have two small ceramic figures of lions from my trip to Taipei.
- a They have beautiful colors including red, green, blue, and yellow.
- b You should visit the National Palace Museum when you are in Taipei.
- c I bought them together from a small shop at a temple I was visiting.

5 My sister has always shown a lot of talent in the performing arts.
- a We've had our differences, and we haven't always agreed on everything.
- b She has acted in school plays since she was about ten years old.
- c I think she's going to follow a career as an actor or dancer.

6 I think artistic talent is something you're born with.
- a I've tried many times to improve my ability at drawing, but it hasn't worked.
- b I have friends who are very talented in art, but they've never taken any special classes.
- c My aunt studied art at the Art Institute of Chicago for four years.

B **Guidance for the Writing Exercise (on page 96)** On the notepad, write the favorite object you chose. Create a topic sentence that states the most important thing you want to say about that object. Then write five supporting details to use in your paragraph.

Favorite object:

Topic sentence:

Details to support my topic sentence:

1.

2.

3.

4.

5.

UNIT 9 Organizing ideas

When you want to describe the benefits and problems of an issue, there are different ways you can organize your ideas. Here are some approaches.

Approach 1: In one paragraph

One way is to describe all the advantages and disadvantages in one paragraph. Following are notes of the details that will be included in the paragraph.

THE ADVANTAGES AND DISADVANTAGES OF SMART PHONES

Advantages: are easy to carry, don't miss calls, keep you connected with family and friends

Disadvantages: bother other people, make people dependent, are easy to lose

This approach is good for a short piece of writing consisting of only a few sentences. However, if you want to develop those ideas in more than just a few sentences, it is easier for the reader to follow if you can organize the details in one of the following ways:

Approach 2: In two paragraphs

In this approach, you can use a first paragraph to describe all the advantages. Then you can use a second paragraph to describe all the disadvantages. Following are notes of the details that will be included in each paragraph.

Paragraph 1: SMART PHONES HAVE ADVANTAGES

are easy to carry, don't miss calls, keep you connected with family and friends

Paragraph 2: BUT THEY ALSO HAVE DISADVANTAGES

bother other people, make people dependent, are easy to lose

Approach 3: In more than two paragraphs

In this approach, you can use a separate paragraph to focus on each different topic. In each paragraph, you can describe both advantages and disadvantages. Following are notes of the details that will be included in each paragraph.

Paragraph 1: (THEY'RE SMALL.) smart phones easy to carry, but also easy to lose

Paragraph 2: (THEY'RE CONVENIENT.) won't miss calls, but you can also bother other people

Paragraph 3: (THEY'VE CHANGED OUR LIVES.) keep people connected with family and friends, but also can make people dependent

A Using Approach 2, organize the ideas into two paragraphs: paragraph 1 is about the benefits of renting a car; paragraph 2 is about the problems. Write 1 or 2 next to each idea.

___ It gives you the freedom to go wherever you want to go whenever you want.

___ You might see places you can't see by bus or train.

___ You could have an accident during your trip.

___ You have more control over whether or not you will have an accident during your trip.

___ You can carry more luggage and other things you might need.

___ To drive safely, you have to become familiar with the local driving rules.

___ If you're traveling with a group of people, it could cost less than paying for bus and train tickets.

___ You may have to understand road signs that are in a different language.

___ If you have to do all the driving, it can be very stressful and tiring.

___ If you're traveling alone or with one other person, it could cost a lot of money in rental fees and gas.

B Now, on a separate sheet of paper, practice using Approach 3. Organize the sentences from Exercise A by topic into three or more separate paragraphs. Don't forget to include a topic sentence.

C Guidance for the Writing Exercise (on page 108) Use your notes on page 107 to write your paragraphs about the benefits and problems of the Internet. Choose Approach 2 or Approach 3 to organize your writing.

UNIT 10 Introducing conflicting ideas: On the one hand; On the other hand

Use On the one hand and On the other hand to present conflicting ideas or two sides of an issue. The following two sentences present the two sides together, one right after the other.

On the one hand, I would want to tell the truth. On the other hand, I wouldn't want to get in trouble.

Remember: You can also present conflicting or contradictory information with Even though, Although, and However.

Even though I'm basically an honest person, I don't always tell the truth.
Although Matt didn't think he broke the dish, it's possible that he did.
Matt wanted to tell the owner of the store what happened. However, Noah didn't agree.

When one paragraph presents one side of an issue and the next one presents the other, writers don't usually use On the one hand in the first paragraph. Instead, they just begin the next paragraph with On the other hand to let the reader know that the conflicting idea will follow. Look at the writing model to the right.

Being honest has many advantages. If you always tell the truth, you don't have to remember an untruth you said before. People who tell the truth don't have trouble sleeping. They can look at themselves in the mirror and feel good.

On the other hand, there are times when telling a lie makes sense. For example, your friend Andrew might ask you if you like his new jacket, and you think it's ugly. If you told him that, it would hurt his feelings. It's possible that not being absolutely truthful might make more sense.

A Reread the Photo Story on page 111. Write a summary of the story in three to five sentences. Answer the questions below.

- Where was Matt?
- Who was he with?
- What happened?
- What did the two friends discuss?

B Answer the questions below. Write three to five sentences about Matt's choices. Then write the consequences of each choice. Use If and the unreal conditional in at least one sentence.

- What should he do?
- What could he do?
- What would most people do?

C Write three to five sentences about what you would do if you were Matt. Answer the questions below.

- What would you do?
- What would happen if you did that?
- What would happen if you didn't?

D Guidance for the Writing Exercise (on page 120) In your paragraphs about Matt's dilemma, use On the one hand, On the other hand, Even though, Although, and However to connect conflicting ideas.

Top Notch Pop Lyrics

▶ 1:16–1:17 Greetings and Small Talk [Unit 1]

You look so familiar. Have we met before?
I don't think you're from around here.
It might have been two weeks ago, but I'm not sure.
Has it been a month or a year?
I have a funny feeling that I've met you twice.
That's what they call déjà vu.
You were saying something friendly, trying to be nice—and now you're being friendly, too.
One look, one word.
It's the friendliest sound that I've ever heard.
Thanks for your greetings.
I'm glad this meeting occurred.

(CHORUS)
Greetings and small talk
make the world go round.
On every winding road I've walked,
this is what I've found.

Have you written any letters to your friends back home?
Have you had a chance to do that?
Have you spoken to your family on the telephone?
Have you taken time for a chat?
Bow down, shake hands.
Do whatever you do in your native land.
I'll be happy to greet you
in any way that you understand.

(CHORUS)

Have you seen the latest movie out of Hollywood?
Have you read about it yet?
If you haven't eaten dinner, are you in the mood for a meal you won't forget?
Bow down, shake hands.
Do whatever you do in your native land.
I'll be happy to greet you
in any way that you understand.

(CHORUS)

▶ 1:35–1:36 Better Late Than Never [Unit 2]

Where have you been? I've waited for you.
I'd rather not say how long.
The movie began one hour ago.
How did you get the time all wrong?
Well, I got stuck in traffic, and when I arrived
I couldn't find a parking place.
Did you buy the tickets? You're kidding—for real?
Let me pay you back, in that case.

(CHORUS)
Sorry I'm late.
I know you've waited here forever.
How long has it been?
It's always better late than never.

When that kind of movie comes to the big screen,
it always attracts a crowd,
and I've always wanted to see it with you—
but it looks like we've missed it now.
I know what you're saying, but actually,
I would rather watch a video.
So why don't we rent it and bring it back home?
Let's get in the car and go.

(CHORUS)

Didn't you mention, when we made our plans, that you've seen this movie recently?
It sounds so dramatic, and I'm so upset,
I'd rather see a comedy!
Well, which comedy do you recommend?
It really doesn't matter to me.
I still haven't seen 'The World and a Day'.
I've heard that one is pretty funny.

(CHORUS)

▶ 2:17–2:18 Checking Out [Unit 3]

Ms. Jones travels all alone.
She doesn't need much space—
a single room with a nice twin bed
and a place for her suitcase.
Her stay is always satisfactory,
but in the morning she's going to be checking out.
Mr. Moon will be leaving soon,
and when he does I'll say,
"Thank you, sir, for staying with us.
How do you want to pay?"
And in the end it isn't hard.
He'll put it on his credit card. He's checking out.
Would you like to leave a message?
Could you call back later?
Do you need some extra towels
or today's newspaper?
Can I get you anything?
Would you like room service?
I'm so sorry.
Am I making you nervous?
Good evening.
I'll ring that room for you.
Is that all?
I'll be glad to put you through.
I'm sorry, but he's not answering.
The phone just rings and rings.
The couple in room 586
have made a king-size mess.
Pick up the laundry. Turn down the beds.
We have another guest
coming with his family.
You'd better hurry or they will be checking out. . .

▶ 2:36–2:37 Wheels around the World [Unit 4]

Was I going too fast
or a little too slow?
I was looking out the window,
and I just don't know.
I must have turned the steering wheel
a little too far
when I drove into the bumper
of that luxury car.
Oh no!
How awful!
What a terrible day!
I'm sorry to hear that.
Are you OK?

(CHORUS)
Wheels around the World
are waiting here with your car.
Pick it up.
Turn it on.
Play the radio.
Wheels around the World—
"helping you to go far."
You can drive anywhere.
Buckle up and go.

Did I hit the red sedan,
or did it hit me?
I was talking on the cell phone
in my SUV.
Nothing was broken,
and no one was hurt,
but I did spill some coffee
on my favorite shirt.
Oh no!
Thank goodness you're still alive!
I'm so happy that
you survived.

(CHORUS)

What were you doing when you hit that tree?
I was racing down the mountain, and the brakes failed me.
How did it happen? Was the road still wet?
Well, there might have been a danger sign,
But I forget.
The hood popped open and the door fell off.
The headlights blinked and the engine coughed.
The side-view mirror had a terrible crack.
The gearshift broke. Can I bring the car back?
Oh no!
Thank goodness
you're still alive!
I'm so happy that
you survived.

(CHORUS)

▶ 3:17–3:18 Piece of Cake [Unit 5]

I need to pick up a few things
on the way back to school.
Feel like stopping at a store with me?
I'd like to, but I think I'll pass.
I don't have time today.
It's already nearly a quarter to three.

(CHORUS)
Don't worry. We'll be fine.
How long can it take?
It's easy. It'll be a piece of cake.

I need a tube of toothpaste and
a bar of Luvly soap,
some sunscreen, and a bottle of shampoo.
Where would I find makeup?
How about a comb?
Have a look in aisle one or two.

(CHORUS)

I have an appointment
for a haircut at The Spa.
On second thought, they're always running late.
My class starts in an hour.
I'll never make it now.
How long do you think we'll have to wait?

(CHORUS)

They say there's someone waiting
for a trim ahead of me.
Can I get you some coffee or some tea?
OK. In the meantime,
I'll be getting something strong
for this headache at the pharmacy!

(CHORUS)

▶ 3:37–3:38 A Perfect Dish [Unit 6]

I used to eat a lot of fatty foods,
but now I just avoid them.
I used to like chocolate and lots of sweets,
but now those days are gone.
To tell you the truth,
it was too much trouble.
They say you only live once,
but I'm not crazy about feeling sick.
What was going wrong?
Now I know I couldn't live without this.
Everything's ready.
Why don't you sit down?

(CHORUS)
It looks terrific,
but it smells pretty awful.
What in the world can it be?
It smells like chicken,
and it tastes like fish—
a terrific dish
for you and me—
a perfect dish for you
and me.

I used to be a big meat eater,
now I'm vegetarian,
and I'm not much of a coffee drinker.
I can't stand it anymore.
I'm avoiding desserts with sugar.
I'm trying to lose some weight.
Some things just don't agree with me.
They're bad for me, I'm sure.
Would you like some?
Help yourself.
Isn't it so good for you health?

(CHORUS)

Aren't you going to have some?
Don't you like it?
Wasn't it delicious?
Don't you want some more?

(CHORUS)

▶ 4:13–4:14 The Colors of Love [Unit 7]

Are you sick and tired of working hard day
and night?
Do you like to look at the world in shades of
black and white?
Your life can still be everything that you were
dreaming of.
Just take a look around you and see all the
colors of love.
You wake up every morning and go through
the same old grind.
You don't know how the light at the window
could be so unkind. If blue is the color that
you choose when the road is rough, you know
you really need to believe in the colors of love.

(CHORUS)
The colors of love
are as beautiful as a rainbow.
The colors of love
shine on everyone in the world.

Are negative thoughts and emotions painful
to express?
They're just tiny drops in the ocean of
happiness.
And these are the feelings you must learn to
rise above.
Your whole life is a picture you paint with the
colors of love.

(CHORUS)

▶ 4:28–4:29 To Each His Own [Unit 8]

He doesn't care for Dali.
The colors are too bright.
He says that Picasso
got everything just right.
She can't stand the movies
that are filmed in Hollywood.
She likes Almodóvar.
She thinks he's really good.
He's inspired by everything
she thinks is second-rate.
She's moved and fascinated
by the things he loves to hate.
He's crazy about art that only
turns her heart to stone.
I guess that's why they say
to each his own.
He likes pencil drawings.
She prefers photographs.
He takes her to the the art museum,
but she just laughs and laughs.
He loves the Da Vinci
that's hanging by the door.
She prefers the modern art
that's lying on the floor.
"No kidding! You'll love it. Just wait and see.
It's perfect in every way."
She shakes her head. "It's not for me.
It's much too old and gray."
She thinks he has the worst taste
that the world has ever known.
I guess that's why they say
to each his own.
But when it's time to say goodbye,
they both feel so alone.
I guess that's why they say
to each his own.

▶ 5:16–5:17 Life in Cyberspace [Unit 9]

I'm just fooling around.
Am I interrupting you?
Well, I wanted to know—
what are you up to?
I tried to send some photos,
but it's been so long
that I almost don't remember
how to log on.
So I'm thinking about getting a
new computer.
I don't know what kind. I should have done
it sooner.
But I heard the Panatel is as good as
the rest.
Check it out. Check it out.
You should really check it out.

(CHORUS)
Let's face it—that's life.
That's life in cyberspace.

When you download the pictures,
then you open the files.
If your computer's slow,
then it can take a little while.
From the pull-down menu,
you can print them, too.
But don't forget to save
everything you do.
Scroll it up. Scroll it down.
Put your cursor on the bar.
Then click on the icon,
and you'll see my new car!
The car goes as fast
as the one I had before.
Check it out. Check it out.
You should really check it out.

(CHORUS)

Am I talking to myself, or are you still there?
This instant message conversation's
going nowhere.
I could talk to Liz.
She isn't nearly as nice.
It isn't quite as much fun.
I've done it once or twice.
What's the problem?
Come on. Give it a try.
If you don't want to be friends,
at least tell me why.
Did you leave to make a call
or go out to get some cash?
Did the photos I sent make your
computer crash?

(CHORUS)

▶ 5:31–5:32 What Would You Do? [Unit 10]

What would you do
if I got a tattoo with your name?
What would you say
if I dyed my hair for you?
What would you do
if I sang outside your window?
What would you think
if I told you I loved you?

(CHORUS)
I hate to say this,
but I think you're making a big mistake.
By tomorrow,
I'm sure you'll be sorry.

What would you do
if I sent you a love letter?
Would you say it was wrong
and send it back to me?
What would you think
if I pierced my ears? Would you care?
Would you think
that I had lost all my modesty?

(CHORUS)

Well, give it some thought.
I know I could make you happy.
Are you kidding?
You'd have to be nuts to ask me.
It's no mistake. I'm sure
that my heart is yours.
I have to find a way
to make you mine.

(CHORUS)

Photo credits: Original photography by Sharon Hoogstraten, David Mager and Libby Ballengee/TSI Graphics. Page 2 (tl) Image Source/Getty Images, (tl) Gogo Images Corporation/Alamy, (tr) WaveBreakMedia/Shutterstock, (tr) Comstock Images/Stockbyte/Getty Images, (bl) DAJ/Getty Images, (bm) WaveBreakMedia/Shutterstock, (br) Jack Hollingsworth/Photodisc/Getty Images; p. 5 (tl) Daniel Grill/Getty Images, p. 6 (The Forbidden Palace) Rabbit75_fot/Fotolia, (Beijing Duck) Zhangsan/Fotolia, (Two men shake hands) Asia Images Group/Getty Images; p. 7 (Taj Mahal) Saiko3p/Fotolia, (Temple) Searagen/Fotolia, (Ceviche) Ildi.Food/Alamy, (Pyramid of Sun) F9photos/Fotolia, Dabldy/Fotolia; p. 8 (tr) Olly/Fotolia, (tr) Aeroking/Fotolia, (mr) Andrey Arkusha/Shutterstock; p. 10 (snail) Sergio Martínez/Fotolia, (1) Michael Spring/Fotolia, (2) Syda Productions/Fotolia, (3)Blend Images/Shutterstock; p. 11 (br) Diego Cervo/Shutterstock; p. 12 (1) Luiz Rocha/Shutterstock, (2) Worakit Sirijinda/Fotolia, (3) Aania/Fotolia, (4) Sam Edwards/Caia Image/Glow Images; p. 13 (The Prado Museum) Anibal Trejo/Fotolia, (Tapas) Paul Brighton/Fotolia, (The Millineum Wheel) QQ7/Shutterstock, (Carnaby Street) Image Source/Getty Images, (Eiffel Tower) Wajan/Fotolia, (Tour Boat) Elenathewise/Fotolia, (Ballet) Ria Novosti/Alamy, (Borscht) Cook_inspire/Fotolia, (Colosseum) Pablo Debat/Fotolia, (Gelato) Eldorado/Fotolia; p. 14 (tl) AF archive/Alamy, (tm) AF archive/Alamy, (tr) Pictorial Press Ltd/Alamy; p. 16 (mr) Allstar Picture Library/Alamy; p. 18 (An action film) AF archive/Alamy, (A horror film) BortN66/Fotolia, (A science-fiction film) Innovari/Fotolia, (An animated film) Natalia Maroz/Shutterstock, (A comedy) KPA Honorar & Belege/United Archives GmbH/Alamy, (A drama) Auremar/Shutterstock, (A documentary) Amar and Isabelle Guillen/Guillen Photo LLC/Alamy, (A musical) Bettina Strenske/Alamy; p. 19 Monkey Business/Fotolia; p. 21 (tl) Gary Conner/Photodisc/Getty Images, (tm) Adam Gregor/Shutterstock, (ml) Eugenia Petrenko/Shutterstock, (mr) Ktsdesign/Fotolia; p. 22 Rich Yasick/E+/Getty Images; p. 23 Nyul/Fotolia; p. 26 (tl) Bjdlzx/E+/Getty Images, (tm) Bjdlzx/E+/Getty Images, (tr) Bjdlzx/E+/Getty Images, (bl) Pejo/Shutterstock, (bml) Tom Wang/Shutterstock, (bmr) Zoonar RF/Thinkstock/Getty Images; p. 28 (tl) EpicStockMedia/Fotolia, (br) Racorn/Shutterstock; p. 32 (tl) Cornelia Pithart/Fotolia, (tl) Ludmilafoto/Fotolia, (tm) Razihusin/Fotolia, (tr) Anterovium/Fotolia, (tr) Nyasha/Fotolia, (bl) Mark Peterson/Corbis News/Corbis, (bl) Comstock/Stockbyte/Thinkstock/Getty Images, (bm) (Woman) Chris Ryan/Ojo Images Ltd/Alamy, (Newspaper) Jocic/Shutterstock, (br) Glow Images/Superstock; p. 33 Degree/eStock Photo/Alamy; p. 34 (The Plaza Hotel) Sandra Baker/Alamy, (Rockefeller center) Marcorubino/Fotolia, (Manhattan Skyline) Rudi1976/Fotolia, (Times Square) Richard Berenholtz/Alamy, (Grand Central Station) Forcdan/Fotolia; p. 37 (1) Image Source/Getty Images, (2) Quavando/Vetta/Getty Images; p. 39 (tl bg) Amy Walters/Shutterstock, (tm bg) Horid85/Fotolia, (tr bg) Horid85/Fotolia; p. 44 (1) Supertrooper/Fotolia, (2) Deusexlupus/Fotolia, (3) Algre/Fotolia, (4) National Motor Museum/Motoring Picture Library/Alamy, (5) Yuri Bizgaimer/Fotolia, (6) Rob Wilson/Shutterstock, (7) Supertrooper/Fotolia, (8) Buzz Pictures/Alamy; p. 45 (1) Tracy Whiteside/Fotolia, (2) Arek Malang/Shutterstock, (3) BikeRiderLondon/Shutterstock, (4) R. Gino Santa Maria/Shutterstock, (5) Andresr/Shutterstock; p. 46 Tomml/E+/Getty Images; p. 47 Carlos_bcn/Fotolia; p. 50 (Haircuts) Lester120/Fotolia, (Facials) Valua Vitaly/Fotolia, (Shaves) Yalcin Sonat/Shutterstock, (Manicures) Vladimir Sazonov/Fotolia, (Pedicures) Tomek Pa/Shutterstock, (Massage) Valua Vitaly/Fotolia, (Yoga) Furmananna/Fotolia, (Kickboxing) Erik Isakson/Getty Images, (Pilates) Andres Rodriguez/Fotolia, (Spinning) Wavebreak media LTD/Alloy/Corbis, (Exercise equipment) Hero Images/Getty Images, (Personal trainers) Visionsi/Fotolia; p. 52 (t) (1) Lan 2010/Fotolia, (2) Akova/Fotolia, (3) Ilya Akinshin/Fotolia, (4) Lan 2010/Fotolia, (5) Darak77/Fotolia, (6) Glovatskiy/Fotolia, (b) (1) Picsfive/Fotolia, (2) Coprid/Fotolia, (3) Mile Atanasov/Fotolia, (4) Igor/Fotolia, (5)Isreal Mckee/Shutterstock, (6) Vadim Ponomarenko/Shutterstock,(bg) Madgooch/Fotolia, (7) Toskov/Fotolia, (8) Stephen Coburn/Shutterstock, (9) Monkey Business/Fotolia, (10) Vipman/Shutterstock, (12) Olya6105/Fotolia, (13) Gresei/Fotolia, (14) Hugh O'Neill/Fotolia, (15) Africa Studio/Fotolia, (16) Urfin/Shutterstock; p. 54 (tr) Hola Images/Alamy, (Female speaking on phone) Minerva Studio/Fotolia; p. 56 (tr) Juanmonino/E+/Getty Images, (bl) Racorn/Shutterstock; p. 57 Igor Gratzer/Shutterstock; p. 58 (l) Fotoluminate LLC/Fotolia, (r) Diego Cervo/Fotolia; p. 59 (1) Holbox/Shutterstock, (2) Tom Cockrem/Stockbyte/Getty Images, (3) Hannamariah/Shutterstock, (4) Eric Lafforgue/Alamy; p. 62 (tl bg) Ilya Zaytsev/Fotolia, (tl) D. Hurst/Alamy, (tr bg) Ilya Zaytsev/Fotolia, (tl) D. Hurst/Alamy, (butter) Coleman Yuen/Pearson Education Asia Ltd, (Fork) Vo/Fotolia, (m bg) Ilya Zaytsev/Fotolia, (Fruit) Koszivu/Fotolia, (Bread,grains,pasta) Nikolay Petkov/Shutterstock, (Vegetables) Ana Blazic Pavlovic/Shutterstock, (Meat,fish,beans) D. Hurst/Alamy, (green napkin) Karandaev/Fotolia, (blue placemat) Aleksandr Ugorenkov /Fotolia; p. 63 (Mushroom diet) Viktor/Fotolia, (Vegan diet) Studio Gi/Fotolia, (Atkins diet) Vladimir Melnik/Fotolia, (Juice Fast) Larisa Lofitskaya/Shutterstock; p. 64 (Sushi) Motorlka/Fotolia, (Mangoes) Volff/Fotolia, (Pasta) Vagabondo/Fotolia, (Ice cream) Unpict/Fotolia, (Asparagus) Africa Studio/Fotolia; p. 67 (Octopus) Denio109/Fotolia, (Shellfish) Maceo/Fotolia, (Tofu) Lilyana Vynogradova/Fotolia, (Steak) Joe Gough/Fotolia, (Broccoli) Ping Han/Fotolia, (Beets) Mitev/Fotolia, (Chocolate) Taigi/Fotolia; p. 68 (tr) Fotandy/Shutterstock, (br) Saje/Fotolia; p. 69 Apollofoto/Shutterstock; p. 70 (a) Shakzu/Fotolia, (Grasshopper) Valeriy Kirsanov/Fotolia, (b) Paul Brighton/Fotolia, (c) Nattawut Thammasak/Fotolia, (d) Africa Studio/Fotolia, (e) Vankad/Fotolia, (f) Uckyo/Fotolia, (Cabbage) Nomad Soul/Fotolia; p. 71 (1,2,3,4) Mariusz Blach/Fotolia, (br) Mourad/Tarek/ Bon Appetit/Alamy; p. 73 (Pad Thai) Narith_2527/iStock/Thinkstock/Getty Images, (Bi Bim Bop) Ain Bagwell/Photodisc/Getty Images, (Chicken Mole) Uckyo/Fotolia, (Potato Soup) Juanmonino/E+/Getty Images, (Tabouleh Salad) M.studio/Fotolia, (Pot Stickers) Chiyacat/Fotolia, (br) Yuris/Shutterstock; p. 74 Lightboxx/Shutterstock; p. 78 Imagesource/Glow Images; p. 79 LightWaveMedia/Shutterstock; p. 80 Pavel L Photo and Video/Shutterstock; p. 81 (tr) Zsschreiner/Shutterstock, (bl) Taka/Fotolia, (br) Eurobanks/Fotolia; p. 82 Monkey Business Images/Shutterstock; p. 83 (t) Rob/Fotolia, (b) Tanya Constantine/Blend/Corbis; p. 85 (1) WaveBreakMedia/Shutterstock, (2) Jeremy Woodhouse/Blend Images/Getty Images, (3) Corey Rich/Aurora/Getty Images; p. 86 (Jewelry) Harshmunjal/Fotolia, (Fashion) Terex/Fotolia, (Pottery) Africa Studio/Fotolia, (Painting) Boyan Dimitrov/Shutterstock, (Photography) Philippova Anastasia/Shutterstock; p. 87 (ml) Boyan Dimitrov/Fotolia, (m) Gurgen Bakhshetsyan/Shutterstock, (mr) Rozaliya/Fotolia, (mr) Nils Volkmer/Shutterstock; p. 89 (Monalisa) Dennis Hallinan/Alamy, (Gold Museum) *Cacique Guatavita, known as El Dorado's raft in gold and emeralds, Colombia, Chibcha civilization (or Muisca)*/De Agostini Picture Library/G. Dagli Orti/Bridgeman Images, (National Palace Museum) *Chinese cabbage, Korean, 19th century (jade) / National Palace Museum, Taipei, Taiwan/* Bridgeman Images, (Museum of Modern Art) GL Archive/Alamy; p. 90 (Wood) Pavel K/Shutterstock, (Glass) Sagir/Shutterstock, (Silver) Nolte Lourens/Fotolia, (Gold ring)Lynnette/Shutterstock; (Cloth) NH7/Fotolia, (Ceramic) Deborah McCague/Shutterstock, (Stone) Winnond/Shutterstock; p. 91 (Vase) Nikonbhoy/Fotolia, (Plate) Piero Gentili/Fotolia, (Dolls) Ketsur/Fotolia, (Figure) Kanvag/Fotolia, (Cups) Mrpuiii/Shutterstock; p. 92 Audrey Benson; p. 93 Africa Studio/Fotolia; p. 94 (Stella) AFP/Newscom, (Vincent) De Agostini Picture Library/Getty Images, (Charles) Picture-alliance/Newscom, (Valentino) Splash News/Newscom, (Frida) Bettmann/Corbis, (Henri) Charles Platiau/Reuters/Newscom, (Ang Lee) Fox 2000 Pictures/Album/Newscom; p. 95 (l) Nicholas Piccillo/Fotolia, (m) Michael Jung/Shutterstock, (r) Arek Malang/Shutterstock; p. 96 (a) Pytralona/Shutterstock, (b) Swisshippo/Fotolia, (c) Nerthuz/Fotolia, (d) www.TouchofArt.eu/Fotolia, (e) Yezep/Fotolia; p. 97 (Accademia Gallery) Akg-Images/Cameraphoto/Newscom, (David) Ndphoto/Shutterstock, (Musee d'Orsay) Brian Jannsen/Alamy, (Apples and Oranges) *Apples and Oranges, 1895-1900 (oil on canvas), Cezanne, Paul (1839-1906)*/Musee d'Orsay, Paris, France/Giraudon/Bridgeman Images, (Peru) Eduardo Rivero/Shutterstock, (India) Сергей Чирков/Fotolia, (China) Stockphoto Mania/Shutterstock, (Sweden) Tobyphotos/Shutterstock; p. 98 (Frank) Yulia Mayorova/Shutterstock, (Kathy) Phototalk/E+/Getty Images, (Nardo) Warren Goldswain/Fotolia; p. 100 (tr) Blue Images/Ivy/Corbis, (Monitor,screen) Antiksu/Fotolia, (Mouse) Violetkaipa/Shutterstock, (Touchpad) Tagore75/Fotolia; p. 102 Nikkytok/Fotolia; p. 103 (Joystick) Geargodz/Fotolia, StockLite/Shutterstock; p. 104 (4) Hero Images/Getty Images; p. 106 Chanpipat/Shutterstock; p. 107 (l) Glow Images/Getty Images, (r) Kitty/Shutterstock; p. 109 (ml) Olix Wirtinger/Fancy/Corbis; p. 115 (Book) Irina Burakova/Fotolia, (Smartphone) Bloomua/Fotolia, (Wallet) Grigoriy Lukyanov/Fotolia, (Coat) Ludmilafoto/Fotolia, (Headphones) Alexander Demyanenko/Fotolia, (Gloves) Spe/Fotolia, (Bag) Nikolai Sorokin/Fotolia; p. 116 (l) Jaroslav Kviz/Profimedia.CZ a.s./Alamy; (m) Tristan Savatier/Moment/Getty Images, (r) AnnaDe/Shutterstock; p. 117 Underwood Photo Archives/Superstock; p. 118 Bikeworldtravel/Fotolia.

Illustration credits: Steve Attoe, pp. 6, 64; Sue Carlson, p. 35; John Ceballos, pp. 25, 37, 49, 121; Mark Collins, pp. 27, 42 (left); Brian Hughes, pp. 24 (bottom), 41; Adam Larkum, p. 61; Pat Lewis, p. 10; Andy Myer, pp. 16 (left, center), 66; Dusan Petricic, pp. 33, 41, 70, 78, 79, 113; Jake Rickwood, p. 24 (top); Geoffrey P. Smith, p. 38; Neil Stewart, p. 119 (center, bottom); Gary Torrisi, p. 46; Anne Veltfort, pp. 16 (right), 31, 42 (right), 66 (top-right), 119 (top).

Text credits: Page 46: *Six Tips for Defensive Driving,* © The Nemours Foundation/KidsHealth. Reprinted with permission; Page 74: *Psychology of Color* from infoplease.com. Reprinted with permission.